SHANGHAI

2nd Edition

**Where to Stay and Eat
for All Budgets**

**Must-See Sights
and Local Secrets**

Ratings You Can Trust

Fodor's Travel Publications   New York, Toronto, London, Sydney, Auckland
www.fodors.com

FODOR'S SHANGHAI
Editor: Stephanie E. Butler

Editorial Contributor: Margaret Kelly
Writers: Lisa Movius, Elyse Singleton, David Taylor

Production Editor: Astrid deRidder
Maps & Illustrations: David Lindroth, Ed Jacobus, Mark Stroud, *cartographers*; Bob Blake, Rebecca Baer, *map editors;* William Wu, *information graphics*
Design: Fabrizio La Rocca, *creative director*; Guido Caroti, Siobhan O'Hare, *art directors*; Tina Malaney, Chie Ushio, Ann McBride, Jessica Walsh, *designers*; Melanie Marin, *senior picture editor*
Cover Photo (Nanjing Street): Alex Mares-Manton/Asia Images/Getty Images
Production Manager: Angela L. McLean

COPYRIGHT
Copyright © 2009 by Fodor's Travel, a division of Random House, Inc.

Fodor's is a registered trademark of Random House, Inc.

All rights reserved. Published in the United States by Fodor's Travel, a division of Random House, Inc., and simultaneously in Canada by Random House of Canada, Limited, Toronto. Distributed by Random House, Inc., New York.

No maps, illustrations, or other portions of this book may be reproduced in any form without written permission from the publisher.

2nd Edition

ISBN 978–1–4000–0821–6

ISSN 1934–5526

SPECIAL SALES
This book is available at special discounts for bulk purchases for sales promotions or premiums. Special editions, including personalized covers, excerpts of existing books, and corporate imprints, can be created in large quantities for special needs. For more information, write to Special Markets/Premium Sales, 1745 Broadway, MD 6-2, New York, New York 10019, or e-mail specialmarkets@randomhouse.com.

AN IMPORTANT TIP & AN INVITATION
Although all prices, opening times, and other details in this book are based on information supplied to us at press time, changes occur all the time in the travel world, and Fodor's cannot accept responsibility for facts that become outdated or for inadvertent errors or omissions. So **always confirm information when it matters,** especially if you're making a detour to visit a specific place. Your experiences—positive and negative—matter to us. If we have missed or misstated something, **please write to us.** We follow up on all suggestions. Contact the Shanghai editor at editors@fodors.com or c/o Fodor's at 1745 Broadway, New York, NY 10019.

PRINTED IN THE UNITED STATES OF AMERICA

10 9 8 7 6 5 4 3 2 1

Be a Fodor's Correspondent

Your opinion matters. It matters to us. It matters to your fellow Fodor's travelers, too. And we'd like to hear it. In fact, we need to hear it.

When you share your experiences and opinions, you become an active member of the Fodor's community. That means we'll not only use your feedback to make our books better, but we'll publish your names and comments whenever possible. Throughout our guides, look for "Word of Mouth," excerpts of your unvarnished feedback.

Here's how you can help improve Fodor's for all of us.

Tell us when we're right. We rely on local writers to give you an insider's perspective. But our writers and staff editors—who are the best in the business—depend on you. Your positive feedback is a vote to renew our recommendations for the next edition.

Tell us when we're wrong. We're proud that we update most of our guides every year. But we're not perfect. Things change. Hotels cut services. Museums change hours. Charming cafés lose charm. If our writer didn't quite capture the essence of a place, tell us how you'd do it differently. If any of our descriptions are inaccurate or inadequate, we'll incorporate your changes in the next edition and will correct factual errors at fodors.com immediately.

Tell us what to include. You probably have had fantastic travel experiences that aren't yet in Fodor's. Why not share them with a community of like-minded travelers? Maybe you chanced upon a beach or bistro or B&B that you don't want to keep to yourself. Tell us why we should include it. And share your discoveries and experiences with everyone directly at fodors.com. Your input may lead us to add a new listing or highlight a place we cover with a "Highly Recommended" star or with our highest rating, "Fodor's Choice."

Give us your opinion instantly at our feedback center at www.fodors.com/feedback. You may also e-mail editors@fodors.com with the subject line "Shanghai Editor." Or send your nominations, comments, and complaints by mail to Shanghai Editor, Fodor's, 1745 Broadway, New York, NY 10019.

You and travelers like you are the heart of the Fodor's community. Make our community richer by sharing your experiences. Be a Fodor's correspondent.

Bon Voyage!

Tim Jarrell, Publisher

CONTENTS

MAPS

Fodor's Features

ABOUT THIS BOOK

Our Ratings

Sometimes you find terrific travel experiences and sometimes they just find you. But usually the burden is on you to select the right combination of experiences. That's where our ratings come in.

As travelers we've all discovered a place so wonderful that its worthiness is obvious. And sometimes that place is so unique that superlatives don't do it justice: you just have to be there to know. These sights, properties, and experiences get our highest rating, **Fodor's Choice**, indicated by orange stars throughout this book.

Black stars highlight sights and properties we deem **Highly Recommended**, places that our writers, editors, and readers praise again and again for consistency and excellence.

By default, there's another category: any place we include in this book is by definition worth your time, unless we say otherwise. And we will.

Disagree with any of our choices? Care to nominate a place or suggest that we rate one more highly? Visit our feedback center at www.fodors.com/feedback.

Budget Well

Hotel and restaurant price categories from ¢ to $$$$ are defined in the opening pages of each chapter. For attractions, we always give standard adult admission fees; reductions are usually available for children, students, and senior citizens. Want to pay with plastic? **AE, DC, MC, V** following restaurant and hotel listings indicate whether American Express, Diner's Club, MasterCard, and Visa are accepted.

Restaurants

Unless we state otherwise, restaurants are open for lunch and dinner daily. We mention dress only when there's a specific requirement and reservations only when they're essential or not accepted—it's always best to book ahead.

Hotels

Hotels have private bath, phone, and TV and operate on the European Plan (aka EP, meaning without meals), unless we specify that they use the Continental Plan (CP, with a continental breakfast), Breakfast Plan (BP, with a full breakfast), or Modified American Plan (MAP, with breakfast and dinner) or are all-inclusive (including all meals and most activities). We always list facilities but not whether you'll be charged an extra fee to use them, so when pricing accommodations, find out what's included.

Many Listings
★ Fodor's Choice
★ Highly recommended
⊠ Physical address
✛ Directions
🕮 Mailing address
☎ Telephone
🖷 Fax
⊕ On the Web
✍ E-mail
🎫 Admission fee
☉ Open/closed times
Ⓜ Metro stations
⊟ Credit cards

Hotels & Restaurants
🏨 Hotel
🛏 Number of rooms
♨ Facilities
🍽 Meal plans
✕ Restaurant
☖ Reservations
🚭 Smoking
🍸 BYOB
✕🏨 Hotel with restaurant that warrants a visit

Outdoors
⛳ Golf
⛺ Camping

Other
☺ Family-friendly
⇨ See also
⊠ Branch address
☞ Take note

Experience Shanghai

THE HEAD OF THE DRAGON

Tai Chi on the Bund

WORD OF MOUTH

"The architecture of Shanghai and definitely the river cruise [give] you a perspective of the old city vs. the new. It was extremely hot and humid and will be more so at the end of August. Have fun—an amazing part of the world."

—merlotnj

SHANGHAI PLANNER

City of the Future

As the most Westernized city in China after Hong Kong, Shanghai is at the forefront of China's modernization. It isn't an ancient Chinese city with loads of historic temples and ruins like Beijing. Almost a quarter of the world's construction cranes stand in this city. Still, architectural remnants of a colonial past survive along the winding, bustling streets that make this city undeniably and intimately Chinese.

When to Go

The best time to visit Shanghai is early fall, when the weather is good and crowds diminish. Although temperatures are scorching and the humidity can be unbearable, summer is the peak tourist season, and hotels and transportation can get very crowded. If possible, book several months in advance for summer travel.

Avoid the two main national holidays, Chinese New Year (which ranges from mid-January to mid-February) and the National Day holiday (during the first week of October), when 1.3 billion people are on the move.

Navigating

Shanghai is divided into east and west sides by the Huangpu River. The metro area is huge, but the city center is a relatively small district in Puxi (west of the river). On the east side lies the district that many think is Shanghai's future—Pudong (east of the river). The city is loosely laid out on a grid and most neighborhoods are easily explored on foot. Massive construction makes pavements uneven and the air dusty, but if you can put up with this, walking is the best way to really get a feel for the city and its people. Taxis are readily available and good for traveling longer distances, and the subway network is expanding every day.

Major east–west roads are named for Chinese cities and divide the city into *bei* (north), *zhong* (middle), and *nan* (south) sections. North–south roads divide the city into *dong* (east), *zhong* (middle), and *xi* (west) segments. The heart of the city is found on its chief east–west streets— Nanjing Lu, Huaihai Lu, and Yanan Lu.

■ TIP→ **Transport cards costing Y10 are available from the metro stations and can be charged with however much money you like. These can be used in taxis, on metros, and on some buses. They aren't discounted, but they'll save you time you would have spent joining queues and fumbling for cash.**

Navigating Vocabulary

Below are some terms you'll see on maps and street signs and in the name of most places you'll go:

Dong is east, **xi** is west, **nan** is south, **bei** is north, and **zhong** means middle. **Jie** and **lu** mean street and road respectively, and **da** means big.

Qiao, or bridge, is part of the place name at just about every entrance and exit on the ring roads.

Men, meaning door or gate, indicates a street that passed through an entrance in the fortification wall that surrounded the city hundreds of years ago. The entrances to parks and some other places are also referred to as *men*. For example, Xizhimen literally means Western Straight Gate.

Getting Around

By Taxi: Taxis are plentiful, cheap, and easy to spot. Your hotel concierge can call for one by phone or you can hail one on the street. Taxi stands are cropping up all over the city, but during peak hours or in rainy weather it's still every person for him- or herself, and fights for the free taxis can get physical. The available ones have a small lit-up sign on the passenger side. If you're choosing a cab from a line, peek at the driver's license on the dashboard. The lower the license number, the more experienced the driver. Drivers with a number below 200,000 can usually get you where you're going.

Most cab drivers don't speak English, so it's best to give them a piece of paper with your destination written in Chinese. (Keep a card with the name of your hotel on it handy for the return trip.) Hotel doormen can help you tell the driver where you're going. It's a good idea to study a map and have some idea of where you are, as some drivers will take you for a ride—a much longer one—if they think they can get away with it.

By Subway: The subway is a great way to get someplace fast without getting stuck in Shanghai's traffic-choked streets. As the subway is improved and extended, more English maps and exit signs are being included. The electronic ticket machines have an English option that provides maps in English so you can pick your destination.

Stations are clean and glass walls are being installed to protect passenger safety. If you aren't sure which exit to take, take any and negotiate your way when aboveground. In-car announcements for each station are given in both Chinese and English. Keep your ticket handy; you'll need to insert it into a second turnstile as you exit at your destination. Transport cards are swiped at entry and exit.

By Ferry: Ferries run around the clock every 10 minutes between the Bund and Pudong's terminal just south of the Riverside Promenade. The per-person fare is Y2 each way.

By Bus: Taking buses is not recommended as they are often crowded, slow, and nearly impossible to negotiate without speaking Chinese.

Opening Hours

Almost all businesses close for Chinese New Year and other major holidays.

Shops: Stores are generally open daily 10 to 7; some stores stay open as late as 10 PM, especially in summer.

Temples & Museums: Most temples and parks are open daily 8 to 5. Museums and most other sights are generally open 9 to 4, six days a week, with Monday being the most common closed day.

Banks & Offices: Most banks and government offices are open weekdays 9 to 5, but some close for lunch (between noon and 2). Bank branches and CITS tour desks in hotels often keep longer hours and are usually open Saturday morning. Many hotel currency-exchange desks stay open 24 hours.

Visitor Centers

China International Travel Service (CITS), an official government agency, maintains offices in many hotels and at some tourist venues.

China International Travel Service (CITS) (⊠ *1277 Beijing Xi Lu, Jing'an* ☎ *021/6289–4510* ⊕ *www.cits.net*).   **Shanghai Tourist Information Services** (⊠ *Yu Garden, 149 Jiujiaochang Lu, Huangpu* ☎ *021/6355–5032* ⊠ *Hongqiao International Airport* ☎ *021/6268–8899*).

TOP SHANGHAI ATTRACTIONS

Yu Garden
(A) When not too crowded, the Garden offers an atmosphere of peace and beauty amid the clamor of the city, with rocks, trees, and walls curved to resemble dragons, bridges, and pavilions.

The Bund
(B) Shanghai's famous waterfront boulevard is lined with art-deco buildings and souvenir stands. It's great for people-watching, being watched yourself, shopping for increasingly chic clothes, and sampling some of Shanghai's most famous restaurants. It's also where you'll get that postcard view of the futuristic skyline in Pudong.

Shanghai Museum
(C) China's best museum houses an incomparable collection of art and artifacts, including paintings, sculpture, ceramics, calligraphy, furniture, and fantastic bronzes.

Shopping on Nanjing Dong Lu
(D) People come from all over China to shop on what was once China's premier shopping street—and it sometimes feels as though they're all here at the same time. Although it's still a little tawdry, like a phoenix rising from the ashes, pedestrian-only Nanjing Dong Lu is undergoing a massive face-lift, and trendy designer boutiques are beginning to emerge alongside pre-1960s department stores and old-fashioned silk shops.

Oriental Pearl Tower or Jinmao Tower
(E) Choose between the 1960s *Jetsons* kitsch of the Pearl Tower or the pagoda-inspired Jin Mao. If you head to the top of either of these two Pudong skyscrapers, you'll be in for a bird's-eye view of

the city and its surroundings. Try to count the cranes working incessantly on restructuring the city's skyline. Cloud Nine is a bar at the top of the Grand Hyatt in the Jin Mao where you can sip a cocktail while looking out at the zillions of twinkling lights. At the time of writing, China's tallest building, the Shanghai World Financial Centre (Mori Tower), was not yet fully opened, but the view from the 101-story building will be awesome.

The Former French Concession
(F) Whether you're an architecture fanatic, a photographer, a romantic, or just plain curious, a wander through these streets is always a wonderful way to pass an afternoon. Fuxing Lu is a good long walk and the streets around Sinan Lu and Fuxing Park have some real architectural treats. Take your time and allow for breaks at cafés or in small boutiques.

Dongtai Lu Antiques Market
(G) This is an ideal spot for souvenir shopping, practicing your Chinese bargaining, and observing Shanghai life at its most charming. On any given day, you might be caught up in part of a wedding, see fat-cheeked babies, or watch old men bent over a game of chess.

Xintiandi
(H) Shopping, bars, restaurants, and museums mix together in restored traditional *shikumen* (stone gate) houses. Xintiandi is a popular location for hanging out and people-watching, and there are a few great boutiques. The small museums have interesting exhibits related to Shanghai's and the Communist Party's history.

GREAT ITINERARIES

Shanghai is fast and tough, so bring good shoes and a lot of patience. Don't expect the grandeur of ancient sights, but rather relish the small details like exquisitely designed art-deco buildings or laid-back cafés. Shanghai hides her gems well, so it's important to be observant and look up and around. The crowds of people and the constant change can make travelers weary, so take advantage of the wide range of eateries and convenient benches.

Best of Shanghai

On Day 1, start at **Yu Garden,** and take a walk through the old city streets and markets surrounding it. Next, head to **the Bund** for a waterfront stroll and a look at some of Shanghai's grandest historic buildings. Segue down **Nanjing Lu,** Shanghai's busiest street, for a spot of shopping. For dinner, check out New Heights at Three on the Bund for its view of the Bund lit up at night.

Head to **People's Square** on Day 2 and make your way to the **Shanghai Museum.** If you aren't suffering museum fatigue, choose from the other worthy offerings in this area, such as the **Urban Planning Exhibition Centre.** In the afternoon take a cab north to **Jade Buddha Temple** and to **M50** on Moganshan Lu to check out China's art scene. That night you can take a relaxing cruise along the Huangpu River or go dancing. Cocktails at Face is a calmer choice for those with sore feet.

Make a trip to Pudong in the morning of Day 3, and go to the top of the **Oriental Pearl Tower** for a bird's-eye view of the city. Relax on the riverfront promenade, or take the kids to the **Shanghai Aquarium** or **Century Park.** After lunch, take the wacky **Bund Tourist Tunnel** back to Puxi. In the afternoon, spend some time walking around the **Former French Concession** for a view of old Shanghai and the city's new chic stores. After dinner at Xintiandi, catch a show of the Shanghai acrobats.

Retail Therapy

Shanghai has possibly the best shopping on the mainland, from designer pieces to knockoff items picked up at market stalls. The Bund and the glamorous Plaza 66 are the up-and-coming designer areas. If you want something more "Chinese," the boutiques in and around Xintiandi offer very stylish fusion pieces. For those on a smaller budget, the Dongtai Lu Antiques Market is near Xintiandi while Taikang Lu offers funkier merchandise. The Shanghai Museum shop is also great for browsing and always has some wonderful treasures to remind you of your trip.

For the History Buff

You won't find much ancient history here—go to Beijing for that—but from the art-deco architectural gems on the Bund to the former homes of political luminaries in the Former French Concession, there are many venues to visit if you want to find out why Shanghai was once called the Paris of the East. Although massively restored, Xintiandi is composed of Shanghai's traditional shikumen homes. Around the Former French Concession area, streets like Shaoxing Lu are still relatively untouched by development. Finally, take a long walk through Hongkou District, down Sichuan Bei Lu where apartment blocks, bridges, and a huge post office still stand—testimony to the past glory of the city.

SHANGHAI WITH KIDS

Today's little emperors have all sorts of fun options for activities, from parks and museums to restaurants. Free English-language magazines such as City Weekend devote pages and sometimes entire issues to kids.

Century Park. Run them ragged in this large green space with pedal cars, cycling, roller-blading, and boating. When they get tired, take a picnic in the designated areas.

Aquaria 21. Kids can go scuba diving in this huge underground theme park with an emphasis on sea life. There are also exhibits on animals like whales and penguins.

Oriental Pearl Tower. Kids can survey the endless sprawl from the space-aged, kitschy, pink "pearls" and then check out the History Museum on the bottom floor. There's a restaurant at the top for lunch with a view.

Science and Technology Museum. Walk through an indoor rain forest and check out the IMAX cinemas along with a wide range of hands-on activities. There are also changing exhibitions that are often free of charge.

Shanghai Urban Planning Exhibition Centre. Marvel at the extensive models of Shanghai. Kids particularly love the IMAX virtual tour of the city. There are various, if somewhat tacky, multimedia displays and lots of maps and photos. In the basement is a street scene from Old Shanghai with shops and cafés.

Bund Tourist Tunnel. Take a psychedelic trip under the river in clear pods and see a light show that includes strobes, lasers, and tinsel. It isn't quite what one expects under a river, but it's good for a giggle.

Shanghai Acrobats. Children are usually delighted to watch the performers twist themselves into all sorts of challenging positions, squeeze into barrels, and spin plates on sticks. Just make sure they don't try this at home.

Super Brand Mall Ice Rink. For the little Chen Lu, Shanghai's giant Super Brand Mall offers ice-skating, cinema, and restaurants. Parents can shop while the kids skate.

Dining with Kids

Now that many expat families are moving to Shanghai, restaurants beyond the usual American fast-food chains have become more child-friendly. Some now have playing areas or children's menus. Also, in many local restaurants, the waitstaff is more than happy to play with kids. Just keep in mind that toilets might be a little dodgy. Blue Frog, Mesa, and O'Malleys are some of the city's most child-friendly restaurants; many of the foreign restaurants on Hongmei Lu also accommodate kids.

Other Experiences Kids Love

■ Take the 911 double-decker bus down Huaihai Lu for a bird's-eye view of the town.

■ Go fast on the Maglev from Pudong.

■ Fly a kite in People's Square.

■ Visit the fish and the birds at the Bird and Flower Market.

■ Cook your own food at a hotpot restaurant.

■ Buy new clothes and toys in the Puan Lu Children's Market.

SIGHTSEEING TOURS

Getting around Shanghai independently is the best way to see the city, and an increasing number of travelers are doing just that. Organized tours are usually rushed and on-again off-again in style, which is a shame as Shanghai really is a great city to walk around. Here are some day-tour options that might help you get your bearings on that stressful first afternoon.

Boat Tours

Huangpu River boat tours afford a great view of Pudong and the Bund, but after that it's mostly ports and cranes.

Huangpu River Cruises launches several small boats for one-hour daytime or nighttime cruises. The company also runs a 3½-hour trip up and down the Huangpu River between the Bund and Wusong, the point where the Huangpu meets the Yangzi River. You'll see barges, bridges, and factories, but not much scenery. All tours depart from the Bund at 239 Zhongshan Dong Lu. You can purchase all tickets at the dock or through CITS; prices range Y50 to Y150. ⊠ *153 Zhongshan Dong Er Lu (the Bund), Huangpu* ☎ *021/6374–4461.*

Shanghai Oriental Leisure Company runs 40-minute boat tours along the Bund from the Pearl Tower's cruise dock in Pudong. Prices range from Y50 to Y70, and tickets can be purchased at the gate to the Pearl Tower. Follow the brown signs from the Pearl Tower to the dock. ⊠ *Oriental Pearl Cruise Dock, 1 Shiji Dadao, Pudong* ☎ *021/5879–1888.*

Shanghai Scenery Co., Ltd. This company owns three boats that run one-hour tours along the Huangpu River starting from Yangzijiang Dock. Day tours cost Y50 and night tours, Y88–Y98. ⊠ *108 Huangpu Rd., Huangpu* ☎ *021/6356–1932* ⊕ *www.shanghaiscenery.com.*

Bus Tours

Grayline Tours has escorted half- and full-day coach tours of Shanghai as well as one-day trips to Suzhou, Hangzhou, and other nearby waterside towns. Prices range from around Y250 to Y1,000. ⊠ *A19, 2F Youth Centre Plaza, 1888 Hanzhong Lu, Putuo* ☎ *021/6150–8061* ⊕ *www.graylineshanghai.com.*

Jinjiang Tours runs a full-day bus tour of Shanghai that includes the French Concession, People's Square, Jade Buddha Temple, Yu Garden, the Bund, and Xintiandi. Tickets cost Y2,400 and the price includes lunch. ⊠ *161 Chang Le Lu, Luwan* ☎ *021/6415–1188* ⊕ *www.jjtravel.com.*

The Shanghai Sightseeing Bus Center has more than 50 routes; 10 include Shanghai's main tourist attractions. One-day trips range from Y30 to Y200. You can buy tickets up to a week in advance. The main ticket office and station, beneath Staircase No. 5 at Shanghai Stadium, has plenty of English signage to help you through the ticketing process. ⊠ *No. 5 Staircase, Gate 12, Shanghai Stadium, 666 Tianyaoqiao Lu, Xuhui* ☎ *021/6426–5555.*

Heritage Tours

Shanghai Jews. This half-day tour is available daily in Hebrew or English and takes visitors to the sites related to Shanghai's Jewish history. The cost is Y400 per person. ☎ *1300/214–6702* ⊕ *www.shanghai-jews.com.*

WHEN IN SHANGHAI . . .

. . . do as the Shanghainese. Or at least try. You may find it a lot harder to adopt the social customs in China than in Rome. Here are a few ways you can show your hosts that you're doing your best to blend.

Indulge in a Steamed Pork Dumpling

You can pick up *xiao long bao* (steamed pork dumpling) on the street—look for the steam coming out from a store or the giant bamboo baskets or at many restaurants. Be careful when you bite into them not to get hot juice in your lap as you'll look like a novice.

Strike a Bargain

There's nothing quite like negotiating a purchase price in a Chinese market. You can learn this valued Chinese skill by bargaining for something inexpensive, so you won't mind if you spend a little too much. Remember that saving face is everything when communicating in China. Smile constantly and remain pleasant. Avoid getting angry and making direct criticisms. Acting noncommittal about the item you desperately want might increase your bargaining power.

Get a Little Bit Closer

Get ready to shove, push, squeeze, and cut in line. You may think that a bus or a subway has no room for you, but then someone else will jump in front of you and find an opening. The Chinese have a different idea of personal space than Westerners, so crowding, bumping, and jostling in public are common. You may be annoyed at first, but if you can think like the Chinese, you may make it onto that crowded ferry without having to wait for the next one.

Give a Gift, Pay a Compliment

Visiting someone you know in Shanghai? If you come bearing a gift, offer it up with both hands to show respect. Expect it to be refused as much as three or four times before finally being accepted. Be persistent in offering it. The receiver may not open it in front of you, so don't insist. If your host or hostess speaks even a little English, be sure to compliment his or her use of it. Your host will probably deny this so be ready to insist gently and repeat the compliment.

Slurp Your Noodles

Your mother would scold you for your bad manners, but China is the perfect place to liberate yourself from rigid table etiquette. Get your head into the bowl, use your chopsticks to bring the noodles into your mouth and then suck them up with noisy gusto. It makes eating so much more fun.

Stare

The smallest of incidents will draw a crowd in China, so if you see a bunch of people massing, typically with hands folded behind their backs, get in there and have a look for yourself. You may find that people also look you up and down in the street, so join in and don't hold back on unabashed people-watching.

Got Phlegm?

Feel free to spit it out on the sidewalk. Although there have been efforts since the SARS scare in 2003 to decrease spitting, it's still quite a common practice, as is blowing your nose on to the street by holding one nostril while voiding the other. Such displays are slowly disappearing, however what is still de rigueur is spitting out bones when eating—either on the floor, your plate, or the table.

FREE THINGS TO DO

From booze to music and art, Shanghai has a lot to offer if you're a bit short on cash or just plain cheap.

Free Art

M50. The galleries at Moganshan Lu are all free. ⊠ *Putuo District, North Shanghai.*

Studio Rouge. This little gallery near the Bund always has the latest in Chinese art. ⊠ *17 Fuzhou Lu, Huangpu 200002* ☎ *021/6323–0833* ⌂ *Building 7, 50 Moganshan Lu, Putuo 200060* ☎ *1380/174–1782 (mobile).*

Wenmiao. On Sunday it only costs Y1 to get into the book market and see the temple. ⊠ *Huangpu District, Old City.*

■TIP➔ **No one will charge you for popping your head into buildings on the Bund such as the Bank of China or Bund 18 to catch a glimpse of the glorious marble interiors.**

Free Drinks

See Shanghai night owls at their wildest at ladies' nights all over town. Drinks for women are mostly free and unlimited (sorry, guys). Check out Barbarossa on Wednesday nights.

Free Shows

Free shows in Shanghai come and go. The best way to get information is to pick up a copy of one of the free English-language magazines at bars, restaurants, shops, and cafés around Shanghai.

Smartened up with a record store and bar, but still grungy and basic, Yuyintang is one of Shanghai's better music venues. On some nights, you'll be able to check out the bands for absolutely nothing.

Dark, sexy JZ club is open late with smooth jazz and blues, often for free.

Free Quintessential Experiences

Set aside some time for random wandering. Shanghai is a great walking city because so many of its real treasures are untouted: tiny alleyways barely visible on the map, garden squares, shopwindows, sudden vistas of skyline or park. With comfortable shoes, walking might become your favorite free activity.

Slip into one of Shanghai's numerous parks or green spaces, such as Fuxing Park or Lu Xun Park, to check out the older generation enjoying their retirement.

Watch elegant tai chi or the sweep of the brush as people practice their calligraphy on the sidewalk in water, not ink.

Take your camera and head to the Bund to get your essential shots of that Pudong skyline with the Oriental Pearl Tower sticking out there like a giant syringe. It's impressive during the day but magical at night.

Get online at the increasing numbers of restaurants and cafés that offer free wireless, including all branches of Wagas.

Get into the Chinese Festival spirit with traditional activities such as seeing the bell ringing at Longhua Temple for New Year, enjoying the lights in the Yu Garden for Lantern Festival at the end of the Chinese New Year, or gazing at the huge harvest moon for Mid-Autumn Festival.

GET A MASSAGE

In China, a massage isn't an indulgence; it's what the doctor orders. According to the tenets of traditional Chinese medicine, massage can help the body's *qi*, or energy, flow freely and remain in balance.

Of course, where you choose to have your massage can tip the scale toward indulgence. Around Shanghai are hundreds of blind massage parlors, inexpensive no-frills salons whose blind masseurs are closely attuned to the body's soft and sore spots. Be careful you haven't wandered into a brothel, though! At the other end of the spectrum lie the hotel spas, luxurious retreats where pampering is at a premium. Here are just a few of the massage outlets in Shanghai that can attend to your needs.

The **Banyan Tree Spa** (⊠ *Westin Shanghai, 88 Henan Zhong Lu, 3rd fl., Huangpu* ☎*021/6335–1888* ⊕*www.banyantree spa.com*), the first China outpost of this ultraluxurious spa chain, occupies the 3rd floor of the Westin Shanghai. The spa's 13 chambers as well as its treatments are designed to reflect *wu sing*, the five elemental energies of Chinese philosophy: earth, gold, water, wood, and fire. Relax and enjoy one of five different massages (Y820 plus service charge), facials, body scrubs, or indulgent packages that combine all three.

With instructions clearly spelled out in English, **Double Rainbow Massage House** (⊠*47 Yongjia Lu, Luwan* ☎*021/6473–4000*) provides a cheap (Y45–Y80), non-threatening introduction to traditional Chinese massage. Choose a masseur, state your preference for soft, medium, or hard massage, then keep your clothes on for a 45- to 90-minute massage. There's no

ambience, just a clean room with nine massage tables.

Dragonfly (⊠*20 Donghu Lu, Xuhui* ☎*021/5405–0008* ⊕*www.dragonfly. com.cn*) is one in a chain of therapeutic retreat centers that has claimed the middle ground between expensive hotel spas and workmanlike blind-man massage parlors. Don the suede-soft treatment robes for traditional Chinese massage (Y135), or take them off for an aromatic oil massage (Y225).

The Three on the Bund complex includes the first **Evian Spa** (⊠*Three on the Bund, Zhongshan Dong Yi Lu, Huangpu* ☎*021/6321–6622* ⊕*www.threeonthebund.com*) outside of France. Its 14 theme rooms offer treatments from head to toe, and nine different massages and a detox package (Y1,300) will ease the effects of pollution and late-night Shanghai partying.

With its exposed-wood beams, unpolished bricks, and soothing fountains, the **Mandara Spa** (⊠*399 Nanjing Xi Lu, Huangpu 200000* ☎*021/5359–4969* ⊕*www. mandaraspa.com*) in the JW Marriott resembles a traditional Chinese water town. Face, beauty, and body treatments include the spa's signature Mandara massage (Y990), a 75-minute treatment in which two therapists administer a blend of five massage styles: Shiatsu, Thai, Lomi Lomi, Swedish, and Balinese.

Ming Massage (⊠*298 Wulumuqi Nan Lu, Xuhui* ☎*021/5465–2501*) is a Japanese-style salon that caters to women, who receive a 20% discount daily from 11 to 4. Cross over the footbridge to one of five small treatment rooms for a foot, body, or combination "Ming" massage (Y178).

GOLF

With its own international tournament—the Volvo China Open—and several courses designed by prestigious names, Shanghai is making its mark on the golf scene. Approximately 20 clubs dot the countryside within a two-hour arc of downtown. All clubs and driving ranges run on a membership basis, but most allow nonmembers to play when accompanied by a member. A few even welcome the public. Most clubs are outside the city, in the suburbs and outlying counties of Shanghai.

Grand Shanghai International Golf and Country Club. This club has a Ronald Fream–designed 18-hole championship course and driving range. ✉ *18 Yangcheng Zhonglu, Yangcheng Lake Holiday Zone, Kunshan City, Jiangsu Province* ☎ *0512/5789–1999* ⊕ *www.grandshanghaigolf.com.cn.*

Shanghai Binhai Golf Club. Peter Thomson designed the Scottish links–style, 27-hole course at this club in Pudong. Another 27 holes are on the books. ✉ *Binhai Resort, Baiyulan Dadao, Nanhui County* ☎ *021/3800–1888 (reservation hotline)* ⊕ *www.binhaigolf.com.*

Shanghai International Golf and Country Club. This 18-hole course designed by Robert Trent Jones Jr. is Shanghai's most difficult. There are water hazards at almost every hole. ✉ *961 Yin Zhu Lu, Zhu Jia Jiao, Qingpu District* ☎ *021/5972–8111.*

Shanghai Links Golf and Country Club. This Jack Nicklaus–designed 18-hole course is about a 45-minute ride east of downtown. It's open to the public on Tuesday for Ladies' Day. ✉ *1600 Lingbai Lu, Tianxu Township, Pudong* ☎ *021/5897–3068* ⊕ *www.shanghailinks.com.cn.*

Shanghai Riviera Golf Resort. The late Bobby J. Martin designed this 18-hole course and driving range. ✉ *277 Yangtze Lu, Nanxiang Town, Jiading District* ☎ *021/5912–6888* ⊕ *www.srgr.cn.*

Shanghai Silport Golf Club. This club hosts the Volvo China Open. Its 27-hole course on Dianshan Lake was designed by Bobby J. Martin; a new 9 holes designed by Roger Packard opened in 2004. ✉ *1 Xubao Lu, Dianshan Lake Town, Kunshan City, Jiangsu Province* ☎ *0512/5748–1111* ⊕ *www.silport.com.cn.*

Shanghai Sun Island International Club. You'll find a 27-hole course designed by Nelson & Haworth plus an excellent driving range at this club. ✉ *2588 Shantai Lu, Zhu Jia Jiao, Qingpu District* ☎ *021/6983–3001* ⊕ *www.sunislandclub.com.*

Tianma Country Club. Tianma is the most accessible course to the public. Its 18 holes have lovely views of Sheshan Mountain. ✉ *3958 Zhaokun Lu, Tianma Town, Songjiang District* ☎ *021/5766–1666* ⊕ *www.tianmacc.com.*

Tomson Shanghai Pudong Golf Club. The closest course to the city center, Tomson has 18 holes and a driving range designed by Shunsuke Kato. Robert Trent Jones Jr. has inked a deal to develop the club's second course. ✉ *1 Longdong Dadao, Pudong* ☎ *021/5833–8888* ⊕ *www.tomson-golf.com.*

QUIRKY SHANGHAI

Learn about China
Get hands-on and dive into some Chinese culture lessons. Cook up a storm or try a hand at calligraphy.

Chinese Cooking Workshop runs cooking workshops in making dim sum and also cooking with a wok. It offers both private and group cooking lessons, and special guest chefs sometimes make appearances. ✉*1st fl., No. 35, 865 Yu Yuan Rd. and Room 2103, Bldg. 10, Lianyang Nianhua, La. 910, Dingxiang Rd., Mingsheng Rd., Pudong* ☎*021/5465–0730* ⊕*www. chinesecookingworkshop.com.*

China Culture Center offers a wide variety of cultural experiences, lectures, and travel schedules. Pull noodles, get into some meditation, or just brush up on your Mandarin while deepening your knowledge of this enigmatic land. ⊕ *www.chinaculturecenter.org.*

Artist **Chen Li Fan** holds calligraphy lessons in Da Marco, an Italian restaurant. ✉*103 Dongzhuanbang Lu* ☎*021/6210–4495.*

Go-Karting
Driving in Shanghai is pretty crazy, so it's best to leave it to the locals. However, the city does host the Grand Prix track, so live out your driving dreams with a go-kart. Checkered flag and Grand Prix babes optional.

DISC Kart. This is definitely not your father's go-kart. A lap on a 160cc cart around the tight indoor track can at times seem more like a demolition derby. ✉*809 Zaoyang Lu, Putuo* ☎*021/6222–2880* ⊕*www.kartingchina.com.*

Shanghai Hauge Racing Car Club. Races are a bit more civilized at this club. You are required to wear a helmet while racing its 50cc to 200cc go-karts around its large

outdoor track. ✉*880 Zhongshan Bei Yi Lu, Hongkou* ☎*021/6531–6800.*

Skiing
Shanghai isn't the first place one would expect to find skiing opportunities, especially since snow falls rarely. However, in the city that has everything, you can be a snow bunny, too.

Shanghai Yin Qi Xing Indoor Skiing Site. This innovative indoor venue brings winter fun to Shanghai's tropical climes. China's biggest indoor ski run has a gentle slope that is good for beginners, who can take snowboarding or skiing lessons in Chinese or Japanese. ✉*1835 Qixing Lu, Minhang* ☎*021/6478–8666* ⊕*www. yinqixing.com.*

Chinese Opera
Popular with the older set, Chinese opera can be squeaky, discordant, and difficult to follow. However, it's an important part of Chinese culture and the costumes and makeup are fantastic. There are different forms of Chinese opera including Kunju, Yueju, and probably the most well-known, Peking (Bejing) Opera. In Shanghai, Yueju Opera is very popular. Classics include *Butterfly Lovers*, a *Romeo and Juliet*–style tale, and *A Dream of Red Mansions* based on the classic Qing Dynasty novel by Cao Xueqin about the fate of a feudal family. Join the weekend crowd at the **Yifu Theatre.** ✉*701 Fuzhou Lu, Huangpu* ☎*021/6351–4668.*

SHANGHAI THEN & NOW

Shanghai, the most notorious of Chinese cities, once known as the Paris of the East, now calls itself the Pearl of the Orient. No other city can better capture the urgency and excitement of China's economic reform, understandably because Shanghai is at the center of it.

A port city, lying at the mouth of Asia's longest and most important river, Shanghai is famous as a place where internationalism has thrived. Opened to the world as a treaty port in 1842, Shanghai for decades was not one city but a divided territory. The British, French, and Americans each claimed their own concessions, neighborhoods where their laws and culture—rather than China's—were the rule.

By the 1920s and '30s, Shanghai was a place of sepia-lighted nightclubs, French villas, and opium dens. Here rich taipans walked the same streets as gamblers, prostitutes, and beggars, and Jews and Russians fleeing persecution lived alongside Chinese intellectuals and revolutionaries.

But now Shanghai draws more parallels to New York City than Paris. The Shanghainese have a reputation for being sharp, open-minded, glamorous, sophisticated, and business-oriented, and they're convinced they have the motivation and attitude to achieve their place as China's powerhouse. Far away from Beijing's watchful political eyes, yet supported by state officials who call Shanghai their hometown, the people have a freedom to grow that their counterparts in the capital don't enjoy. That ambition can be witnessed firsthand across Shanghai's Huangpu River, which joins the Yangzi at the northern outskirts of the city. Here lies Shanghai's most important building project—Pudong New Area, China's 21st-century financial, economic, and commercial center. Pudong, literally "the east side of the river," is home to Shanghai's stock-market building, one of the tallest hotels in the world, the city's international airport, and the world's first commercial "Maglev" (magnetic levitation) train. Rising from land that just a few years ago was dominated by farm fields is the city's pride and joy, the Oriental Pearl Tower—a gaudy, flashing, spaceship-like pillar—the tallest building in Asia. As Shanghai prepares to host the 2010 World Expo, Pudong is again immersed in a decade-long round of construction.

IMPORTANT DATES IN SHANGHAI'S HISTORY

1842	Signing of the Treaty of Nanjing at the end of the First Opium War gives the British the right to settle in selected Chinese cities, including Shanghai
1895	After defeating the Chinese in the Sino-Japanese War, the Japanese gain the right to engage in trade and set up factories in Shanghai
1922	The first meeting of the Chinese Communist Party is held in Shanghai
1937	Shanghai is bombed by the Japanese amidst their growing control of China

Puxi, the west side of the river and the city center, has also gone through staggering change. Charming old houses are making way for shiny high-rises. The population is moving from alley housing in the city center to spanking-new apartments in the suburbs. Architecturally spectacular museums and theaters are catching the world's attention. Malls are popping up on every corner. In 1987 there were about 150 high-rise buildings in the city. Today there are more than 3,000, and the number continues to grow. Shanghai is reputed to be home to one-fifth of all the world's construction cranes.

Shanghai's open policy has also made the city a magnet for foreign investors. As millions of dollars pour in, especially to Pudong, Shanghai has again become home to tens of thousands of expatriates. Foreign influence has made today's Shanghai a consumer heaven. Domestic stores rub shoulders with the boutiques of Louis Vuitton, Christian Dior, and Ralph Lauren. Newly made businessmen battle rush-hour traffic in their Mercedes and Lexus cars. Young people keep the city up until the wee hours as they dance the night away in clubs blasting techno music. And everyone walks around with a cell phone. It's not surprising that the Shanghainese enjoy one of the highest living standards in China. Higher salaries and higher buildings, more business and more entertainment—they all define the fast-paced lives of China's most cosmopolitan and open people.

1941	The Japanese take the International Settlement and intern foreign residents in prison camps
1945	Japan surrenders and the American military occupies Shanghai
1949	The People's Republic of China is born and the Communist People's Liberation Army enters Shanghai
1976	The death of Chairman Mao and the arrest and trial of the Gang of Four lead to the end of the Cultural Revolution
1978	Deng Xiaoping starts the process of opening up and reforming China
1990	Shanghai is officially chosen to be China's main hope for its economic future
2002	Shanghai wins the bid for the World Expo 2010

HOLIDAYS & FESTIVALS

Festivals in China are hard to pin down as the traditional ones are organized by the Chinese lunar calendar. This means they are often on different dates every year. For major holidays such as National Day, the government announces the official holiday period close to the event, which can be frustrating for those wishing to make travel plans. If you want to travel during major holiday times, remember to book well ahead and expect to pay a higher rate.

Chinese New Year: This is the biggest holiday of the year and usually occurs in January or February. Families get together to eat dumplings, and children are given new clothes and red envelopes with money inside. Fireworks displays are put on by the city, and you'll find traditional dance performances at the large temples. Things can get a little quiet commercially, however, as some businesses close during the weeklong holiday.

Lantern Festival: This falls soon after Chinese New Year. Lanterns in all shapes and sizes including rabbits and lotus flowers are lit. Special treats to eat include sweet dumplings called *yuanxiao* and *tangyuan*.

Qing Ming Festival: The tomb-sweeping festival takes place on the 4th or 5th of April each year and is now an official public holiday. On this day, Chinese people are supposed to visit their ancestors' graves and do a bit of maintenance.

May Day: This is the Chinese form of Labor Day and takes place in the first week of May, although the government has reduced the weeklong holiday to avoid overcrowding on transport and at tourist sites. Expect fireworks and massive crowds everywhere. Some businesses may also close as the owners take their own holiday.

Children's Day: It seems like every day is Children's Day for some of China's little emperors. However, they also get their own special day on June 1 with parties and special deals at various child-friendly establishments.

Dragon Boat Festival: Around 2,000 years ago, a poet named Qu Yuan threw himself into the river in protest against the emperor. To commemorate him, people now race dragon boats and eat *zongzi* (sticky rice dumplings). The date of this festival varies every year but is often in May or June and is one of China's new public holidays.

Seven Sisters Festival: The Chinese equivalent of Valentine's Day usually occurs in July or August. It is celebrated with romantic gifts and dinners but is not as commercialized as February 14th.

Mid-Autumn Festival: Based on a legend of a woman in the moon called Chang'e, families reunite to eat mooncakes and gaze upon the full moon during this festival. It usually takes place in September or October.

National Day: On October 1, 1949, Mao Zedong stood on Tiananmen Square and proclaimed that the people of China had stood up. This was the birth of the People's Republic of China. It's commemorated each year with a weeklong holiday. In Beijing, there are military parades in Tiananmen Square, but in Shanghai the action is limited to large crowds, a plethora of Chinese flags, and fireworks.

ON THE HORIZON

Shanghai changes almost daily. Go away for a holiday and your favorite café might have been completely renovated or your neighborhood convenience store torn down to accommodate yet more apartment blocks. The Pudong skyline was changed from rural to sci-fi in a mere decade. The future will bring even more developments and delights. So what's in the works now? Here's a taste:

The **Shanghai World Financial Center** being built in Pudong across the street from the Jinmao Tower is almost complete. Although it resembles a giant bottle opener in shape, at a planned 101 stories high, it's going to be one of the tallest buildings in the world. However, it may not loom large for long; next door a 1,903 foot tall, 118-story building is already going up.

The cultural behemoth that is the **World Expo** will hit Shanghai in 2010. Construction has been going crazy to clear and prepare the site in time for the event, and tickets are already on sale. Shanghai's slogan for the event—which showcases cultures from all over the world—is "Better City, Better Life." The blue mascot, Haibao, who looks like Gumby and Smurfette's rockabilly love child, is popping up everywhere. Shanghai's transport will soon improve dramatically as construction on the Shanghai Metro continues to expand with eight lines in action and a planned 11 lines to be built and in service by 2010. The Shanghai–Beijing high-speed rail link, reducing the journey from 14 hours to five, is set to be passenger-ready by 2010.

On Chongming Island in the Yangzi, the **Dongtan Eco-City** and areas for ecological tourism are being developed. By 2010, the demonstrator phase of Dongtan Eco-City is projected to have a population of 10,000 and be the world's first purpose-built ecologically sustainable city.

Rumors are still rife that Shanghai will get its own **Disneyland,** but this isn't due to happen until at least 2012. In the meantime, there's rumor of a **Universal Studios** to pave the way, although nothing much has happened since the government signed an agreement in 2002.

21ST ★
CENTURY
CHINA

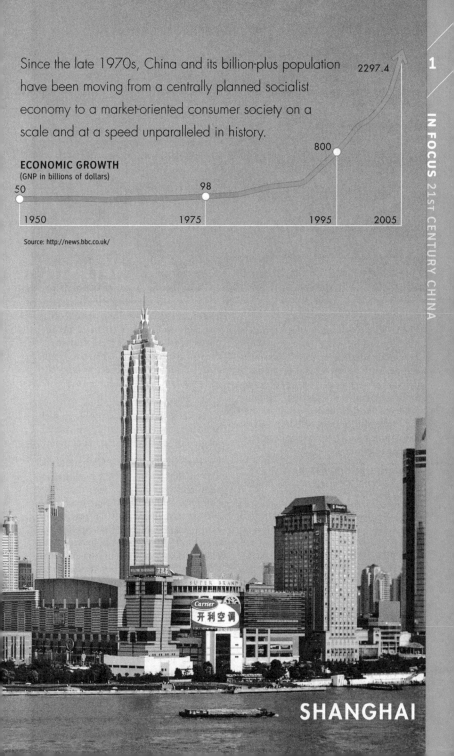

Since the late 1970s, China and its billion-plus population have been moving from a centrally planned socialist economy to a market-oriented consumer society on a scale and at a speed unparalleled in history.

ECONOMIC GROWTH
(GNP in billions of dollars)

2297.4

800

98

50

1950   1975   1995   2005

Source: http://news.bbc.co.uk/

SHANGHAI

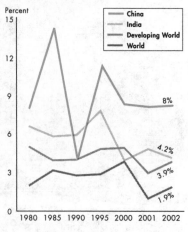

BEIJING

A Chinese Century?

The SARS hiccup aside, China's economy has been red-hot since joining the World Trade Organization in 2001. One of the engines driving the global economy, it helped revive Japan's sagging economy and the slumping international shipping industry. Worldwide commodities markets have also been boosted by China's increasing hunger for everything from copper to coffee.

GDP-ANNUAL GROWTH RATE

Percent

China
India
Developing World
World

15

12

9   8%

6

4.2%

3   3.9%

1.9%

0
1980 1985 1990 1995 2000 2001 2002

Source: World Bank/Earth Trends

The country that was long written off as just a cheap exporter is now a net importer. It's the fourth-largest economy in the world after the United States, Japan, and Germany, whose economies are growing at less than half the rate.

Such development is nothing short of remarkable, but national problems such as energy, the environment, and wealth inequality are threatening the country.

Internationally, it's how China and the United States cooperate on global issues, and how they manage their own complex relationship, that may have the greatest impact on the rest of the century. Since Nixon first opened the door in 1972, the two countries have managed to forge a working relationship. But Yuan revaluation, trade issues, energy supply (especially oil), and both countries' military role in the Asia-Pacific region are all issues that could sour this budding friendship.

(top) Architectural stars (or starchitects) like Rem Koolhaas, Li Hu, Paul Andreu, and Jacques Herzog and Pierre de Meuron (Olympic Stadium, above) are descending on Beijing for construction of state-of-the-art Olympic venues. (right) Hong Kong skyline.

HONG KONG

Fueling the Chinese Dream

China is now the number–two energy consumer in the world, after the United States. Its consumption has exploded by an average of 5% yearly since 1998. This thirst for fuel is evident on roads all over the country. The land of the bicycle is now car-crazy. Three million vehicles were recently sold, and higher sales are predicted in the coming years.

Back in 2005, the country consumed 320 million tons of crude oil, roughly one third of which was imported. It's expecting to import 500 million tons by 2020, two thirds of its projected total imports.

Where will China get this oil? Much comes from countries with troubled relations with the West such as Iran and Sudan, but it is also working on importing more from traditional U.S. suppliers such as Saudi Arabia.

There's also a growing demand for electricity, 75% of which comes from coal. In the coming 25 years, the greenhouse gases produced by China's coal burning will probably exceed that of all industrial nations combined. And the country will continue to rely on coal for electricity in the years to come, despite large hydropower projects and a plan to increase the number of nuclear power plants.

Aside from developing clean, renewable energy sources, China needs to improve its poor energy efficiency—it uses nine times the energy Japan does to produce one GDP unit. But plans are being made to improve energy efficiency by 20% by 2010.

WORLD OIL CONSUMPTION

USA 24.8%

Rest of the World 50.7%

China 7.9%

Japan 6.9%

Russia 3.5%

Germany 3.3%

India 2.9%

Source: http://www.nationmaster.com/

Can China Go Green?

A devastated environment is a major result of China's economic transformation. For example, because of deforestation around the capital, Beijing is threatened by the encroaching Gobi Desert, which dumped 300,000 tons of sand on the city in one week in 2006. Industrial carelessness and lack of regulation result in accidents such as the 50-mile benzene spill in a river near Harbin in late 2005.

Cities have been smoggy for decades because of pollution from factories, vehicles, and especially coal. But air quality is now becoming obscured by water issues. In mid-2006 the Water Resources Ministry reported that 320 million urban residents—more than the population of the United States—did not have access to clean drinking water.

Much of this is the result of a development-at-any-cost mentality, particularly in the wake of economic reform. Companies and factories, many of which are foreign-owned, have only recently had to deal with environmental laws— "scoff laws"—that are often circumvented by bribing local officials. And average citizens don't have freedom of speech or access to political tools to fight environmentally damaging projects.

Is the central government waking up? In 2006 the vice-chairman of China's increasingly outspoken State Environmental Protection Agency put it bluntly: "We will face tremendous problems if we do not change our development patterns."

Mind the Gap

China has come a long way from the days when everyone had an "iron rice bowl," or a state-appointed job that was basically guaranteed regardless of one's abilities or work performance.

Since 1980, the country has quadrupled per capita income and raised more than 220 million of its citizens out of poverty. A belt of prosperity is emerging along the coast, but hundreds of millions still live on less than $1 per day.

(left) Owning a car is the new Chinese dream. (top right) The Three Gorges Dam will be the largest in the world, supplying the hydroelectric power of 18 nuclear plants. (bottom right) China's cities are some of the most polluted in the world.

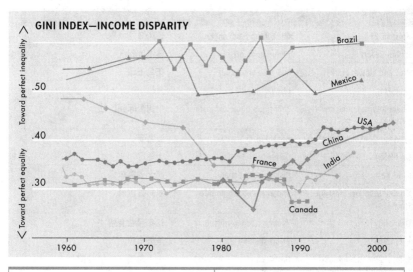

GINI INDEX—INCOME DISPARITY

Toward perfect inequality ∧

Toward perfect equality ∨

.50 .40 .30

Brazil
Mexico
USA
China
France
India
Canada

1960   1970   1980   1990   2000

Economists use a statistical yardstick known as the Gini coefficient to measure wealth inequality in a society, with zero being perfect equality and one being perfect inequality. The World Bank estimates that China's national Gini coefficient rose from 0.30 to 0.45 from 1982, a 50% jump in two decades. In 2006, some academics estimated China's current Gini coefficient to be closer to, or even higher, than Latin America's 0.52.

As economic inequality has grown, so has discontent, particularly in rural areas. The country recorded 87,000 public protests in 2005, an increase of 11,000 over the year before.

Many of these protests are incited by the acts of local, particularly rural, officials whose corruption policies are sometimes beyond Beijing's sphere of influence.

Most protests are focused on specific incidents or officials rather than general dissent against the government, but the growing frequency of such events is not going unnoticed by the central government. In 2005, 8,400 officials were arrested on corruption-related charges.

CHINA IN NUMBERS

	CHINA	U.S.
Area in sq km:	9,560,960	9,631,420
Population	1.3 bil	300 mil
Men (15–64 yrs)	482 mil	100 mil
Women (15–64 yrs)	456 mil	101 mil
Population growth	0.59%	0.91%
Life expectancy: men	70.8	75
Life expectancy: women	74.6	80.8
GDP per head	$1,090	$37,240
Health spending, % GDP	5.8	14.6
Doctors per 1000 pop.	1.6	3.0
Hospital beds per 1000 pop.	23.12	6.43
Infant mortality rate per 1000 births	2.1	5.7
Education spending, % GDP	95.1%	99%
Adult literacy: men	86.5%	
Adult literacy: women		99%
Internet users	111 mil	204 mil

ENGLISH NAME	PINYIN	CHINESE CHARACTERS
Aquaria 21	Chángfēng hǎidǐ shìjiè	长风海底世界
Binhai Resort	Bīnhai dùjià qū	滨海度假区
Bird and Flower Market	huā niǎo shì chǎng	花鸟市场
Blue Frog	Lánwā	蓝蛙
China International Travel Service	Zhōngguó guójì lǚxíngshè	中国国际旅行社
Chinese Cooking Workshop	Bōsàidùn	波塞顿
Da Marco	Dàmakě	大马可
DISC Kart	Díshìke sàichēchǎng	迪士卡赛车场
Double Rainbow Massage House	Shuāngchǎihong ànmúo	双彩虹按摩
Dragonfly	Yōuting bǎojiàn huìsuǒ	悠亭保健会所
Evian Spa	Yīyún shuǐliáo	依云水疗
Grand Shanghai International Golf and Country Club	Dàshànghai gúojì gāoěrfū dùjiàcūn	大上海国际高尔夫度假村
Grayline Tours	huīxiàn lǚyóu	灰线旅游
Hangzhou	Hángzhōu	杭州
Hongqiao International Airport	Shànghai hóng qiáo guó jì jī chǎng	上海虹桥国际机场
Huangpu River Cruises	Pǔjiang yóulan	浦江游览
Jinjiang Tours	Jīnjiāng lǚyóu	锦江旅游
Maglev	Mǎ gē lè fú	玛格勒福
Mandara Spa	Màndámèng shuǐliáo	蔓达梦水疗
Mesa	Méisà	梅萨
Ming Massage	Míngyī ànmó	明一按摩
O'Malley's	Ōumǎlì	欧玛莉
People's Square	rénmín guǎngchǎng	人民广场
Shanghai Acrobats	Shànghǎi zajìtuán	上海杂技团
Shanghai Binhai Golf Club	Shànghǎi bīnhǎi gāoěrfū jùlèbù	上海滨海高尔夫俱乐部
Shanghai Hauge Racing Car Club	Shànghǎi qǔyáng kǎdīngchē jùlèbù	上海曲阳卡定车俱乐部
Shanghai International Golf and Country Club	Shànghǎi gǔjì gāoěrfū xiāngcūn jùlèbù	上海国际高尔夫球乡村俱乐部
Shanghai Jews	Shànghǎi yoūtàirén	上海犹太人
Shanghai Links Golf and Country Club	Shànghǎi lìnkěsī gāoěrfū xiāngcūn jùlèbù	上海林克司高尔夫乡村俱乐部
Shanghai Oriental Leisure Company	Shànghǎi mìngzhū shuǐshàng yúlè fāzhān yǒuxiàn gōngsī	上海明珠水上娱乐发展有限公司

ENGLISH NAME	PINYIN	CHINESE CHARACTERS
Shanghai Riviera Golf Resort	Shànghǎi dōngfāng bālí gāoěrfū xiāngcūn jùlèbù	上海东方巴黎高尔夫乡村俱乐部
Shanghai Scenery Co.	Shànghǎi fēngcǎi	上海风采
Shanghai Sightseeing Bus Centre	Shànghǎi lǚyóu jísàn zhōngxīn	上海旅游集散中心
Shanghai Silport Golf Club	Shànghǎi xūbǎo gāoěrfū jùlèbù	上海旭宝高尔夫俱乐部
Shanghai Stadium	Shànghǎi tǐ yù guǎn	上海体育馆
Shanghai Sun Island International Club	Shànghǎi tàiyǎngdǎo gāoěrfū jùlèbù	上海太阳岛高尔夫俱乐部
Shanghai Tourist Information Services	Shànghǎi lǚyóu zīxún fúwù zhōngxīn	上海旅游咨询服务中心
Shanghai World Financial Centre	Shànghǎi shìjiè jīnróng zhōngxīn	上海世界金融中心
Shanghai Yin Qi Xing Indoor Skiing Site	Shànghǎi yǐnqīxīn shìnèi huáxuěchǎng	上海银七星室内滑雪场
Super Brand Mall Ice Rink	Sīkǎitè Zhèngdà zhēnbīng líubīngchǎng	司凯特正大真冰溜冰场
Suzhou	Sūzhōu	苏州
Tianma Country Club	Shànghǎi tiānmǎ gāoěrfū xiāngcūn jùlèbù	上海天马高尔夫乡村俱乐部
Tomson Shanghai Pudong Golf Club	Tāngchén Shànghǎi Pǔdōng gāoěrfū qiúchǎng	汤臣上海浦东高尔夫球场
Yangcheng Lake Holiday Zone	Yángchénghú dùjiàqū	阳澄湖度假区
Yifu Theatre	Yìfū wǔtái	逸夫舞台
Districts		
Changning District	Chángníng qū	长宁区
Huangpu District	Huǎngpǔ qū	黄浦区
Jing'an District	Jìng'ān qū	静安区
Lujiazui	Lùjiazuǐ lù	陆家嘴路
Luwan District	Lúwān qū	卢湾区
Minhang District	Mǐnháng qū	闵行区
Pudong South Road	Pǔdóng nán lù	浦东南路
Putuo District	Pǔtuó qū	普陀区
Puxi	Pǔxī	浦西
Xuhui District	Xúhuì qū	徐汇区
Zhabei District	Zháběi qū	闸北区

ENGLISH NAME	PINYIN	CHINESE CHARACTERS
Important Streets		
Duolun Road	Duōlún lù	多伦路
Fangbang Road	Fāngbāng lù	方浜路
Fuzhou Road	Fúzhōu lù	福州路
Guangdong Road	Guǎngdōng lù	广东路
Jinling Road	Jinlíng lù	金陵路
Julu Road	Jùlù lù	巨鹿路
Maoming Road	Màomíng lù	茂名路
Moganshan Road	Mògānshān lù	莫干山路
Nanjing Road	Nánjīng lù	南京路
Nanjing Xi Lu (Nanjing West Road)	Nánjīng xī lù	南京西路
Renmin Dadao (Renmin Ave)	Rénmin dàdào	人民大道
Shaanxi Nan Lu (Shaanxi South Road)	Shǎnxi nǎn lŭ	陕西南路
Xintiandi	Xīntiāndì	新天地
Zhongshan Dong Yi Lu (Zhongshan East No. 1 Road)	Zhōngshān dōng yī lù	中山东一路
Zhongshan Xi Lu (Zhongshang West Road)	Zhōngshān xī lù	中山西路

Neighborhoods

Yuyuan Garden

WORD OF MOUTH

"Shanghai may not be an old city in Chinese terms, but it has a fascinating history nonetheless, with strong links to the 19th century European incursions into China and the Communist revolution. There are interesting reminders of those times—the French Concession and the Bund, [and] the former houses of Sun Yatsen and Zhou Enlai . . . The fine art museum at Renmin Park is also well worth a visit."

—Neil_Oz

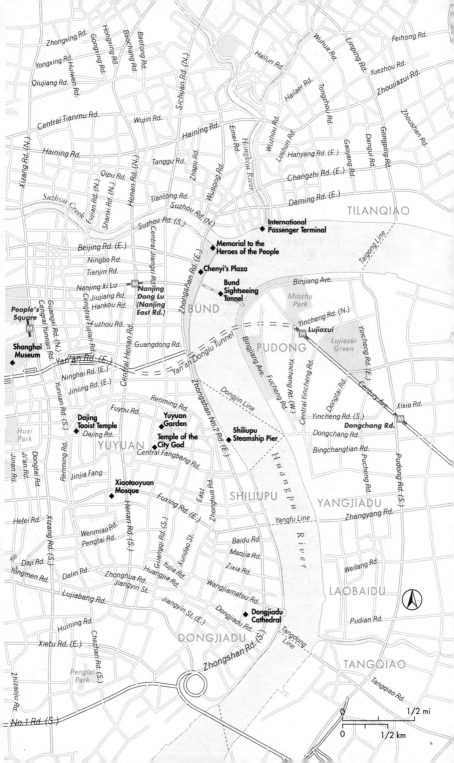

SHANGHAI, OR "CITY ABOVE THE SEA," lies on the Yangzi River delta, and until 1842 it was a small fishing village. After the first Opium War the village was carved up into autonomous concessions administered concurrently by the British, French, and Americans. Each colonial presence brought with it its particular culture, architecture, and society, marking the beginning of Shanghai's openness to Western influence.

In its heyday, Shanghai had the best art, the greatest architecture, and the strongest business in Asia. With dance halls, brothels, glitzy restaurants, international clubs, and a racetrack, it catered to the rich. The Paris of the East was known as a place of vice and indulgence. Amid this glamour and degradation the Communist Party held its first meeting in 1921.

In the 1930s and '40s, the city weathered raids, invasions, and occupation by the Japanese. By 1943, at the height of World War II, most foreigners had fled. After the war's end, Nationalists and Communists fought a three-year civil war for control of China. The Communists declared victory in 1949 and established the People's Republic of China.

Between 1950 and 1980 Shanghai's industries soldiered on through periods of extreme famine and drought, reform, and suppression. Politically, the city was central to the Cultural Revolution and the Gang of Four's base. The January Storm of 1967 purged many of Shanghai's leaders, and Red Guards set out to destroy the "Four Olds": old ways of idea, living, traditions, and thought.

In 1972, with the Cultural Revolution still going, Shanghai hosted the historic meeting between Premier Zhou Enlai and U.S. president Richard Nixon. They signed the Shanghai Communiqué, which encouraged China to open talks with the United States and the rest of the world.

In 1990 China's leader, Deng Xiaoping, chose Shanghai as the center of the country's commercial renaissance, and it has again become one of China's most open cities ideologically, socially, culturally, and economically.

Today, beauty and charm coexist with kitsch and commercialism. From the colonial architecture of the Former French Concession to the forest of cranes and the neon-lit high-rises of Pudong, Shanghai is a city of paradox and change.

■TIP➜Shanghai is a sprawling city with large districts. We have created a series of smaller neighborhoods, centered on the main attractions. You still need to know the official districts when dealing with hotels, taxis, and tourist resources, so official districts are listed at the end of each entry.

2

OLD CITY

Sightseeing
★★★
Nightlife
★
Dining
★★
Lodging
★★
Shopping
★★★★

Tucked away in the east of Puxi are the remnants of Shanghai's Old City. Once encircled by a thick wall, a fragment of which still remains, the Old City has a sense of history among its fast disappearing old *shikumen* (stone gatehouses), temples, and markets. Delve into narrow alleyways where residents still hang their washing out on bamboo poles and chamber pots are still in use. Burn incense with the locals in small temples, sip tea in a teahouse, or get a taste of Chinese snacks and street food. This is the place to get a feeling for Shanghai's past, but you'd better get there soon, as the wrecker's ball knows no mercy.

WHAT'S HERE

Wenmiao is a short cab ride (or a 30-minute walk) from the **Huangpi Nan Lu** metro station. You can see in the surrounding areas where whole blocks of Shanghai's architectural heritage have been razed in the name of progress. **Wenmiao** is on a small street lined with trinket shops popular with students. The interior of the temple is cool and calm except during the Sunday book market. You can walk from here to the **Yu Garden** complex. The side streets are buzzing with life. Old people recline in chairs and fan themselves in the summer heat, and dogs and children play in the streets under haphazardly strung washing lines. Sadly, many of these buildings bear the character that indicates that they are soon to be demolished.

If you enter the Yu Garden area at **Dajing Lu,** you'll come across what is left of the **Old City Wall** that once encircled the city. Inside the Yu Garden complex itself are several sights, but be prepared for crowds, particu-

GETTING ORIENTED

BUND

Yan'an Rd. (E.)

Ninghai Rd. (E.)

Yunnan Rd. (S.)

Jinling Rd. (E.)

Xizang Rd. (S.)

Henan Rd. (S.)

Yan'an Dongliu Tunnel

Jinling Rd. (E.)

Renming Lu

Dongjin Line

Fuyou Rd.

Chen Xiangge Temple ◆

Dajing Taoist Temple ◆

Old City Wall ◆ Dajing Rd.

Yu Garden ◆

Gucheng Park

YUYUAN

Huxinting Tea House ◆

Shiliupu Steamship Pier ◆

Temple of the City God ◆

Fangbang Lu

Renming Lu

Jinjia Fang

Zhongshan No.2 Rd. (E.)

Dongtai Rd.

Xiaotaoyuan Mosque ◆

Fuxing Rd. (E.)

Henan Rd. (S.)

East St.

Zhonghua Rd.

SHILIUPU

Zhonghua Rd.

NANSHI

Bai Yun Guan Temple ◆

Wenmiao Rd.

Pengtai Rd.

LAO XIMEN

Xilin Rd.

Daji Rd.

Dalin Rd.

Zhonghua Rd.

Jiangyin St.

Guangqi Rd. (S.)

Qiaojia Rd.

Yujia Rd.

Xundao St.

Zhonghua Rd.

Miezhu Rd.

Watcango Jiao St.

Baidu Rd.

Maojia Rd.

Zixia Rd.

Huangjia Rd.

Wangjiamatou Rd.

Lujiabang Rd.

Jiangyin St. (E.)

Dongjiadu Rd.

Dongjiadu Cathedral ◆

Huining Rd.

DONGJIADU

Xietu Rd. (E.)

Guohuo Rd.

Lujiabang Rd.

Duojia Rd.

Sanmenxia Rd.

Chezhan Rd. (S.)

Penglai Park

Zhongshan No.1 Rd. (S.)

Zhongshan Rd. (S.)

Waima Rd.

| 0 | | 1/4 mi |
| 0 | | 1/4 km |

GETTING HERE

At press time, Shanghai's ever-expanding metro system had not yet reached Old City, but you can see it being built. However, it's a short walk east from Nanjing Dong Lu station on Line 2, and a slightly longer, but interesting, walk south from Huangpi Nan Lu on Line 1. ■TIP→ **Be warned that taxis are nearly impossible to find in this area when you want to leave.**

TOP REASONS TO GO

Shanghai's backstreets: Step back in time by wandering through the narrow alleys before their imminent destruction.

Wenmiao: Shanghai's only Confucian temple has a buzzing Sunday book market and great street food just outside.

Yu Garden: Get your souvenir shopping done at this hectic mix of souvenir shops, old buildings, and teahouses.

Huxingting Teahouse: Choose from a wide selection of teas, listen to Chinese classical music, and watch the consumer madness below.

South Bund Soft Spinning Material Market: Drape yourself in silks and brocades and have a little something whipped up by a tailor.

QUICK BITES

The **Huxinting Teahouse** (✉*257 Yuyuan Lu, Huangpu* ☎*021/6373–6950 downstairs, 021/6355–8270 upstairs*) is Shanghai's oldest. Although tea is cheaper on the 1st floor, be sure to sit on the top floor by a window overlooking the lake.

On the west side of the central man-made lake in Yu Garden is **Nanxiang Steamed Bun Restaurant** (✉*85 Yuyuan Lu, Huangpu* ☎*021/6326–5265*), a great dumpling house famed for its *xiao long bao* (steamed pork dumplings).

MAKING THE MOST OF YOUR TIME

This area could take a very long afternoon or morning as it's a good one to do on foot, especially if you're interested in photography. Browsing the shops in and around the Yu Garden might add a couple of hours, although a confirmed shopaholic could extend that time period indefinitely. If you take a cab between areas, half a day should be sufficient.

SAFETY

Pickpockets are the main problem in Old City. Keep your belongings close at hand and zip valuables away, especially in crowded areas.

NEAREST PUBLIC RESTROOMS

Although not exactly public, the toilet in McDonald's on Fuyou Lu and Lishui Lu is the closest you will get to a decent bathroom. It's clean enough on a good day, but bring your own toilet paper.

A GOOD WALK

More a wander than a walk, it's well worthwhile to head into the remaining backstreets around the Yu Garden to see life in the shikumen gatehouses. Just take a side street and off you go.

A BRIEF HISTORY

This area of the city has been inhabited for over 2,000 years. It started out as a fishing town, but when Shanghai was carved up by foreign powers, one part of the central city remained under Chinese law and administration. Surrounded by the ring road of Renmin Lu/Zhonghua Lu, these old winding back alleys eventually became notorious as gangster- and opium-filled slums until the Communists cleaned up the area. Today the vices have disappeared for the most part and only the narrow meandering lanes and a dwindling number of tiny, pre-1949 shikumen houses are still standing. Rapid development means that the Old City is fast losing its historical buildings and laneways to be replaced by ugly apartment blocks.

larly on the weekend when you can hardly move. It's worth a look, although to be honest, the garden is terribly crowded and not the finest example of a Chinese garden (the ones in Suzhou are more interesting). Stop at the elegant **Huxinting Teahouse** for a rest from the madness and then wend your way around the shops to the **Cheng Huang Miao**, the larger of the two temples, and a Taoist one to boot. If you're lucky, you might catch a live performance of music or dance on your way.

You can do your souvenir shopping at the myriad of shops that surround the bazaar, but one of the best places to check out is the **Cang Bao Antiques Building** on **Fangbang Lu**. On the way, stop off at the tiny **Chen Xiangge Temple**, which is run by nuns. For modern items ranging from Hello Kitty slippers to rather large and sensible looking underwear, visit the large markets on **Fuyou Lu**.

If you have the energy, walk the **Renmin/Zhonghua** loop road around until you get to **Dongjiadu Lu** where you'll find **Dongjiadu Cathedral**, built in 1849. Finally, about 1640 feet south is the new **South Bund Soft-Spinning Material Market**, where you can browse among bolts of silks and other fabrics and have clothes made.

WHAT TO SEE

Chen Xiangge Temple. If you find yourself passing by this tiny temple on your exploration of the Old City, you can make an offering to Buddha with the free incense sticks that accompany your admission. Built in 1600 by the same man who built Yu Garden, it was destroyed during the Cultural Revolution and rebuilt in the 1990s. The temple is now a nunnery, and you can often hear the women's chants rising from the halls beyond the main courtyard. ⊠*29 Chenxiangge Lu, Huangpu* ☎*021/6320–0400* ✉*Y5* ♡*Daily 7–4.*

Old City Wall. The Old City used to be completely surrounded by a wall, built in 1553 as a defense against Japanese pirates. Most of it was torn down in 1912, except for one 50-yard-long piece that still stands at Dajing Lu and Renmin Lu. You can walk through the remnants and check out the rather simple museum nearby, which is dedicated to the history of the Old City (the captions are in Chinese). Stroll through the tiny neighboring alley of Dajing Lu for a lively panorama of crowded market life in the Old City. ✉*269 Dajing Lu, at Renmin Lu, Huangpu* ☎*021/6326–6171* ✆*Y5* ⏱*Daily 9–4:30.*

Temple of the City God. *(Chenghuang Miao)* Lying at the southeast end of the bazaar. This Taoist Temple of the City God was built during the early part of the Ming Dynasty and was later destroyed by fire in 1924. The main hall was rebuilt in 1926 and has been renovated many times over the years. Inside are gleaming gold figures, and atop the roof you'll see statues of crusading warriors—flags raised, arrows drawn. ✉*Xi Dajie Lu, Huangpu* ☎*021/6386–8649* ✆*Y10* ⏱*Daily 8:30–4:30.*

Fodor'sChoice
★

Yu Garden. Since the 18th century, this complex, with its traditional red walls and upturned tile roofs, has been a marketplace and social center where local residents gather, shop, and practice *qi gong* in the evenings. Although a bit overrun by tourists and not as impressive as the ancient palace gardens of Beijing, Yu Garden is a piece of Shanghai's past, and one of the few old sights left in the city.

To get to the garden itself, you must wind your way through the bazaar. The garden was commissioned by the Ming Dynasty official Pan Yun-duan in 1559 and built by the renowned architect Zhang Nanyang over 19 years. When it was finally finished it won international praise as "the best garden in southeastern China." In the mid-1800s the Society of Small Swords used the garden as a gathering place for meetings. It was here that they planned their uprising with the Taiping rebels against the French colonists. The French destroyed the garden during the first Opium War, but the area was later rebuilt and renovated.

Winding walkways and corridors bring you over stone bridges and carp-filled ponds and through bamboo stands and rock gardens. Within the park are an **old opera stage,** a **museum** dedicated to the Society of Small Swords rebellion, and an **exhibition hall,** opened in 2003, of Chinese calligraphy and paintings. One caveat: the park is almost always thronged with Chinese tour groups, especially on weekends. As with most sights in Shanghai, don't expect a tranquil time alone. ✉*218 Anren Lu, bordered by Fuyou Lu, Jiujiaochang Lu, Fangbang Lu, and Anren Lu, Huangpu* ☎*021/6326–0830 or 021/6328–3251* ⊕*www. yugarden.com.cn* ✆*Y40* ⏱*Gardens daily 8:30–5.*

XINTIANDI & THE CITY CENTER

Sightseeing
★★★★
Nightlife
★★★
Dining
★★★★
Lodging
★
Shopping
★★★★

Xintiandi is Shanghai's showpiece restoration project. Reproduction shikumen houses contain expensive bars, restaurants, and chic boutiques. It's at its most magical on a warm night when locals, expats, and visitors alike pull up a chair at one of the outside seating areas and watch the world go by. Nearby, the area around People's Square has some magnificent examples of modern and historical architecture and a smattering of some of Shanghai's best museums. The adjoining People's Park is a pleasant green space where it's possible to escape the clamor of the city for a while.

WHAT'S HERE

As you come out of **People's Square** metro station, look up at the varied skyline including the UFO-like **Radisson** building and the art-deco **Park Hotel.** You have to admit, Shanghai really knows how to do skyscrapers.

Once aboveground, head for the **Shanghai Museum,** the city's largest. It's best explored when energy levels are still high. Be prepared for long lines now that admission is free. Wander among ancient bronzes and divine ceramics, and pick up some gifts at the great museum store. After that, at the **Shanghai Urban Planning Center,** children will particularly enjoy the virtual tour of Shanghai, and the master-plan model of the city is truly mind-boggling. As you go toward the art museum, gaze up at the **Grand Theatre,** which is particularly splendid when it's lit up at night. Head down **Huangpi Bei Lu** and then into **Nanjing Xi Lu.** Here you'll find the **Shanghai Art Museum** in what was once the main building at the racetrack. **Kathleen's 5** is a good place to stop for refreshment. After touring the art gallery, slip into **People's Park.** In summer, you'll find a pond full of magnificent lotus blooms with the Moroccan-style building of **Barbarossa** behind. Keep this in mind for an afternoon beverage. Inside the park, you'll find peace and greenery, old people chatting, young couples, and the **Museum of Contemporary Art**, which has exhibitions of local and overseas artists.

Head down **Huangpi Bei/Nan Lu** to arrive at **Xintiandi**. If you want to shop for souvenirs, then **Dongtai Lu Antiques Market** is close by. Antiques might be a bit hard to find, but there are some great trinkets.

At **Xintiandi**, the **Shikumen Museum** and the **Site of the First National Congress of the Communist Party** are both places that give interesting insights into Shanghai's history. Inside the **Shikumen Museum** you can see what the interiors of these traditional Shanghainese houses may have looked like in the 1920s and '30s. If you fall in love with the furniture, which you will, you can always head out to one of the antiques showrooms in the Hongqiao and Gubei area to get something similar. The **Site of the First National Congress of the Communist Party** edges slightly toward propaganda at times, but is quite informative about the people and events that led to the forming of the Communist Party.

Xintiandi has some great shops including the lovely **Shanghai Trio** and **Shanghai Tang,** one of China's own designer brands. It's also a pleasant place for dinner with a varied selection of restaurants, so grab a chair and indulge in a bit of people-watching.

WHAT TO SEE

Fodor's Choice ★ **Dongtai Lu Antiques Market.** A few blocks east of Xintiandi, antiques dealers' stalls line the street. You'll find porcelain, Victrolas, jade, and anything else worth hawking or buying. The same bowls and vases pop up in multiple stalls, so if your first bargaining attempt isn't successful, you'll likely have another opportunity a few stores down. Prices have shot up over the years, and fakes abound, so be careful what you buy. ⊠ *Off Xizang Lu, Huangpu* ☉ *Daily 10–6.*

Grand Theater. The spectacular front wall of glass shines as brightly as the star power in this magnificent theater. Its three stages host the best domestic and international performances, including the debut of *Les Misérables* in China in 2002 and *Cats* in 2003. The dramatic curved roof atop a square base is meant to invoke the Chinese traditional saying, "the earth is square and the sky is round." ■TIP➔ **See it at night.** ⊠ *300 Renmin Dadao, Huangpu* ☎ *021/6386–8686* ⊕ *www.shgtheatre.com.*

Park Hotel. This art-deco structure overlooking People's Park was originally the tallest hotel in Shanghai. Completed in 1934, it had luxury rooms, a nightclub, and chic restaurants. Today it's more subdued, and the lobby is the most vivid reminder of its glorious past. It was also apparently an early inspiration for famous architect I. M. Pei (of the glass pyramids at the Louvre). ⊠ *170 Nanjing Xi Lu, Huangpu* ☎ *021/6327–5225* ⊕ *www.parkhotel.com.cn.*

GETTING ORIENTED

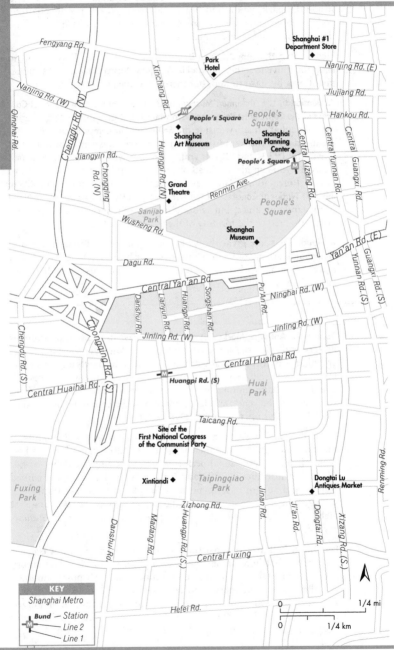

Fengyang Rd.

Nanjing Rd. (W)

Qinhai Rd.

Chengdu Rd.

Xinchang Rd.

Jiangyin Rd.

Chongqing Rd. (N)

Huangpi Rd. (N)

Grand Theatre

Sanijab Park

Wusheng Rd.

Dagu Rd.

Park Hotel

People's Square

Shanghai Art Museum

Renmin Ave.

People's Square

Shanghai Urban Planning Center

People's Square

Shanghai Museum

Shanghai #1 Department Store

Nanjing Rd. (E)

Jiujiang Rd.

Hankou Rd.

Central Xizang Rd.

Central Yunnan Rd.

Central Guangxi Rd.

Yan'an Rd. (E)

Yunnan Rd. (S)

Guangxi Rd. (S)

Central Yan'an Rd.

Danshui Rd.

Lianyun Rd.

Huangpi Rd.

Songshan Rd.

Pu'an Rd.

Ninghai Rd. (W)

Jinling Rd. (W)

Chengdu Rd. (S)

Jinling Rd. (W)

Chongqing Rd. (S)

Central Huaihai Rd.

Huangpi Rd. (S)

Central Huaihai Rd. (S)

Huai Park

Taicang Rd.

Site of the First National Congress of the Communist Party

Fuxing Park

Xintiandi

Taipingqiao Park

Zizhong Rd.

Danshui Rd.

Madang Rd.

Huangpi Rd. (S)

Jinan Rd.

Ji'an Rd.

Dongtai Rd.

Xizang Rd. (S)

Renming Rd.

Dongtai Lu Antiques Market

Central Fuxing

Hefei Rd.

KEY

Shanghai Metro

Bund — Station

Line 2

Line 1

0   1/4 mi

0   1/4 km

TOP REASONS TO GO

Shanghai Museum: This well-thought-out, well-labeled museum has a comprehensive selection of items from China's past and particularly impressive porcelain and bronze collections.

Xintiandi: Although pricey, this enclave is still worth a look for the reconstructed buildings, and it's also home to some great restaurants and boutiques.

Shanghai Art Museum: Housed in the rather lovely old racetrack building, there's a good mix of local and international exhibitions here.

Shanghai Urban Planning Center: Get a fascinating look at the massive changes in Shanghai and the government's plans for its future.

Dongtai Lu Antiques Market: Often more peaceful than the Yu Garden, you'll find a good range of souvenir shopping among real old Shanghai houses.

QUICK BITES

Ye Shanghai (⌧ *338 Huangpi Nan Lu, Luwan* ☎*021/ 6311–2323*) is a good bet at Sunday dim-sum brunch both for price and quality, and on other days, it's a stylish introduction to Shanghainese food.

Vegetarian Lifestyle (⌧ *77 Songshan Lu, Luwan* ☎*021/ 6384–8000*) makes the list of Shanghai's best restaurants mainly for the lightness and creativity of its food. If greasy Chinese food is getting to you, this is the place to come. However, since it's Buddhist, there's no alcohol, smoking, or stimulating spices—which is not necessarily a bad thing!

Barbarossa (⌧ *231 Nanjing Xi Lu [inside People's Park], Huangpu* ☎*021/6318–0220*), in a custom-built casbah in People's Park, is a romantic place to view the sunset during its daily happy hour from 5 to 8 PM. There is a choice of seating options from a terrace overlooking the water to a small rooftop where you can gaze at the sky. We would say gaze at the stars, but after all, this is Shanghai.

MAKING THE MOST OF YOUR TIME

The sights in this area are divided into two neat clusters—those around People's Square and those around Xintiandi. You can easily walk between the two in about 20 minutes. Visiting all the museums in the People's Square area could take a good half day. Xintiandi's sights don't take very long at all, so you could go before dinner, check out the museums, and then settle down for a pre-dinner drink and people-watch.

GETTING HERE

People's Square metro station is at present the main point of convergence for Shanghai's metro lines. The underground passageways can be confusing, so it's best to take the first exit and then find your way aboveground. Xintiandi is a block or two south of Line 1's Huangpi Nan Lu metro station.

SAFETY

Be careful in the mad press of people and traffic when crossing the roads around People's Square. There are people employed to supervise the crossings, and if the police catch you jaywalking, you might get fined.

NEAREST PUBLIC RESTROOMS

Dotted around the outside of People's Square are rather grand looking and well-maintained public toilet buildings.

A BRIEF HISTORY

Shikumen (stone gatehouses) were terraced buildings in lanes built in the 1920s and '30s, and although few survive, they once used to be found all over Shanghai. **People's Square** was once the Shanghai racetrack, built in 1862 and after Japanese occupation in 1941 was a place where the Japanese kept foreigners interned. It was also used by the Red Guard during the Cultural Revolution as a site for "struggle sessions," where people deemed to be antirevolutionary were forced to give self-criticisms and admit to crimes, and often subjected to torture.

People's Park. In colonial days, this park was the northern half of the city's racetrack. Today the 30 acres of flower beds, lotus ponds, and trees are crisscrossed by a large number of paved paths. There's also an art gallery, the **Museum of Contemporary Art,** and a bar and restaurant, **Barbarossa,** inside. ⊠ *231 Nanjing Xi Lu, Huangpu* ☎ *021/6327–1333* 🎫 *Free* ☉ *Daily 6–6 in winter and 5–7 in summer.*

Fodor'sChoice
★

People's Square. Once the southern half of the city's racetrack, Shanghai's main square has become a social and cultural center. The **Shanghai Museum** is inside it, and the Municipal Offices, Grand Theater, and Shanghai Urban Planning Center surround it. During the day, visitors and residents stroll, fly kites, and take their children to feed the pigeons. In the evening, kids roller-skate, ballroom dancers hold group lessons, and families relax together. Weekends here are especially busy. ⊠ *Best place to enter is at Xizang Lu/Renmin Dadao Huangpu.*

Shanghai Art Museum. At the northwest corner of People's Park, the former site of the Shanghai Library was once a clubhouse for old Shanghai's sports groups, including the Shanghai Race Club. The building is now the home of the state-run Shanghai Art Museum. Its permanent collection includes paintings, calligraphy, and sculpture, but its rotating exhibitions have favored modern artwork. There's a museum store, café, and a rooftop restaurant. ⊠ *325 Nanjing Xi Lu, at Huangpi Bei Lu, Huangpu* ☎ *021/6327–2829* ⊕ *www.sh-artmuseum.org.cn* 🎫 *Varies, depending on exhibition. Generally Y20* ☉ *Daily 9–4.*

Fodor'sChoice
★

Shanghai Museum. Truly one of Shanghai's treasures, this museum has the country's premier collection of relics and artifacts. Eleven galleries exhibit Chinese artistry in all its forms: paintings, bronzes, sculpture, ceramics, calligraphy, jade, Ming and Qing Dynasty furniture, coins, seals, and art by indigenous populations. Its bronze collection is one of the best in the world, and its dress and costume gallery showcases intricate handiwork from several of China's 52 minority groups. If you opt not to rent the excellent acoustic guide, information is well presented in English. You can relax in the museum's pleasant tearoom or buy postcards, crafts, and reproductions of the artwork in the bookshop. ⊠ *201 Renmin Da Dao, Huangpu* ☎ *021/6372–3500* ⊕ *www.shanghaimuseum.net* 🎫 *Free, Y20 for Chinese acoustic guide, Y40 for foreign-language acoustic guide* ☉ *Daily 9–4.*

Shanghai Urban Planning Center. To understand the true scale of Shanghai's building boom, visit the Master Plan Hall of this museum. Sprawled out on the 3rd floor is a 6,400-square-foot planning model of Shanghai—the largest model of its kind in the world—showing the metropolis as city planners expect it to look in 2020. You'll find familiar existing landmarks like the Pearl Tower and Shanghai Center as well as future sites like the so-called Flower Bridge, an esplanade over the Huangpu River being built for Expo 2010. ✉*100 Renmin Dadao, Huangpu* ☎*021/6372–2077* ⊕*www.supec.org* ✉*Y30 unless there is a special exhibition* ☉*Mon.–Thurs. 9–5, Fri.–Sun. 9–6, last ticket sold 1 hr before closing.*

Site of the First National Congress of the Communist Party. The secret meeting on July 31, 1921, that marked the first National Congress was held at the Bo Wen Girls' School, where 13 delegates from Marxist, Communist, and Socialist groups gathered from around the country. Today the site is surrounded by Xintiandi, Shanghai's center of conspicuous consumption. The upstairs of this restored shikumen is a well-curated museum explaining the rise of communism in China. ✉*374 Huangpi Nan Lu, Luwan* ☎*021/5383–2171* ✉*Free, audio tour Y10* ☉*Daily 9–4.*

FodorśChoice ★ **Xintiandi.** By World War II, around 70% of Shanghai's residents lived in shikumen or "stone gatehouses." Over the last two decades, most have been razed in the name of progress, but this 8-acre collection of stone gatehouses was renovated into an upscale shopping-and-dining complex and renamed Xintiandi, or "New Heaven on Earth." The restaurants are busy from lunchtime until past midnight, especially those with patios for watching the passing parade of shoppers. Just off the main thoroughfare is the visitor center and the **Shikumen Museum** (✉*House 25, North Block, 123 Xingye Lu, Luwan* ☎*021/3307–0337*), a shikumen restored to 1920s style and filled with furniture and artifacts collected from nearby houses. Exhibits explain the European influence on shikumen design, the history of the Xintiandi renovation, as well as future plans for the entire 128-acre project. ✉*181 Taicang Lu, Luwan* ⊕*Bordered by Taicang Lu, Madang Lu, Zizhong Lu, and Huangpi Nan Lu* ☎*021/6311–2288* ⊕*www.xintiandi.com* ✉*Museum Y20* ☉*Museum daily 10:30–10:30.*

THE BUND & NANJING DONG LU

Sightseeing
★★★

Nightlife
★★★★

Dining
★★★★

Lodging
★★★★

Shopping
★★

The city's most recognizable sightseeing spot, the Bund, on the bank of Shanghai's Huangpu River, is lined with massive foreign buildings that predate 1949. Some of these buildings have been developed into hip "lifestyle" complexes with spas, restaurants, bars, galleries, and designer boutiques. The Bund is also an ideal spot for that photo of Pudong's famous skyline. Leading away from the Bund, Nanjing Dong Lu is slowly returning to being the stylish street it once was, and it's a popular shopping spot for the locals. Some of the adjacent streets still have a faded glamour. The best time to visit is at night to stroll the neon-lit pedestrian road.

WHAT'S HERE

People's Square station is the best place to begin. Head out exit three, following the signs to **Raffles City.** You can indulge in a bit of retail therapy in this mall before stepping out into **Xizang Nan Lu.** At **Nanjing Dong Lu,** gaze up at the austere art-deco grandeur of the **Shanghai No. 1 Department Store.** You can take this famous shopping street to get to the **Bund.** It may currently look a bit down on its luck, but, as is clear from the massive construction going on, it is currently undergoing quite a face-lift. If your feet are complaining, jump on the tourist train.

Try to look upward to catch glimpses of the wonderful architecture above the shop signs and in between the neon.

Before you head under the road to the promenade, stop to check out the **Peace Hotel.** The Northern Building is the more distinctive with its green-tiled pitched roof. At the moment, it is closed for renovation, with no set date for reopening, but you can still check out the exterior.

It's a rather impressive view either looking back at the old colonial buildings or at the sweep of modern construction across the river in **Pudong**. At the north end of the Bund is **Huangpu Park**, once banned to Chinese, and now just a little grotty. Inside is the **Memorial to the Heroes of the People**. Heading south toward the ferry terminal, you'll pass a large statue of Chen Yi, Shanghai's first post-1949 mayor.

Nearby, a former observation tower sits, having been moved 73 feet to make way for construction (which is in full swing surrounding the tower). Just past the ferry terminal is the **I Love Shanghai** bar, where, if it's open, you can pick up an I LOVE SHANGHAI T-shirt.

> **TREAT YOURSELF**
>
> Housed in the Westin Hotel, which incidentally is one of Shanghai's nicest, the **Banyan Tree Spa** is a decadent way to indulge with single treatments such as massages right up to deluxe packages. The spa has elegantly decorated treatment rooms representing the five Chinese elements. ⊠ *Level 3, The Westin, 88 Henan Zhong Lu, Huangpu* ☎ *021/6335–1888* ⊕ *www.banyantreespa.com.*

Back along the other side of the road are the monumental buildings that make the Bund so famous. Several of them have been done up in recent years to create homes for trendy expensive bars, boutiques, and restaurants. One of the nicest places to sit and enjoy the view is **New Heights** at **Three on the Bund**, or you can check out **Laris**, also in the same building.

Some streets in Shanghai still specialize in certain merchandise, and **Fuzhou Lu** was once Shanghai's books and stationery street. There are still quite a few bookstores and some great buildings along this street. Pop into the little gallery **Studio Rouge** to see what's happening in Chinese art and get your feet reshod in embroidered shoes at **Suzhou Cobblers**. For some great milk tea and decorative ceilings, go to the **Xinwang Teahouse** on **Shandong Lu** and **Hankou Lu**. At the end of **Fuzhou Lu**, you'll end up back at your starting point, People's Square, from where you can take the metro to your next location.

Alternatively, you can head to the **Banyan Tree Spa** at the **Westin** in the **Bund Centre** to have yourself spoiled rotten.

WHAT TO SEE

Bank of China. Here, old Shanghai's Western architecture (British art deco in this case) mixes with Chinese elements. In 1937 it was designed to be the highest building in the city and surpassed the neighboring Cathay Hotel (now the Peace Hotel) by a hair, except for the green tower on the Cathay's roof. ⊠ *23 The Bund, Zhongshan Dong Yi Lu, Huangpu* ☎ *021/6329–1979.*

Fodor's Choice ★ **The Bund.** Shanghai's waterfront boulevard best shows both the city's pre-1949 past and its focus on the future. Today the municipal government has renovated the old buildings of this most foreign face of the city, highlighting them as tourist attractions, and even tried for a while

GETTING ORIENTED

The simplest way to get here is to take metro Line 2 to Nanjing Dong Lu station, and then head east for the Bund or west for the main shopping area of Nanjing Dong Lu. Alternatively, you can get off at People's Square station and walk east.

The Bund: This icon of Shanghai is fast becoming a stretch of sophisticated shopping, dining, and drinking.

Peace Hotel: Victor Sassoon's famous hotel is a museum piece of art-deco design both inside and out. While under renovation, only the facade is visible.

M on the Bund: The food may not always be great, but it was the first restaurant with a wonderful view over the river. Its chic Glamour Bar on the floor below hosts a wonderful array of local and international musicians, writers, and other interesting people.

Three on the Bund: Possibly the hippest lifestyle complex on the Bund. The restaurant and bar on the top, New Heights, is a lovely place to while away an evening.

Fuzhou Lu: A stroll down this street might turn up a few good books, a quirky shoe store, and some spottings of old-style buildings. It's also a pleasant alternative to get from the Bund to People's Square while avoiding Nanjing Dong Lu.

Map labels:
- Central Henan Rd.
- Central Jiangxi Rd.
- Central Sichuan Rd.
- Beijing Rd. East
- People's Hero Memorial Column
- Huangpu Park
- Chenyi's Plaza
- Nanjing Rd. (E.)
- Peace Hotel
- Bank of China
- Bund Sightseeing Tunnel
- Jiujiang Rd.
- Hankou Rd.
- Zhongshan Rd. East
- BUND
- Former HSBC Building
- Huangpu
- PUDONG
- Central Henan Rd.
- Central Jiangxi Rd.
- Central Sichuan Rd.
- Guangdong Rd.
- Yan'an Donglu Tunnel
- Huangpu River
- Binjiang Ave.
- Yan'an Rd. (E.)
- Bund Museum

KEY

Shanghai Metro
- — Station
- Line 2
- Line 1

QUICK BITES

Laris (✉ 6/F Three on the Bund, 17 Guangdong Lu, Huangpu ☎ 021/6321–9922), with its all-white interior, is a beautiful place to have lunch, and it has a decent set menu that won't break the bank. The food is modern fusion and pretty tasty to boot. If you want a good view, book in advance.

M on the Bund (✉ 7/F 5 The Bund, 20 Guangdong Lu, Huangpu ☎ 021/6350–9988) is something of a Shanghai institution as it was the first foreign restaurant to take up shop on the Bund. The food is hit-or-miss, but the Glamour Bar is an attractive place to gather.

MAKING THE MOST OF YOUR TIME

This excursion is a relatively easy stroll as it takes about 20 minutes to walk up Nanjing Dong Lu. You can also combine this area with either a trip to Pudong or to the sights around People's Square to make a day's worth of exploring.

SAFETY

As in any tourist area, there are pickpockets. Not so much a safety issue as an annoyance are the "art students" who invite you to see a display of paintings; avoid this at all costs as not only will you be subject to the hard sell, but the paintings are also overpriced and usually of poor quality. Also be wary of the money changers who loiter outside the Bank of China. Some may be reputable, but some may not.

A GOOD WALK

Join in with the throng and stroll the Bund promenade from Huangpu Park to the ferry terminus. Despite the other people, it can be quite romantic, especially at night.

A BRIEF HISTORY

The district's name is derived from the Anglo-Indian and literally means "muddy embankment." In the early 1920s the Bund became the city's foreign street: Americans, British, Japanese, French, Russians, Germans, and other Europeans built banks, trading houses, clubs, consulates, and hotels in styles from neoclassical to art deco. As Shanghai grew to be a bustling trading center in the Yangzi Delta, the Bund's warehouses and ports became the heart of the action. With the Communist victory, the foreigners left Shanghai, and the Chinese government moved its own banks and offices here.

to sell them back to the very owners it forced out after 1949. Currently, the area is undergoing a massive transformation including the closure of half the lanes of traffic along the waterfront and a revamp of the northern area near Suzhou Creek.

On the riverfront side of the Bund, Shanghai's street life is in full force. The city rebuilt the promenade, making it an ideal gathering place for both tourists and residents. In the morning, just after dawn, the Bund is full of people ballroom dancing, doing aerobics, and practicing kung fu, qi gong, and tai chi. The rest of the day people walk the embankment, snapping photos of the Oriental Pearl Tower, the Huangpu River, and each other. Be prepared for the aggressive souvenir hawkers; while you can't completely avoid them, try ignoring them or telling them *"bu yao,"* which means "Don't want." In the evenings lovers come out for romantic walks amid the floodlit buildings and tower. ✉ *5 blocks of Zhongshan Dong Yi Lu between Jinling Lu and Suzhou Creek, Huangpu.*

Former Hong Kong and Shanghai Bank Building (HSBC). One of the Bund's most impressive buildings—some say it's the area's pièce de résistance—the domed structure was built by the British in 1921–23, when it was the second-largest bank building in the world. After 1949 the building was turned into Communist Party offices and City Hall; now it is used by the Pudong Development Bank. In 1997 the bank made the news when it uncovered a beautiful 1920s Italian-tile mosaic in the building's dome. In the 1950s the mosaic was deemed too extravagant for a Communist government office, so it was covered by white paint, which protected it from being found by the Red Guards during the Cultural Revolution. It was then forgotten until the Pudong Development Bank renovated the building. If you walk in and look up, you'll see the circular mosaic in the dome—an outer circle painted with scenes of the cities where the HSBC had branches at the time: London, Paris, New York, Bangkok, Tokyo, Calcutta, Hong Kong, and Shanghai; a middle circle made up of the 12 signs of the zodiac; and the center painted with a large sun and Ceres, the Roman goddess of abundance. ✉ *12 The Bund, Zhongshan Dong Yi Lu, Huangpu* ☎ *021/6161–6188* ✉ *Free* ⊙ *Weekdays 9–5:30, weekends 9–5.*

Huangpu Park. The local government paved over what once was a lovely green garden to create this park. During colonial times Chinese could not enter the park; a sign at the entrance allegedly said, NO DOGS OR CHINESE ALLOWED. From its location at the junction of Suzhou Creek and the Huangpu River, it offers views of both sides of the river. Beneath the park's **Memorial of the Heroes of the People** obelisk is a sweeping relief of China's liberation. ⊠*North end of Bund, beside the river, Huangpu* ☎*021/5308–2636* ✉*Free* ⊙*Apr–Oct., daily 5* AM*–10* PM*; Nov.–Mar., daily 6* AM*–6* PM*.*

★ **Peace Hotel** *(Heping Fandian).* This hotel at the corner of the Bund and Nanjing Lu is among Shanghai's most treasured old buildings. If any establishment will give you a sense of Shanghai's past, it's this one. Its high ceilings, ornate woodwork, and art-deco fixtures are still intact, and hopefully will remain so once the current renovations have finished, and the ballroom evokes old Shanghai cabarets and gala parties.

The south building was formerly the Palace Hotel. Built in 1906, it is one of the oldest buildings on the Bund. The north building, formerly the Cathay Hotel, built in 1929, is more famous historically. It was known as the private playroom of its owner, Victor Sassoon, a wealthy landowner who invested in the opium trade. The Cathay was actually part of a complete office and hotel structure collectively called Sassoon House. Victor Sassoon himself lived and entertained his guests in the green penthouse. The hotel was rated on a par with the likes of Raffles in Singapore and the Peninsula in Hong Kong. It was *the* place to stay in old Shanghai; Noël Coward wrote *Private Lives* here. Though the hotel is closed for renovation, as of this printing, you can still see the hotel's art deco exterior. ⊠*20 Nanjing Dong Lu, Huangpu .*

FORMER FRENCH CONCESSION

Sightseeing
★★★
Nightlife
★★★★
Dining
★★★★
Lodging
★★★
Shopping
★★★★

With its tree-lined streets and crumbling old villas, the Former French Concession is possibly Shanghai's most atmospheric area. It's a wonderful place to go wandering and make serendipitous discoveries of stately architecture, groovy boutiques and galleries, or cozy cafés. Here, much of Shanghai's past beauty remains, although many of the old buildings are in desperate states of disrepair. One of the major roads through this area, Huaihai Lu, is a popular shopping location with shops selling international and local brands. It's also where many of Shanghai's restaurants, bars, and clubs are located, so if you are looking for an evening out, head to this area.

WHAT'S HERE

From **Huangpi Lu** or **Shaanxi Nan Lu** station, head down **Huaihai Lu** to **Sinan Lu.** On shady **Sinan Lu,** you'll find wonderful old villas set in small gardens and lots of trees. Farther down Sinan Lu is the entrance to **Sun Yat-sen's Former Residence,** where you'll be taken through a rather hurried guided tour; however, it's a good opportunity to get a look inside an old house. To the west down **Gaolan Lu** is **Fuxing Park,** a pleasant place during the day, but it really comes alive on weekend nights due to the massive karaoke parlor located there. Down the road is the home of the former prime minister during Mao's time, Zhou Enlai. Here you can wander around by yourself. Turn right down **Taikang Lu,** and you'll come across the growing artistic community that has set up there with studios and some funky design shops. Take a break in the courtyard at **Kommune,** which serves an excellent breakfast.

Head in the general direction of the intersection of **Maoming Lu** and **Huaihai Lu** through tranquil backstreets where modern development has been relatively subdued. On Maoming Lu, once a notorious bar street, there's an entrance to the former **Morriss Estate,** now **Ruijin Park,** which is a lovely spot to settle at one of the cafés or bars for a quiet drink. **Face,** a bar in an old mansion within the grounds, is particularly charming and also serves afternoon tea. At the intersection, there is the **Cathay Cinema,** a restored art-deco movie theater which is still in use. Those interested in architecture can continue down Maoming Lu to check out the **Jinjiang Hotel** and the **Lyceum Theatre.**

You might want to walk down Huaihai Lu to browse the shops with the crowds, or slip down **Changle Lu** or **Julu Lu** to avoid them. At **Fenyang Lu,** you can pop into the **Arts and Crafts Research Institute,** which although somewhat dusty and lackluster, is still an opportunity to see people working on traditional Chinese crafts such as paper cutting.

Happy hour in the garden at **Sasha's,** a stately old home once belonging to businessman TV Soong (brother of Soong Qingling and Soong Meiling who were married to Sun Yat-sen and Chiang Kai-shek, respectively), is a very pleasant experience and the lounge-bar is cozy when the weather is cold. On Hengshan Road is the **International Cathedral,** which still holds services. If you want to check your e-mail, the **Shanghai Library** has Internet access in the basement for Y4 per hour.

Finally, head down Huaihai Lu to check out the **Former Residence of Soong Qingling.**

WHAT TO SEE

Cathay Cinema. Once part of millionaire Victor Sassoon's holdings, the art-deco Cathay Cinema was one of the first movie theaters in Shanghai. The building still serves as a theater, showing a mix of Chinese and Western films. ✉ *870 Huaihai Zhonglu, at Maoming Nan Lu, Luwan* ☎ *021/5404–0415* ✆ *www.guotaifilm.com.*

Fuxing Park. The grounds of this European-style park—known as French Park before 1949—provide a bit of greenery in crowded Shanghai. Here you'll find people practicing tai chi and lovers strolling hand in hand. ✉ *105 Fuxing Zhong Lu, Luwan* ☎ *021/5386–1069* ✉ *Free* ⊙ *Daily 6 AM–6 PM.*

International Cathedral. This small ivy-covered cathedral dates to Shanghai's Concession days. Today it's called the Hengshan Community Church and holds weekly Protestant services. ✉ *53 Hengshan Lu, Xuhui* ☎ *021/6437–6576.*

Lyceum Theatre. In the days of old Shanghai, the Lyceum was the home of the British Amateur Drama Club. The old stage got a face-lift in 2003 and is still in use as a concert hall. ✉ *57 Maoming Nan Lu, Luwan* ☎ *021/6217–8530.*

Shanghai Arts and Crafts Research Institute. It's a little dusty, run-down, and bare-bones, but you can watch Shanghai's artisans as they create

GETTING ORIENTED

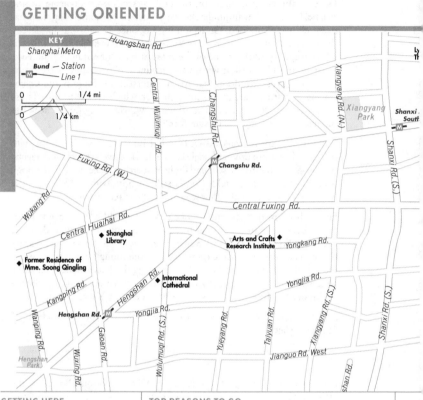

KEY
Shanghai Metro
Bund — Station
—Ⓜ— Line 1

0   1/4 mi
0   1/4 km

Huangshan Rd.
Central Wulumuqi Rd.
Changshu Rd.
Xiangyang Rd. (N.)
Xiangyang Park
Shanxi South
Fuxing Rd. (W.)
Ⓜ Changshu Rd.
Wukang Rd.
Central Fuxing Rd.
Shanxi Rd. (S.)
Central Huaihai Rd.
◆ Shanghai Library
Arts and Crafts ◆ Research Institute
Yongkang Rd.
◆ Former Residence of Mme. Soong Qingling
Kangping Rd.
Hengshan Rd.
◆ International Cathedral
Yongjia Rd.
Wanping Rd.
Hengshan Rd. Ⓜ
Yongjia Rd.
Gaoan Rd.
Wuxing Rd.
Wulumuqi Rd. (S.)
Yueyang Rd.
Taiyuan Rd.
Xiangyang Rd. (S.)
Shanxi Rd. (S.)
Jianguo Rd. West
Hengshan Park

GETTING HERE

Any of the four Line 1 metro stops (Huangpi Nan Lu, Shaanxi Nan Lu, Changshu Lu, or Hengshan Lu) will land you somewhere in the French Concession area. There are usually plenty of taxis except on rainy days or at peak hours.

TOP REASONS TO GO

Walking tree-lined avenues: Tree-lined streets with old buildings make for a pleasant walk. Poke your head into compounds and snap photos of the architecture while it's still there.

Taikang Lu: This fast-growing artistic community of bars, cafés, studios, and boutiques situated around a network of laneways makes for an alternative to Shanghai's malls and shopping streets.

Ruijin Park: Relax in an elegant park that was formerly the Morriss Estate. Face is best of the bars and cafés inside, and afternoon tea facing the lawn here is respite from Shanghai's endless activity.

QUICK BITES

Face (✉ *Building 4, Ruijin Guest House, 118 Ruijin Er Lu, Xuhui* ☎ *021/6466–4328*) is a bar and restaurant in an old mansion set in Ruijin Park. Decorated with Asian antiques including opium beds for lounging, it has an air of colonial decadence. Cocktails or afternoon tea are the most chic ways to enjoy the atmosphere.

Secret Garden (✉ *333 Changle Lu, Xuhui* ☎ *021/5405–0567*) is hidden away, but is worth seeking out to enjoy elegantly presented Chinese food among antique-style furniture, silk cushions, and candlelight in an old villa.

MAKING THE MOST OF YOUR TIME

This is really a lovely area to walk around, so it might be best to leave cabs behind and go on foot. The only site that is at a distance is Soong Qingling's Former Residence, which is a bit farther down Huaihai Lu. It's a pleasant way to while away a morning or an afternoon.

NEAREST PUBLIC RESTROOMS

Your best bets are the malls on Huaihai Lu such as at Times Square or Hong Kong Plaza. Don't forget the toilet paper.

A GOOD WALK

The walk from **Shaanxi Nan Lu** or **Huangpi Nan Lu** metro station to the **Taikang Lu** artists' community is a good one because it encompasses many of Shanghai's different personalities—the consumerism of **Huaihai Lu**, the old-world avenue of **Sinan Lu**, and the funky and alternative feel of Taikang Lu. Without stopping at the sites, this walk should take about 30 minutes.

A BRIEF HISTORY

The French were first granted permission to settle in Shanghai by the Qing in 1844. Although originally established by the French and run by their municipal government, by the 1930s the area was largely populated by Russians and Chinese. It also became a place of gangster activity including opium trade and prostitution. Today the area is a charming historic district known for its atmosphere and beautiful old architecture.

traditional Chinese arts and crafts. Works you can purchase include everything from paper-cuts to snuff bottles, but prices can be a bit high compared to quality. Formerly, the old French mansion housed an official of the Concession's pre-1949 government. ⊠ *79 Fenyang Lu, Xuhui* ☎ *021/6437–0509* ✉ *Y8* ☾ *Daily 9–5.*

Soong Qingling's Former Residence. While she first came to national attention as the wife of Dr. Sun Yat-sen, Soong Qingling became revered in her own right for her dedication to the Communist Party. Indeed, many mainland Chinese regard her as the "Mother of China." (On the other hand, Soong's sister, Meiling, married Chiang Kai-shek, who was the head of the Nationalist government from 1927 to 1949, at which point the couple fled to Taiwan.) This three-story house, built in 1920 by a German ship owner, was Soong's primary residence from 1948 to 1963. It has been preserved as it was during her lifetime and includes her 4,000 books in the study and furniture in the bedroom that her parents gave as her dowry. The small museum next door has some nice displays from Soong Qingling and Sun Yat-sen's life, including wedding pictures from their 1915 wedding in Tokyo. ⊠ *1843 Huaihai Zhonglu, Xuhui* ☎ *021/6437–6268* ⊕ *www.shsoong-chingling.com* ✉ *Y20* ☾ *Daily 9–4:30.*

Sun Yat-sen's Former Residence. Dr. Sun Yat-sen, the father of the Chinese republic, lived in this two-story house for six years, from 1919 to 1924. His wife, Soong Qingling, continued to live here after his death until 1937. Today it's been turned into a museum, and tours are conducted in Chinese and English. ⊠ *7 Xiangshan Lu, Luwan* ☎ *021/6437–2954* ✉ *Y20* ☾ *Daily 9–4:30.*

2

NANJING XI LU & JING'AN

Sightseeing
★

Nightlife
★★★

Dining
★★★

Lodging
★

Shopping
★★★★

Shanghai's glitziest malls and some five-star hotels are along the main street in this area, Nanjing Xi Lu. So, if you're into designer threads, luxury spas, or expensive brunches, you can satisfy your spending urges and max out your credit here. For those of a more spiritual bent, Jingan Temple, whose reconstruction is finally pretty much finished, is one of Shanghai's largest temples. The small Jingan Park across the street is popular with couples. Behind the temple is an interesting network of backstreets.

WHAT'S HERE

Sights are a bit thin on the ground in this area, but if you like international designer labels, this is where you can work the plastic. Coming out from **Jingan Si** metro station on Line 2, you'll be close to **Jingan Temple.** Across the street is **Jingan Park,** which has an Indonesian restaurant, Bali Laguna, in a rather romantic setting if you can ignore the **Yanan Lu** flyover behind you.

Behind the temple is the **Paramount,** a restored dance hall with two daily sessions of dancing at various prices. If you don't have a partner, don't worry—you can rent one. Behind the Paramount and Jingan Temple is a network of backstreets that make for interesting wandering.

Farther up **Nanjing Xi Lu,** you'll pass shiny malls with high-end designer stores, and five-star hotels as well as the monumental Soviet-inspired **Shanghai Exhibition Center.**

GETTING ORIENTED

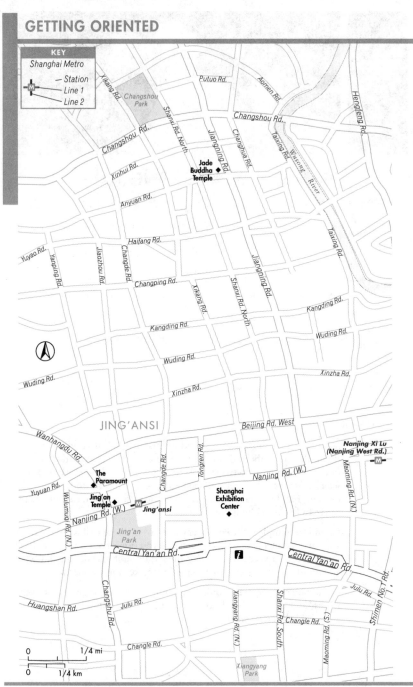

KEY

Shanghai Metro

- **M** Station
- — Line 1
- — Line 2

Changshou Park

Putuo Rd.

Aomen Rd.

Hengfeng Rd.

Xikang Rd.

Shanxi Rd. North

Changshou Rd.

Changshou Rd.

Jiangning Rd.

Changhua Rd.

Taixing Rd.

Wusong River

Xinhui Rd.

Jade Buddha Temple ◆

Anyuan Rd.

Haifang Rd.

Yuyao Rd.

Yanping Rd.

Jiaozhou Rd.

Changde Rd.

Changping Rd.

Xikang Rd.

Shanxi Rd. North

Jiangning Rd.

Taixing Rd.

Kangding Rd.

Kangding Rd.

Wuding Rd.

Wuding Rd.

Xinzha Rd.

Wuding Rd.

Xinzha Rd.

Xinzha Rd.

JING'ANSI

Beijing Rd. West

Wanhangdu Rd.

Changde Rd.

Tongren Rd.

Nanjing Xi Lu (Nanjing West Rd.) **M**

Maoming Rd. (N.)

The Paramount ◆

Nanjing Rd. (W.)

Yuyuan Rd.

Wulumuqi Rd. (N.)

Jing'an Temple ◆

M Jing'ansi

Shanghai Exhibition Center ◆

Nanjing Rd. (W.)

Jing'an Park

Central Yan'an Rd.

Central Yan'an Rd.

Shimen No.1 Rd.

Julu Rd.

Changshu Rd.

Huangshan Rd.

Julu Rd.

Xiangyang Rd. (N.)

Shanxi Rd. South

Changle Rd.

Maoming Rd. (S.)

Changle Rd.

Xiangyang Park

0 ⊢——————⊣ 1/4 mi

0 ⊢——————⊣ 1/4 km

2

GETTING HERE

Metro Line 2 takes you to **Jingan Si** station. If you want to take a taxi afterward, joining the line at the **Shanghai Centre/Portman Ritz-Carlton** is a good idea, especially when it's raining.

TOP REASONS TO GO

Jingan Temple: Although not Shanghai's best temple, this is the main sight in this area and one of Shanghai's larger inner-city temples.

Designer shopping: If you have the funds, the designer shopping here is currently the best in Shanghai; all the big, high-end brands fill posh-looking malls.

QUICK BITES

Situated in Jingan Park, **Bali Laguna** (⊠ *1649 Nanjing Xi Lu, inside Jingan Park, Jing'an* ☎ *021/6248–6970*) is a romantic setting overlooking a small pool that is particularly pretty at night when the lights twinkle and reflect in the water. The food does not live up to the atmosphere, so stick to the drinks.

Bi Feng Tang (⊠ *1333 Nanjing Lu, Jing'an* ☎ *021/6279–0738*) serves up cheap Cantonese-style food with lots of choices. It's open until 5 AM so it's perfect for midnight snacking. The menu is big on dim sum and you might get to sit in one of the replica boats.

Element Fresh (⊠ *Rm 112, Shanghai Centre, 1376 Nanjing Xi Lu, Jing'an* ☎ *021/6279–8682*) is very popular for its large breakfasts, great salads, and fresh juices. Be prepared to wait for a table on weekends and during office lunch hours.

MAKING THE MOST OF YOUR TIME

This area can be covered very quickly—in an hour or so—as there isn't much to see. **Jingan Si** metro is on Line 2, so if you don't get caught up in a shopping frenzy, head to **People's Square, Nanjing Dong Lu,** and the **Bund** afterward.

SAFETY

There are often a few beggars along this strip, but they aren't overly aggressive and not really a threat to your safety. It's entirely up to you whether you give them money or not—some are in real need and others are professionals who belong to "beggar rackets."

NEAREST PUBLIC RESTROOMS

Malls are your best bets for decent clean toilets. The ones in CITIC Square are particularly recommended.

SOUVENIRS

The main reason to come to **I Love Shanghai** (⊠ *155 Zhongshan Dong Er Lu, Huangpu* ☎ *021/ 6355–8058*) is to get your I Love Shanghai T-shirt. While you're here relax and enjoy one of the drink specials.

A BRIEF HISTORY

In the past, home to Shanghai's ultrarich such as the Kadoories and the Hardoons, Nanjing Xi Lu was once Bubbling Well Road and also the site of some of Shanghai's more famous clubs of the 1930s. Jingan Park was once Bubbling Well Cemetery. The street and the cemetery take their name from a well that used to exist in the area and was apparently first used in the 3rd century AD. The first temple was built at this site around the same time, but the one you see today is a shiny new reproduction that's typical of the Chinese habit of tearing down buildings and replacing them with reconstructions.

WHAT TO SEE

Jingan Temple. Originally built about AD 300, the Jingan Temple has been rebuilt and renovated numerous times. The temple's Southern-style halls, which face a central courtyard, gleam with new wood carvings of elephants and lotus flowers, but the hall interiors have stark, new concrete walls, and feel generally antiseptic. The temple's main draw is its copper Hongwu bell, cast in 1183 and weighing in at 3.5 tons. ✉1686 Nanjing Xi Lu, next to the Jingan Si subway entrance, Jing'an ☎021/6256–6366 ✉Y10 ☉Daily 7:30–5.

Paramount. Socialites referred to the Paramount, built in 1933, as the finest dance hall in Asia. Now, at night, the domed roof of this art-deco dance hall glows blue and inside people dance the afternoon and the night away. ✉218 Yuyuan Lu, Jing'an ☎021/6249–8866 ✉Varies depending on the dance session time ☉Daily.

Shanghai Exhibition Center. This mammoth piece of Russian architecture was built as a sign of Sino-Soviet friendship after 1949. Today, it hosts conventions and special touring exhibitions. The complex has a restaurant that caters largely to tour groups. ✉1000 Yanan Zhonglu, Jing'an ☎021/6279–0279 ☉Daily 9–4.

2

PUDONG

Sightseeing
★★★
Nightlife
★
Dining
★★
Lodging
★★★
Shopping
★★★

Shanghai residents used to say that it was better to have a bed in Puxi than an apartment in Pudong, but the neighborhood has come a long way in recent years from a rural area to one that represents a futuristic city of wide boulevards and towering skyscrapers topped by the almost complete Mori Tower, fondly referred to as "the bottle-opener." Apartments here are some of the most expensive in Shanghai. Although a little on the bland side, it is home to expat compounds designed in a medley of bizarre architectural styles, international schools, and malls. However, there are quite a few sites here worth visiting, particularly if you have children.

WHAT'S HERE

As you stagger out from the bewildering light show of the **Bund Tourist Tunnel,** head toward the **Oriental Pearl Tower.** Directions are not a problem, as you really couldn't miss it if you tried. Its oversized pink "pearls" loom over the shoreline. You can head up to the top of this tower to see the view of Shanghai stretching out forever on a pollution-free day—which is a rarity. However, it is expensive, so you might want to save your money for the **Jinmao Tower.** Close to the Oriental Pearl Tower is the **Shanghai Ocean Aquarium** where the kids can have a great time hanging with the fish. Across the road in an obscure office building is a branch of **Wagas** for morning heart-starter coffee or its afternoon tea special.

You'll probably need to take a taxi to see the rest of the sights. Head over to the **Science and Technology Museum** where the whole family can

GETTING ORIENTED

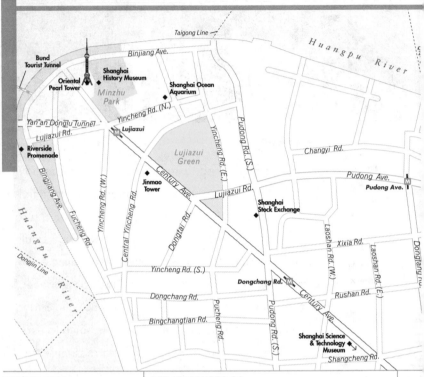

GETTING HERE

The Bund Tourist Tunnel is a strange and rather garish way of making the journey under the Huangpu River to Pudong. You might get a few laughs from the light displays. Otherwise, you can take the metro on Line 2 to Lujiazui, or catch the ferry from the Bund.

TOP REASONS TO GO

Oriental Pearl Tower: Shanghai's iconic tower stands out against the Pudong skyline like something from a '60s space cartoon.

Jinmao Tower: The most elegant skyscraper in Shanghai combines Chinese classical architecture and modern materials.

Shanghai Science and Technology Museum: An absorbing and hands-on place, this is a great place to take children.

Century Park: This huge park in Pudong has a variety of areas and activities including boats, bicycles, and trains.

2

KEY
Shanghai Metro
— Station
— Line 2

MAKING THE MOST OF YOUR TIME

Pudong is not a walking-friendly area as there are large, rather featureless distances between the sights. You can either take the metro to get around or jump in a cab. If you visit all the sights, you could easily spend a day out here. For some Puxi residents, it's like a journey to another country.

SAFETY

Pudong is a pretty safe area and the only thing to keep a look out for is the cars as you cross the impossibly wide boulevards.

NEAREST PUBLIC RESTROOMS

All the major sites have facilities. Some are located past the ticket booth, but the ones at the Shanghai Aquarium are in the foyer before you go in.

A GOOD WALK

An evening stroll along the Riverside Promenade provides a good view back across to the Bund. There is a choice of bars and cafés should you feel peckish or thirsty.

QUICK BITES

The beer at **Paulaner Brauhaus** (✉ *Binjiang Fengguangting 2967, Fudu Duan, Pudong* ☎ *021/6888–3935*) is particularly good. It's located on the Riverside Promenade, and at night, you get a spectacular view across to the Bund.

Wagas (✉ *Rm G102, 1233 Lujiazui Huan Lu, Pudong* ☎ *021/5879–4235*) is one of a chain of Australian-owned groovy cafés that have made many a homesick expat happy. Serving decent-sized pastas, sandwiches, burgers, salads, and some great cakes, it also has a range of special deals at different times of the day.

Super Brand Mall (✉ *168 Lujiazui Lu, Pudong* ☎ *021/6887-7888*) has a large food hall with a wide enough variety of restaurants, including the popular American fast-food chains such as KFC, to satisfy all stomachs.

enjoy the hands-on experiences offered or take a look at a film in one of the IMAX cinemas. Alternatively, if the weather is good, opt for **Century Park** where you can picnic, cycle, or just stroll.

Back toward the Huangpu River are the Jinmao Tower where for a much cheaper price than the Oriental Pearl Tower, you can go to the dazzlingly high 88th-floor observation deck. If you are there in the evening, the **Cloud Nine** bar at the **Grand Hyatt**, although lacking in atmosphere, is a top spot for a drink and a view of the lights. The cover charge (which includes drinks) is a bit steep though.

The **Superbrand Mall**—formerly Asia's largest— overlooks the Huangpu and has 10 floors of movies, restaurants, and shops. Once you have shopped 'til you drop, cross over the street to the **Riverside Promenade** where you can stroll or grab a bite at one of the restaurants there. At night the view across to the Bund is really lovely.

WHAT TO SEE

Bund Tourist Tunnel. For a look at Shanghai kitsch at its worst, you can take a trip across—actually, under—the Huangpu in plastic, capsular cars. The accompanying light show is part Disney, part psychedelia, complete with flashing strobes, blowing tinsel, and swirling hallucinogenic images projected on the concrete walls. The five-minute ride will make your head spin; you'll wonder if the Chinese central government isn't giving Shanghai just a little too much money. ⊠*Entrances are on the Bund at Nanjing Dong Lu and in Pudong near the Riverside Promenade* ☎*021/5888–6000* ✆*Y40 one way, Y50 round-trip* ☼*Mon.– Thurs. 8 AM–10:30 PM, Fri. and Sat. 8 AM–11 PM.*

Century Park. This giant swathe of green in Pudong is a great place to take children as it has a variety of vehicles for hire, good flat paths for rollerblading, and pleasure boats. On a fine day, pack a picnic as there are designated picnic areas as well as woods and grass to play on. ⊠*1001 Jinxiu Lu, Pudong* ☎*021/3876–0588* ⊕*www.centurypark. com.cn* ✆*Y10* ☼*Daily 7 AM–6 PM.*

★ **Jinmao Tower** *(Jinmao Dasha).* This gorgeous 88-floor (8 being the Chinese number implying wealth and prosperity), industrial, art-deco pagoda houses what is currently the highest hotel in the world—the Grand Hyatt Shanghai takes up the 53rd to 87th floors. The 88th-floor observation deck, reached in 45 seconds by two high-speed elevators, offers a 360-degree view of the city. The Jinmao combines the classic 13-tier Buddhist pagoda design with postmodern steel and glass. Check out the Hyatt's dramatic 33-story atrium or the Cloud Nine bar on the 87th floor. ⊠*88 Shiji Dadao, Pudong* ☎*021/5047–0088* ✆*Observation deck Y70* ☼*Daily 8:00 AM–10 PM.*

★ **Oriental Pearl Tower.** The tallest tower in Asia (1,535 feet) has become the pride and joy of the city, a symbol of the brashness and glitz of today's Shanghai. This UFO-like structure is especially kitschy at night, when it flashes with colored lights against the classic beauty of the Bund. Its three spheres are supposed to represent pearls (as in "Shanghai, Pearl of the Orient"). An elevator takes you to observation decks in the tower's three spheres. Go to the top sphere for a 360-degree bird's-eye view of the city, or grab a bite in the Tower's revolving restaurant. On the bottom floor is the Shanghai History Museum. ⊠*1 Shiji Da Dao, Pudong* ☎*021/5879–1888* ✉ *Y150 including the museum* ☉*Daily 8 AM–9:30 PM.*

Riverside Promenade. Although the park that runs 2,750 yards along the Huangpu River is sugary-sterile in its experimental suburbia, it still offers the most beautiful views of the Bund. You can stroll on the grass and concrete and view a perspective of Puxi unavailable from the west side. If you're here in the summer, you can ENJOY WADING, as a sign indicates, in the chocolate-brown Huangpu River from the park's wave platform. ⊠*Bingjiang Dadao, Pudong* ✉*Free.*

★ **Shanghai History Museum.** This impressive museum in the base of the Pearl Tower recalls Shanghai's pre-1949 history. Inside you can stroll down a re-created Shanghai street circa 1900 or check out a streetcar that used to operate in the concessions. Dioramas depict battle scenes from the Opium Wars, shops found in a typical turn-of-the-20th-century Shanghai neighborhood, and grand Former French Concession buildings of yesteryear. ⊠*1 Shiji Dadao, Pudong* ☎*021/5879–1888* ✉*Y35* ☉*Daily 8–9:30.*

☾ **Shanghai Ocean Aquarium.** As you stroll through the aquarium's 12,000-foot-long, clear, sightseeing tunnel, you may feel like you're walking your way through the seven seas—or at least five of them. The aquarium's 10,000 fish represent 300 species, five oceans, and four continents. You'll also find penguins and species representing all 12 of the Chinese zodiacal animals, such as the tiger barb, sea dragon, and seahorse. ⊠*1388 Lujiazui Ring Rd., Pudong* ☎*021/5877–9988* ⊕*www.sh-aquarium.com* ✉*Y120 adults, Y80 children* ☉*9 AM–6 PM.*

☾ **Shanghai Science and Technology Museum.** This museum, a favorite attraction for kids in Shanghai, has more than 100 hands-on exhibits in its six main galleries. Earth Exploration takes you through fossil layers to the earth's core for a lesson in plate tectonics. Spectrum of Life introduces you to the animal and plant kingdoms within its simulated rain forest. Light of Wisdom explains basic principles of light and sound through interactive exhibits, and simulators in AV Paradise put you in a plane cockpit and on television. Children's Technoland has a voice-activated fountain and miniature construction site. In Cradle of Designers, you can record a CD or assemble a souvenir. Two IMAX theaters and an IWERKS 4-D theater show larger-than-life movies, but mostly in Chinese. All signs are in English; the best times to visit are weekday afternoons. ⊠*2000 Shiji Dadao, Pudong* ☎*021/6854–2000* ⊕ *www.sstm.org.cn* ✉*Y60; there are separate prices for the IMAX and IWERKS* ☉*Tues.–Sun. 9–5:15.*

A BRIEF HISTORY

Up until 1990, Pudong was an endless expanse of rural area with squat ramshackle housing, fields, and run-down warehouses. Check out the Shanghai Urban Planning Center photos if you can't visualize it looking at the massive banks of glass and steel that now glitter from across the Huangpu. Its lightning transformation happened after the Chinese government announced that Shanghai was to play an important role in China's economic development and that Pudong was to be a Special Economic Zone. Nowadays, scores of expats live in the area and some of the largest business interests are located there. For some Puxi dwellers, though, it remains an unexplored land.

2

NORTH SHANGHAI

Sightseeing
★★
Nightlife
★
Dining
★
Lodging
★
Shopping
★★

Although often neglected in favor of their more glamorous neighboring areas, the northern Shanghai districts of Putuo, Hongkou, and Zhabei still offer some interesting sights. Hongkou District, particularly, is still relatively undeveloped and unchanged, and buildings from the past are still visible behind cheap clothing stores. An area with an interesting history, it has the most sights worth seeing as well as the lush green sweep of Lu Xun Park. The old buildings and warehouses around Suzhou Creek, which feeds into the Huangpu, are slowly being turned into a hip and happening arty area, particularly the M50 development. Also in Putuo District is another one of Shanghai's main temples, the Jade Buddha Temple.

WHAT'S HERE

Just across the Suzhou Creek from the Bund is the **Pujiang Hotel,** which was once the site of the very fashionable Astor House, and **Broadway Mansions,** an imposing art-deco apartment block, now **Shanghai Mansions** and a hotel. As you go down **Sichuan Bei Lu,** you will see many architectural gems including the old **Post Office.** If you have been to the **Shanghai Urban Planning Center** and looked at the past and present photos, you will notice that much around this area has not changed.

Toward the end of this long road is **Duolun Lu,** a "cultural" street where famous writers such as **Lu Xun** used to wander. At the entrance of the street is a rather harsh looking modern-art gallery, the **Doland Gallery of Modern Art,** which holds a range of exhibitions. If you continue down

GETTING ORIENTED

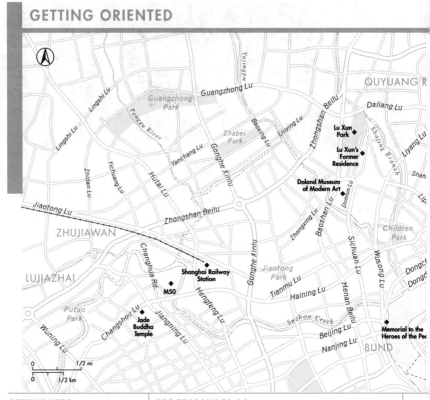

GETTING HERE

For the Jade Buddha Temple and M50, you can hop off the metro Line 3 or 4 at Zhongtan Lu, and then it's a short walk to M50 and a longer one to Jade Buddha. You can take the Pearl Line to East Baoxing Lu and Hongkou Stadium for Lu Xun Park and Duolun Lu. The best way to get around these areas is by taxi.

TOP REASONS TO GO

Lu Xun Park: A great place for people-watching and for kids to let loose for a bit, the park buzzes with activity all day long.

Doland Museum of Modern Art: Shanghai's first modern-art museum still holds an eclectic mix of exhibitions.

M50: Full of small and firmly established galleries, M50 is being developed as Shanghai's new art center and is one of the best places to see what is happening in Chinese contemporary art in Shanghai.

Jade Buddha Temple: This serene temple (outside festivals and holidays) is home to a precious Buddha statue.

2

NEAREST PUBLIC RESTROOMS

Inside the gate of Lu Xun Park are some reasonable public toilets. The toilet entrance fee is 5 mao.

A GOOD WALK

If you're a good walker, it's an interesting but long journey down Sichuan Bei Lu, a block or two from the Pujiang Hotel (Astor House), to Lu Xun Park, as some of the area has changed little over the years. Also, wandering around the backstreets of the area around Lu Xun Park will turn up some architectural gems.

QUICK BITES

Bandu Music Cafe (⊠ *Building 11, 50 Moganshan Lu, Putuo* ☎ *021/6276–8267*) is relaxed during the day and a spot to pick up Chinese classical folk music. At night, especially on Saturday, there are often free performances.

MAKING THE MOST OF YOUR TIME

North Shanghai's sights are in three distinct areas. The galleries at M50 open later in the morning, so it may be best to head to some other sites first. Be aware that many of them are closed on Monday. Qipu Lu also gets very busy as the day goes on and is unbearable on weekends.

SAFETY

Qipu Lu in particular is notorious for pickpockets. In the crowded narrow corridors of some of the markets, it's very easy for someone to slip an unnoticed hand into your pocket.

Duolun Lu, you will see some fine examples of old Shanghai architecture including a great church, built in "temple-style" complete with Chinese upturned eaves. There are some interesting junk/antique stores along here, so take time to browse.

At the end of Duolun Lu, head for the **Lu Xun Park,** named after China's most famous writer, who lived in the area at various times in his life. In the park, you will find locals engaged in all sorts of activities as well as Lu Xun's tomb and a museum. If you are a real fan, you can head to his former residence in **Shanyin Lu,** which is worth checking out for the atmospheric laneway it is situated in alone.

Nearby are remnants of Shanghai's Jewish settlement at the **Ohel Moishe Synagogue** and **Huoshan Park.** Shanghai was one of the few places willing to accept Jewish refugees fleeing from persecution under the Nazi rule.

While you are in the area, you might want to go to **Qipu Lu,** a large indoor market, which is a mecca for cheap clothing, shoes, and accessories.

WHAT TO SEE

Duolun Lu. Designated Shanghai's "Cultural Street," Duolun Road takes you back in time to the 1930s, when the 1-km-long (½-mi-long) lane was a favorite haunt of writer Lu Xun and fellow social activists. Bronze statues of those literary luminaries dot the lawns between the well-preserved villas and row houses, whose first floors are now home to antiques shops, cafés, and art galleries. As the street takes a 90-degree turn, its architecture shifts 180 degrees with the seven-story, stark, gray **Shanghai Doland Museum of Modern Art.** ⊠ *Off Sichuan Bei Lu, Hongkou.*

★ **Jade Buddha Temple.** Completed in 1918, this temple is fairly new by Chinese standards. During the Cultural Revolution, in order to save the temple when the Red Guards came to destroy it, the monks pasted portraits of Mao Zedong on the outside walls so the Guards couldn't tear them down without destroying Mao's face as well. The temple is built in the style of the Song Dynasty, with symmetrical halls and courtyards, upturned eaves, and bright yellow walls. The temple's great treasure is its 6½-foot-tall seated Buddha made of white jade with a robe of precious gems, originally brought to Shanghai from Burma. Other Buddhas, statues, and frightening guardian gods of the temple populate the halls, as well as a collection of Buddhist scriptures and paintings. The monks who live and work here can sometimes be seen worshipping. It's madness at festival times. ⊠ *170 Anyuan Lu, Putuo* ☎ *021/6266–3668* ⊕ *www.yufotemple.com* ⊠ *Y30* ⊙ *Daily 8–4:30.*

Lu Xun Park and Memorial. Lu Xun (1881–1936)—scholar, novelist, and essayist—is considered the founder of modern Chinese literature. He is best known for his work *The True Story of Ah Q.* The park holds his tomb and a statue of the writer, as well as a **museum** of manuscripts, books, and photos related to his life and career. The park is usually full of pockets of people chatting, playing badminton, or doing a myriad of other activities. ⊠ *2288 Sichuan Bei Lu, Hongkou* ☎ *021/6540–2288*

🖼Free ⊙ *Park daily 5* AM–7 PM; *memorial and museum daily 9–5, last entrance at 4.*

M50. This is a cluster of art galleries and artists' studios by Suzhou Creek is home to some of Shanghai's hottest galleries, where you will see works from China's best artists as well as new and not-so-well-known ones. There are also a couple of shops selling music and art supplies and a branch of Shirtflag. Don't be shy about nosing around—there are galleries on many floors of these old factories and warehouses and sometimes artists will be around for a chat. ✉ *50 Moganshan Lu, Putuo* 🖼*Free* ⊙ *Daily although most galleries are closed on Mon. Opening times vary depending on the gallery.*

Ohel Moishe Synagogue and Huoshan Park. Currently called the Jewish Refugee Memorial Hall of Shanghai, the Ohel Moishe Synagogue served as the spiritual heart of Shanghai's Jewish ghetto in the 1930s and '40s. In this sanctuary-turned-museum, whose restoration was completed in 2008, visitors can see a reconstruction of the main room of the synagogue and see artworks inspired by the story of Jews in Shanghai. An outside building has photos, newspaper clippings, and a film (narrated in Chinese).

Around the corner, down a lane just as well preserved, Huoshan Park bears a memorial tablet in the immigrants' honor. ✉ *62 Changyang Lu, Hongkou* 🕾*021/6541–5008* 🖼*Y50* ⊙ *Mon.–Sat. 9* AM–4 PM.

Shanghai Doland Museum of Modern Art. Opened in December 2003, this is Shanghai's first official venue for modern art. The six-story museum's 14,400 square feet of exhibition space include a tiny shop selling art books and a metal spiral staircase that's a work of art in itself. The exhibitions, which change frequently, are cutting edge for Shanghai. It's showcased electronic art from American artists, examined gender issues among Chinese, and featured musical performances ranging from Chinese electronica to the *dombra*, a traditional Kazak stringed instrument. ✉ *27 Duolun Lu, Hongkou* 🕾*021/6587–2530* 🖼*Varies according to the exhibition* ⊙ *Daily 10–5:30.*

A BRIEF HISTORY

Hongkou was originally the American Settlement, but later joined with the British to form the International Settlement. At the turn of the 20th century Shanghai was not only an international port but also an open one, where anyone could enter regardless of nationality. As the century wore on and the world became riddled with war, Jews, first fleeing the Russian Revolution and then escaping Hitler, arrived in Shanghai from Germany, Austria, Poland, and Russia. From 1937 to 1941 Shanghai became a haven for tens of thousands of Jewish refugees. In 1943 invading Japanese troops forced all the city's Jews into the "Designated Area for Stateless Refugees" in Hongkou District, where they lived until the end of the war. Today you can still see evidence of their lives in the buildings and narrow streets of the area.

Farther north, Zhabei District was decimated during the fighting with the Japanese in Shanghai during the 1930s. The now leafy green area of Zhabei Park was also used as an execution ground for Communists in the 1920s.

XUJIAHUI & SOUTH, HONGQIAO & GUBEI

Sightseeing
★★
Nightlife
★
Dining
★★
Lodging
★★
Shopping
★★★

Buyers throng into the large malls in the shopping precinct at Xujiahui, which shines with neon and billboard advertisements. Down the road are the districts of Hongqiao and Gubei where wealthy expats live in high-walled compounds and drive huge SUVs. You're likely to find a larger concentration of Western-style restaurants and supermarkets here.

WHAT'S HERE

Worship at the temple of commerce at Xujiahui. Then head off to worship at another temple, but this time a much more spiritual one at **Longhua.** Here you can light your free incense and pray to Buddha, see the monks wandering around or ring the giant bell for good fortune. The Longhua Pagoda across the way is not accessible to tourists, but is photogenic. Next door is the serene Longhua Martyrs Cemetery in commemoration of those who died for the Communist Cause including those executed in the Guomindang round-up in 1927. Farther away from the center you can wander among the plants of the Shanghai Botanic Gardens.

WHAT TO SEE

Longhua Martyrs Cemetery. A tranquil place now, this cemetery has had a bloody history. It has been the execution site of many Communists, particularly during the Guomingdang crackdown in 1927. Now it's full of large Soviet-style sculpture. The most chilling sight is the grassy execution area accessed by a tunnel where the remains of murdered Communists were found with leg irons still on in the 1950s. ✉*180*

GETTING ORIENTED

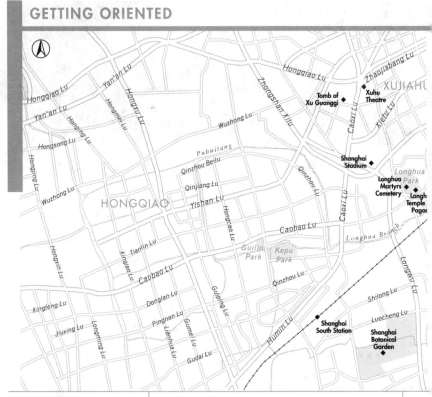

GETTING HERE

Metro Line 1 takes you right into the depths of the Grand Gateway Mall at Xujiahui. The other sights are fairly far-flung, so it might be a good idea to jump into a taxi. If you are going to places like the Shanghai Botanical Gardens from the center of town, be prepared for a large taxi bill. Otherwise, you can get off at Shanghai South Railway Station.

SAFETY

Temples can get very crowded during festivals and this can be very unpleasant due to the pushing and shoving.

TOP REASONS TO GO

Longhua Temple and Pagoda: Take your free incense at the door and pray in the four directions with the locals at one of Shanghai's larger temple complexes—and the only one that is still fully active.

Longhua Martyrs Cemetery: Besides being historically interesting, there is also some amazing Soviet-style sculpture work in this pleasant garden.

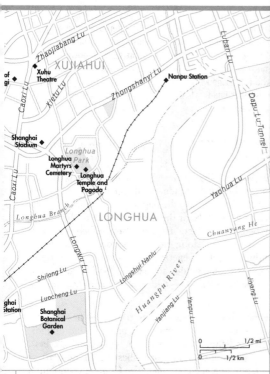

MAKING THE MOST OF YOUR TIME

There isn't much to see out in the southern suburbs, so there's no need to make it a large part of your trip. Getting here will take the longest time. The sights themselves will take an hour or two, unless you are deeply interested in botany and wish to linger at the Shanghai Botanical Gardens. Likewise, if you like malls and shopping, you could spend a lot of time wandering around Grand Gateway and the like at Xujiahui. Avoid Xujiahui on the weekends if possible.

TOURING TIP

Make sure to take the walk through the chilling tunnel to the bluntly named Martyrs Dying Ground at the Longhua Martyrs Cemetery. You will emerge at the extremely poignant sight where many people lost their lives. It may not be the most cheerful event of your day, but it will certainly fill you with a sense of awe at the senselessness of these events in history.

QUICK BITES

Da Marco (✉ *1/F, Grand Gateway, 1 Hongqiao Lu, Xujiahui* ☎ *021/6447-7577*) serves classic Italian cooking in a cheerful and bright environment. Rub shoulders with Shanghai's Italian expat community in this citywide favorite.

Hongmei Jie/Hongmei Entertainment street (✉ *Lane 3338 Hongmei Lu, Gubei*), stretching from Hongmei Lu to Hongxi Lu, is a pedestrian-only street that offers a wide range of food choices from Chinese to great bread shops to bars with a wide variety of beers.

Longhua Vegetarian Hall (✉ *Longhua Temple, 2853 Longhua Lu, Xuhui* ☎ *021/6456-6085*) is where you can pull up a Formica table and a stool and get some temple food. This is a basic vegetarian place mostly serving noodles.

A BRIEF HISTORY

Xu Guangqi, a Catholic convert living in Shanghai during the 16th and 17th centuries, and his family once owned large parts of the Xujiahui area. They donated much of the land to the Jesuits who established a cathedral and various other buildings, such as orphanages and monasteries. Xuhui College, which was built in 1850, offered the first fully Western curriculum in China. Once the Communists seized power from the Nationalists, Catholicism was no longer tolerated and the Jesuits left China for safer places like Macau.

Longhua Lu, Xuhui ☎*021/6468–5995* ⊕*www.slmmm.cn* ✉*Y1* ⊙*Daily 6–5, museum 9–4.*

★ **Longhua Temple** *(Longhua Si)*. Shanghai's largest temple has as its centerpiece a seven-story, eight-sided pagoda. While the temple is thought to have been built in the 3rd century, the pagoda dates from the 10th century; it's not open to visitors. Near the front entrance of the temple stands a three-story bell tower, where a 3.3-ton bronze bell is rung at midnight every New Year's Eve. Along the side corridors of the temple you'll find the Longhua Hotel, a vegetarian restaurant, and a room filled seven rows deep with small golden statues. ✉*2853 Longhua Lu, Xuhui* ☎*021/6456–6085 or 021/6457–6327* ✉*Y10 with free incense* ⊙*Daily 7–4:30.*

Shanghai Botanical Gardens. Spread over 200 acres, the garden has separate areas for peonies and roses, azaleas, osmanthus, bamboo and orchids, and medicinal plants. Its Penjing Garden is among the world's best. *Penjing* translates as "pot scenery," and describes the Chinese art of creating a miniature landscape in a container. The Chinese Cymbidium Garden has more than 300 varieties on bonsai. Within the Grand Conservatory are towering palms and more than 3,500 varieties of tropical plants. ✉*1111 Longwu Lu, Xuhui* ☎*021/5436–3369* ⊕*www.shbg. org* ✉*Y15 for entrance through main gate only* ⊙*Daily 7–5.*

Soong Qingling Mausoleum. Unlike her beleaguered sister, Soong Meiling, who married the wrong guy, Chiang Kai-shek, and escaped to Taiwan, Soong Qingling is a heroine in China. She was buried in the Wanguo Cemetery in 1981 and the cemetery was renamed in her honor. Now you can visit her grave, along with that of her maid and her parents. ✉*21 Songyuan Lu, Xuhui* ☎*021/6275–8080* ✉*Y3* ⊙*Daily 8:30–4.*

Xujiahui Cathedral. Built by the Jesuits in 1848, this Gothic-style cathedral still holds regular masses in Chinese. Stained-glass artist Wo Ye designed the new windows for the entire cathedral. ✉*158 Puxi Lu, Xuhui* ☎*021/6438–2595* ⊙*Daily 5–5.*

Giant Buddha Statue, Leshan

THE AGE OF EMPIRES

When asked his opinion on the historical impact of the French Revolution, Chairman Mao quipped, "It's too early to tell." Though a bit tongue in cheek, China does measure its history in millennia, and in its grand timeline, interactions with the West have been mere blips.

According to historical records, Chinese civilization stretches back to the 15th century BC—markings found on turtle shells carbon dated to around 1500 BC bear some similarity to modern Chinese script. China then resembled city-states rather than a unified nation. Iconic figures such as Lao Tzu (the father of Taoism), Sun Tzu (author of the *Art of War*), and Confucius lived during this period. Generally, 221 BC is accepted as the beginning of Imperial China, when the city-states united under various banners.

Over the next 2,200 years (give or take a few), China alternated between periods of harmony and political upheaval. Its armies conquered new territory and were in turn conquered by external invaders (most of whom wound up themselves being assimilated).

By the early 18th century, the long, slow decline of the Qing—the last of China's Imperial dynasties—was already in progress, making the ancient nation ripe for exploitation by rising European powers. The Imperial era ended with the forced abdication of child Emperor Puyi (whose life is chronicled in Bernardo Bertolucci's *The Last Emperor*), and it's here that the history of modern China, first with the founding of the republic under Sun Yat-sen and then with the establishment of the People's Republic under Mao Zedong, truly begins.

(left) Oracle shell with early Chinese characters. (top, right) The Great Wall stretches 4,163 miles from east to west. (bottom, right) Confucius was born in Qufu, Shandong.

circa 1500 BC
Writing Appears

The earliest accounts of Chinese history are still shrouded in myth and legend, and it wasn't until 1959 that stories were verified by archaeological findings. For millennia, people formed communities in the fertile lands of what is now central China. The first recorded Chinese characters are said to have been developed 3,500 years ago. Though sometimes referred to as the Shang Dynasty, this period was more of a precursor to modern Chinese dynasties than a truly unified kingdom.

722–475 BC
The Warring States Period

China was so far from unified that these centuries are collectively remembered as the Warring States Period. As befitting such a contentious time, military science progressed, iron replaced bronze, and weapons material improved. Some of China's greatest luminaries lived during this period, including the father of Taoism, Lao-tzu, Confucius, and Sun-Tzu, one of the greatest military tacticians and the author of the infamous *Art of War*, which is still studied in military academies around the world.

221–207 BC
The First Dynasty

The Qin Dynasty eventually defeated all of the other warring factions thanks to their cutting-edge military technology, namely the cavalry. The Qin were also called Ch'in, which may be where the word China first originated. The first Emperor, Qin Shi-huang, unified much of the lands and established a legal code and vast bureaucracy to hold it together. The Qin dynasty also standardized the written and spoken language and introduced a common currency.

The Warring States Period	The First Dynasty		Buddhism Arrives
300BC	0		300AD

2

IN FOCUS THE AGE OF EMPIRES

(left) Terracotta warriors in Xian, on the Silk Road. (top right) Buddha statue, Maijishan Cave in Tianshui, Gansa. (bottom left) Sun Tzu, author of The *Art of War*.

In order to protect his newly unified country, Qin Shi-huang ordered the creation of the massive Great Wall of China, which was built and rebuilt over the next 1,000 years. He was also a sculpture enthusiast and commissioned a massive army of stone soldiers to follow him into the afterlife. Buried with him, these terra-cotta warriors would remain hidden from the eyes of the world for two thousand years, until they were found by a farmer digging in a field just outside of Xian. These warriors are among the most important archaeological finds of the 20th century.

220–265 BC Buddhism Arrives

Emperor Qin's dreams of a unified China fell apart, and eventually the kingdom split into three warring factions. But what was bad for stability turned out to be good for literature. The Three Kingdoms Period is still remembered in song and story. *The Romance of the Three Kingdoms* is as popular among Asian bookworms as the *Legend of King Arthur* is among Western readers. It's still widely read and has been translated into almost every language. Variations of the story have been adapted for manga, television series, and video games.

The Three Kingdoms period was filled with court intrigue, murder, and massive battles that, while exciting to read about centuries later, weren't much fun at the time. Armies ravaged the countryside, and most people lived and died in misery. Perhaps it was the carnage and disunity of the time that turned the country into a magnet for forces of harmony; it was during this period that Buddhism was first introduced into China, traveling over the Himalayas from India, via the Silk Road.

(left) Genghis Khan conquered much of China. (top, right) Islamic lecture at madrassa classroom inside Dongguan mosque, Xinning. (bottom, right) Kublai Khan was the first Mongol Emperor of China.

618–845 Religion Diversifies

Chinese spiritual life continued to diversify. Nestorian Monks from Asia Minor arrived bearing news of Christianity, and Saad ibn Abi Waqqas (a companion of the Prophet Muhammad) supposedly visited the Middle Kingdom to spread the word of Islam. During this era, Wu Zetian, onetime concubine, seized power from the Tang Dynasty and became the first (and only) woman to assume the title of emperor. She ruled for 25 years through puppet emperors and finally, for 15 years as Emperor Shengshen.

1271–1368 Ghengis Invades

In Xanadu did Kublai Khan a stately pleasure dome decree . . .

Or so goes the famed Coleridge poem. But Kublai's grandfather Temujin (better known as Ghengis Khan) had bigger things in mind. One of the greatest war tacticians in history, he united the restive nomads of Mongolia's grassy plains and eventually sacked, looted, and pillaged much of the known west and most of the Chinese landmass. By the time Ghengis died in 1227, his grandson was well-tutored and ready to take on the rest of China.

By 1271, Kublai had established a capital in a land-locked city that would only much later become known as Beijing. This marks the beginning of the first (but not last) non-Han dynasty. Kublai Khan kept fighting southward and by 1279, Guangzhou fell to the Mongols, and Khan became the ultimate monarch of China. Though barbarians at heart, the Mongols must be credited for encouraging the arts and a number of early public works projects, including extending the highways and grand canals.

2

(left) Statue of admiral Zheng He. (top right) Forbidden City in Beijing (bottom right) Child emperor Puyi.

1368–1644 Ming Dynasty

Many scholars believe that the Mongols' inability to relate with the Han is what ultimately pushed the Han to rise up and overthrow them. The reign of the Ming Dynasty was the last ethnically Han Dynasty to rule over a unified China. At its apex, the Bright Empire encompassed a landmass easily recognized as China, even by today's mapmakers. The Ming Emperors built a huge army and navy, refurbished the agricultural system, and printed many books using movable type long before Gutenberg. In the 13th century, Emperor Yongle began construction of the famous Forbidden City in Beijing, a veritable icon of China.

Also during the Ming Dynasty, China's best known explorer, Zheng He, plied the seven seas in massive treasure fleets that dwarfed in size and range the ships of Christopher Columbus. A giant both in stature and persona, Admiral Zheng (who was also a eunuch) spent two decades expanding China's knowledge of the world outside of its already impressive borders. He traveled as far as India, Africa, and (some say) even the coast of the New World.

1644–1911 Qing Dynasty

The final dynasty represented a serious case of minority rule. They were Manchus from the northeast. The early Qing dynasty was a brutal period as forces loyal to the new emperor crushed those loyal to the old. The Qing Dynasty peaked in the mid-to-late 18th century but soon after, its military powers began to wane. In the 19th century, Qing control weakened and prosperity diminished. By 1910 China was fractured, a baby sat on the Imperial throne, and the Qing Dynasty was on its deathbed.

(left) Portrait of Marshal Chiang Kai-shek with his wife. (top, right) Mao Zedong on December 6, 1944. (bottom, right) Sun Yat-sen.

The Opium Wars

1834–1860

European powers were hungry to open new territories up for trade, but the Qing weren't buying. The British East India Company, strapped for cash, realized they could sell opium in China at huge profits. The Chinese government quickly banned the nefarious trade and in response, a technologically superior Britain declared war. After a humiliating defeat in the first Opium War, China was forced to cede Hong Kong. Other foreign powers followed with territorial demands of their own.

Republican Era

1912–1949

China's Republican period was chaotic and unstable. The revolutionary Dr. Sun Yat-sen —revered by most Chinese as the father of modern China—was unable to build a cohesive government without the aid of regional warlords and urban gangsters. When he died of cancer in 1925, power passed to Chiang Kai-shek, who set about unifying China under the Kuomintang. What began as a unified group of both left- and right-wingers quickly deteriorated, and by the mid-1920s, civil war

between the Communists and Nationalists was brewing.

The '30s and '40s were bleak decades for the Chinese people, caught between a vicious war with Japan and periodic clashes between Kuomintang and Communist forces. After Japan's defeat in 1945, China's civil war kicked into high gear. Though the Kuomintang were armed with superior weapons and backed by American money, the majority of Chinese people rallied behind the Communists. Within four years, the Kuomintang were driven off the mainland to Taiwan, where the Republic of China exists to the present day.

(top left) Illiterate soldiers are taught about Mao's *Little Red Book* in Beijing December 1966. (top right) Central Shenzhen, Guangdong (bottom left) Poster of Mao's slogans.

1949–Present

The People's Republic

On October 1, 1949, Mao Zedong declared from atop Beijing's Gate of Heavenly Peace that "The Chinese People have stood up." And so the People's Republic of China was born. The Communist party set out to overhaul China's ancient feudal system, emphasizing class struggle, redistribution of wealth, and elimination of foreign dominance. The next three decades would see a massive, often painful transformation of Chinese society from feudalism into the modern age.

The Great Leap Forward was a disaster—Chinese peasants were encouraged to cram 100 years of industrial development into as many weeks. Untenable decisions led to industrial and agricultural ruin, widespread famine, and an estimated 30 million deaths. The trauma of this period, however, pales in comparison to The Great Proletarian Cultural Revolution. From 1966–1976, fear and zealotry gripped the nation as young revolutionaries heeded Chairman Mao's call to root out class enemies. During this decade, millions died, millions were imprisoned, and much of China's accumulated religious, historical, and cultural heritage literally went up in smoke.

Like a phoenix rising from its own ashes, China rose from its own self-inflicted destruction. In the early 1980s, Deng Xiao-ping took the first steps in reforming China's stagnant economy. With the maxim "To Get Rich is Glorious," Deng loosened central control on the economy and declared Special Economic Zones, where the seeds of capitalism could be incubated. Two decades later, the nation is one of the world's most vibrant economic engines. Though China's history is measured in millennia, her brightest years may well have only just begun.

PLACES TO VISIT	PINYIN	CHINESE
Bank of China	Zhōngguó yínháng	中国银行
Banyan Tree Spa	Yuèróngzhuāng	悦榕庄
Bund	Wàitān	外滩
Bund 18	Wàitān shí bā hào	外滩十八号
Bund Centre	Wàitān zhōngxīn	外滩中心
Bund Tourist Tunnel	Wàitān rénxìng guānguāng suìdào	外滩人行观光隧道
Former Hong Kong and Shanghai Bank Building	Pǔdōng fāzhǎn yínháng	浦东发展银行
Fuzhou Road	Fúzhōu lù	福州路
Hankou Road	Hànkǒu lù	汉口路
Henan Zhong Road	Hénán zhōnglù	河南中路
Huangpu Park	Huángpǔ gōngyuán	黄埔公园
Huangpu River	Huángpǔjiāng	黄浦江
I Love Shanghai	Wǒaìshànghǎi	我爱上海
Jinling Road	Jīnlíng lù	金陵路
Laris	Lùwéixuān	陆唯轩
Memorial of the Heroes of the People	Rénmínyīngxióng jìniànbēi	人民英雄纪念碑
Nanjing Dong (East) Road	Nánjīng dōng lù	南京东路
New Heights	Xīnshìjiǎo	新视角
Peace Hotel	Hépíng fàndiàn	和平饭店
Raffles City	Láifúshì guǎngchǎng	来福士广场
Shandong Road	Shāndōng lù	山东路
Shanghai No.1 Department Store	Dìyī bǎihˇuo	第一百货
Studio Rouge	Hóngzhài dāngdài yìshù huàláng	红寨当代艺术画廊
Number Three on the Bund	Wàitān sān hào	外滩三号
Xinwang Tea House	Xīnwàng chá cāntīng	新旺茶餐厅
Xizang Nan (South) Road	Xīzàng nan lù	西藏南路
Zhongshan Dong (East) Yi Road	Zhōngshān dōng yī lù	中山东一路
Zhongshan Er Road	Zhōngshān èr lù	中山二路

Shopping

3

Shanghai Super Brand Mall

WORD OF MOUTH

"[Friends] had suggested shopping on Taikong Street and in the Art Alley, so that's where we headed next. In fact, they were right— it was great shopping! There were all sorts of little shops and galleries selling clothing and jewelry, and various art materials, frames, paintings, sculpture, and antiques along with charming little cafes."

—wiselindag

SHOPPING PLANNER

Start Shopping!

When in Shanghai, do as the locals do and hit the shops hard. Ask people in the street their favorite hobby, and if they don't say basketball or PC games, they will probably say shopping. New stores open each day—from glittering luxury behemoths to tiny boutiques with barely any breathing room.

Great Souvenirs

- Revolutionary propaganda depicting Chairman Mao
- Handmade shoes
- A mah-jongg set
- Old advertising posters
- Yixing teapots
- An inflatable Shanghai Oriental Pearl Tower
- Baijiu (and the accompanying hangover)
- Brightly colored Wuxi clay dolls
- Cricket cage
- Silk brocade with dragon or bamboo motifs
- Miao embroidery

Top Places to Shop

Duolun Lu is a pedestrian street in Shanghai's historic Hongkou. Not only is it lined with examples of old architecture and home to a modern-art gallery, but its stalls and curio stores are ripe for browsing.

Moganshan Lu, a complex near Aomen Lu, once housed poor artists. It is now being developed and repackaged as M50, a hot new art destination with galleries, cafés, and stores moving in to make this a happening place to shop and hang out.

Taikang Lu is a former factory district that's now home to artists and designers. It has a hip and laid-back vibe, particularly on weekdays, and is fast becoming Shanghai's SoHo. You won't find Andy Warhols at the International Artists Factory, but there is definitely some worthwhile shopping.

In **Xintiandi,** exclusive and expensive stores are housed in reproduction traditional shikumen buildings. Get ready to work that plastic.

Xujiahui, where six major shopping malls and giant electronics complexes in Puxi converge, looks like it's straight out of Tokyo. Shop 'til you drop, or play with the gadgets and compare prices at the electronics shops.

Yu Garden, a major tourist haunt in the Old Town area of Shanghai, can be overwhelming, but hard bargaining brings rewards. The amount and variety of goods for sale here is phenomenal. It is continually expanding as vendors move out of old buildings in the surrounding areas.

Also check out these streets that specialize in specific traditional products: **Fenyang Lu** and **Jinling Lu** for musical instruments; **Changle Lu** and **Maoming Lu** for *qipao* (Chinese-style dresses); and **Fuzhou Lu** for books and art supplies, including calligraphy supplies.

Avoid Scams

Fake antiques are often hidden among real treasures and vice versa. Some stores may tell you whether a piece is old or new, but you only have their word to prove it. Also be aware of age; the majority of pieces date from the late Qing Dynasty (1644–1911). Technically, only items dated after 1795 can be legally exported. In some stores, only domestic customers may purchase these items to prevent illegal exportation.

China is famous for its silk, but some unscrupulous vendors will try to pass off synthetics at silk prices. Ask the shopkeeper to burn a small scrap from the bolt you're considering. If the burned threads bead up and smell like plastic, the fabric is synthetic. If the threads turn into ash and smell like burned hair, the fabric is real silk. (The same goes for wool.) For brocade silk, fair market prices range from Y30 to Y40 a meter; for synthetics, Y10 to Y28. You'll pay more in retail shops.

On tourist stretches such as the Yu Gardens and Nanjing Dong Lu, you may be approached by young people claiming to be students who invite you to an "art exhibition." Unless you are in the market for imitation artwork at high prices, decline and keep moving. You may also be approached by people wanting to sell you fake bags, watches, etc. Likewise, keep moving.

Check for fake pearls before purchasing. Real pearls will feel gritty when you bite them, and they also feel cool to the touch. Taking a knife to the surface to see if it scrapes off or burning the pearl are common tactics used by vendors to show that it is real.

Real jade makes a distinctive chiming sound when struck and will stick slightly to your hand when under water.

Shopping Hours

Shanghai gets up late and opening hours really vary. Local supermarkets open early, but malls don't usually open until 10 and boutiques at 11 AM. The upside is stores tend to stay open later, with many closing at 10 PM. Markets generally start earlier, at around 8:30 or 9:30 AM, and close at around 6 PM. Most stores are open seven days a week.

■ TIP→ **Shopping here is a voyage of discovery that is best done on foot so as to discover the little surprises, especially in areas like the Former French Concession.**

Sample Costs in Shanghai

Item Price (in yuan)

DVD on the street Y8

DVD in a store Y10

Mao's Little Red Book (new) Y40

Fake designer sunglasses Y30

Silk brocade Y35 per meter

Pearls Y40 for a basic strand

Updated by
Elyse Singleton

Because of Shanghai's commercial status as China's most open port city, it has the widest variety of goods to be found in the nation after Hong Kong. Ritzy chrome shopping malls stand alongside dingy state-run stores and around the corner from local markets, inundating the intrepid shopper with both foreign name brands and domestic goods. Take some time to do some window-shopping on Huaihai Lu, one of China's premier shopping streets.

OLD CITY

SOUVENIRS

Old Street of Yu Gardens. Souvenir shops, tourists, and vendors touting for business fill this street. Some of the merchandise is of dubious taste, but there are still some shops selling unusual or good-quality products. **Shop 368** sells pretty embroidered shoes, belts, and spangles; **Shop 385** has overpriced yet tempting retro pieces; **Shop 408** sells old books, some dating back to the Ming Dynasty; **Shop 430** sells opera costumes, including amazing headdresses and the obligatory fake beards. ✉ *Fangbang Lu, Huangpu.*

XINTIANDI & CITY CENTER

ANTIQUES

★ **Dong Tai Antique Shop.** Friendly owner Mr. Liu sells a range of lamps, gramophones, fans, and other electrical equipment salvaged from Shanghai's glorious past. Some of his stock has been bought by chic restaurants like M on the Bund, and most are in some kind of working order. A small glass lamp base will set you back about Y100 if you stand your ground. ✉ *11 Dongtai Lu, Luwan* ☎ *021/6385–8793.*

BOOKS & ART SUPPLIES

Chaterhouse Books. An oasis for the starved reader, this bookstore stocks a good range of magazines in English and other languages and English books, including children's books and a comprehensive selection of travel guides. ⊠*Shop B1-K Shanghai Times Square, 99 Huaihai Zhong Lu, Luwan* ☎*021/6391–8237* ⊕*www.chaterhouse.com. cn* ⊠*Shop 68, 6F Super Brand Mall, 168 Lujiazui Xi Lu, Pudong* ☎*021/5049–0668* ⊠*Shop 202B, 2F Shanghai Centre, 1376 Nanjing Xi Lu, Huangpu* ☎*021/6279–7633.*

GIFTS

Shanghai Museum Shop. The selection of books on China and Chinese culture at the main store is impressive, and there are some children's books. Expensive reproduction ceramics are available as well as smaller gift items such as magnets, scarves, and notebooks. Cool purchases like a Chinese architecture–ink stamp (Y90) make great gifts. A delicate bracelet with Chinese charms costs Y150. ⊠*Shanghai Museum, 201 Renmin Dadao, Huangpu* ☎*021/6372–3500* ⊠*123 Taicang Lu, Luwan* ☎*021/6384–7900.*

NANJING DONG LU & THE BUND

ANTIQUES

Shanghai Antique and Curio Store. A pleasant departure from the touristy shops in the area, this government-owned store is an excellent place to gauge whether you are being taken for a ride elsewhere. Goods start with small pieces of embroidery, and range from ceramics to wedding baskets (traditionally used to hold part of the bride's dowry). Be aware that some of the pieces may not be taken out of the country, as a sign in the ceramics store warns. ⊠*240 Guangdong Lu, Huangpu* ☎*021/6321–5868.*

ART

★ **Studio Rouge.** A small but well-chosen collection of mainly photography and paintings by emerging and established artists crowds this simple space. Look for Studio Rouge M50 in Moganshan Lu; it houses the works of more international artists. ⊠*17 Fuzhou Lu, Huangpu* ☎*021/6323–0833* ⊠*Building 7, 50 Moganshan Lu, Putuo* ☎*1380/174–1782 (mobile).*

BOOKS & ART SUPPLIES

Foreign Languages Bookstore. On the first floor, find a selection of English-language books about China and Chinese language. Head to the fourth floor for English-language classic novels and children's books. Prices start at Y10 for paper-cut cards. ⊠*390 Fuzhou Lu, Huangpu* ☎*021/6322–3200* ⊕ *www.sbt.com.cn.*

Yangzhenhua Bizhuang. Calligraphy supplies at excellent prices—fine brushes start at just Y2—can be purchased at this long-established shop. It still has the original glass counters and dark-wood shelves and a staff that relaxes at the back with tea and pumpkin seeds. ⊠*290 Fuzhou Lu, Huangpu* ☎*021/6322–3117.*

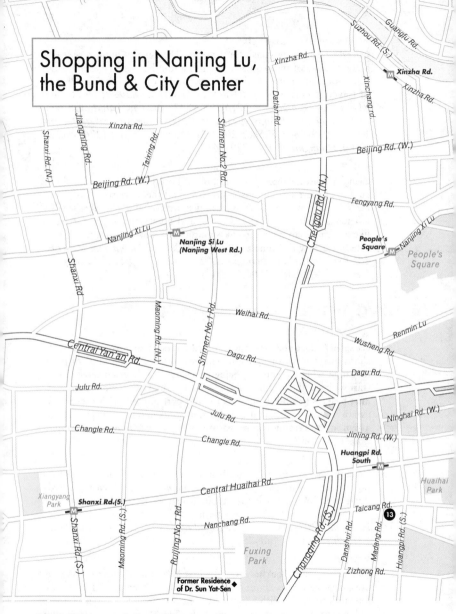

Shopping in Nanjing Lu, the Bund & City Center

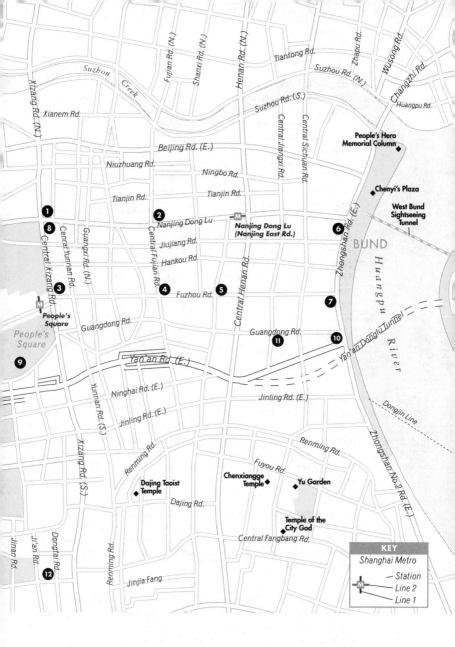

ULTIMATE SHOPPING TOUR

Shopping in Shanghai requires comfortable shoes and regular stops for sustenance. To beat the crowds (which increase as the day progresses), start at around 9 AM at **Yu Garden.** It is the best place in Shanghai for standard Chinese items such as chopsticks, name chops (stone stamps carved with names and characters), painted bottles, and teapots.

Avoid the stores inside the bewildering main complex and concentrate on slightly cheaper ones around **Fangbang Lu.** Dive into side streets and forage among the large buildings on the edges, such as the market at **Fuyou Gate.**

Revive with steamed buns from street vendors and grab a taxi to **Dongtai Lu** (about Y20) for more eclectic Chinese items such as cricket cages, old qipao, and odd pieces from the 1930s and '40s. Enjoy the surroundings: old men playing chess and babies in spilt pants toddling about. Stop at **Xintiandi,** a short walk away, for lunch and window-shopping.

You can walk from here to **Taikang Lu** to take in the wonderful buildings along Sinan Lu, but it's a long haul, especially with all those bags, so take a cab if you're not up to the walk. Taikang Lu has a more modern and arty edge. Buy T-shirts at **insh** or **Shirtflag,** or listen to Miao women singing as they embroider at the **Harvest Studio.** Finally, collapse in a heap at **Kommune,** a café in the yard off Lane 210.

CERAMICS

Blue Shanghai White. The eponymous colored ceramics here are designed and hand-painted by the owner, and are made in Jingdezhen, once home to China's imperial kilns. Some larger pieces are made with wood salvaged from demolition sites around Shanghai, such as a wooden bureau with ceramic drawer fronts. Prices start at Y60 for a cup to Y30,000 for a screen with ceramic panels. ☒*17 Fuzhou Lu, Room 103, Huangpu* ☎*021/6323–0856* ⊕*www.blueshanghaiwhite.com.*

CHINESE MEDICINE

Shanghai No. 1 Dispensary. If you've got an illness, this place has something to cure it. The flagship store on Nanjing Dong Lu carries Eastern and Western medicines from ginseng to hairy antler, and aspirin to acupuncture needles. ☒*616 Nanjing Dong Lu, Huangpu* ☎*021/6322–4567.*

CLOTHING & SHOES

Bund 18. The glamorous collection of shops here sell high-end designer clothing and accessories such as Marni, Ermenegildo Zegna, Cartier, and Giorgio Armani. The boutique **Younik** stands out by specializing in Shanghai-based designers, including Lu Kun. ☒*18 Zhongshan Dong Yi Lu, Huangpu* ☎*021/6323–7066* ⊕*www.bund18.com.*

★ **Suzhou Cobblers.** Beautifully embroidered handmade shoes and slippers with quirky designs such as cabbages are sold alongside funky bags made from rice sacks. Children's shoes are also available. Also sold here are sweet knitted toys and children's sweaters. ☒*17 Fuzhou Lu, Room*

101, Huangpu ☎*021/6321–7087*
⊕*www.suzhou-cobblers.com.*

Three on the Bund. Like Bund 18
(above), Three on the Bund is a
luxury complex that stocks mainly
European-designer brands. ⊠*3
Zhongshan Dong Yi Lu, Huangpu*
☎*021/6323–0101* ⊕*www.threeon
thebund.com.*

DEPARTMENT STORES

Shanghai No. 1 Department Store.
Shanghai's largest state-owned
store attracts masses of Chinese
shoppers, especially on weekends.
It sells everything from porce-

lain dinnerware to badminton racquets and is popular with much of
Shanghai's male population who want no-nonsense, one-stop shopping. ⊠*830 Nanjing Dong Lu, Huangpu* ☎*021/6322–3344* ⊕*www.
shdsno1.com.*

MALLS

Brilliance Shimao International Plaza. This mall near People's Square stocks
some high-end designers, such as Givenchy, mixed in with midrange
ones such as Lacoste and Esprit, as well as China's first NikeID studio.
⊠*829 Nanjing Dong Lu, Huangpu* ☎*021/3313–4718.*

Raffles City. Near People's Square, Raffles City has midrange foreign and
local designer stores including funky street wear such as Miss Sixty,
Roxy, and FCUK. It also has a movie theater showing both Chinese and
foreign films, and a food court in the basement with snacks and drinks.
⊠*268 Xizang Zhong Lu, Huangpu* ☎*021/6340–3600* ⊕*www.raffles
city-shanghai.com.*

PEARLS & JEWELRY

★ **Amy Lin's Pearls and Jewelry.** Friendly owner Amy Lin has sold pearls to
European first ladies and American presidents but treats all her customers like royalty. Her shop amongst the fake bags at Fenshine Plaza has
inexpensive trinket bracelets, strings of seed pearls, and stunning Australian seawater pearl necklaces. ⊠ *Shop 30, 3F, Fenshine Fashion and
Accessories Plaza, 580 Nanjing Xi Lu, Huangpu* ☎*021/5228–2372*
⊕*www.amy-pearl.com.*

Ling Ling Pearls & Jewelry. Traditional pearl necklaces and inexpensive
fashion jewelry that is hipper than the competition stand out here.
Contemporary-looking pearl-and-stone combinations are priced high,
but large discounts are often given sans haggling. The shop is located in
Pearl City, among the other pearl and jewelry sellers. ⊠*2F, Pearl City,
558 Nanjing Dong Lu, 2nd fl., Huangpu* ☎*021/6322–9299.*

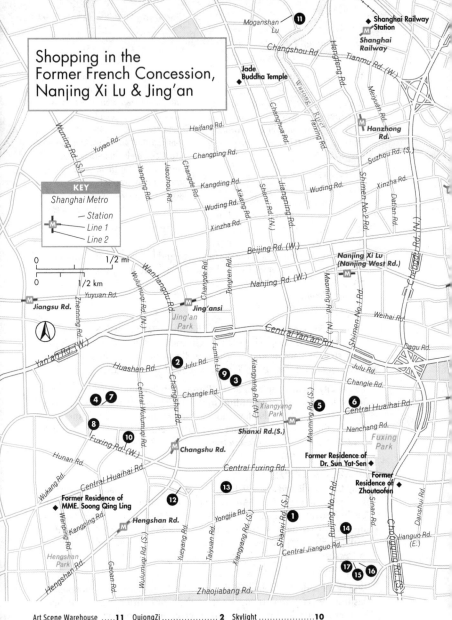

Shopping in the Former French Concession, Nanjing Xi Lu & Jing'an

KEY
Shanghai Metro
— Station
Line 1
Line 2

FORMER FRENCH CONCESSION

ANTIQUES

Brocade Country. The English-speaking owner, Liu Xiao Lan, has a Miao mother and a broad knowledge of her pieces. The Miao sew their history into the cloth and she knows the meaning behind each one. Many pieces are antique-collector's items and Ms. Liu has also started designing more wearable items. Antique embroidery can cost an arm and a leg, but smaller embroidery pieces are affordable and flat and easy to slip into a suitcase. ⊠*616 Julu Lu, Jing'an* ☎*021/6279–2677.*

Jin. This packed little store sells furniture that's up to 100 years old. Compared to the larger antiques warehouses, prices are quite competitive. Good buys include tiny little stools at Y80 and cute embroidered cats and shoes. The shop doesn't arrange shipping. ⊠*614 Julu Lu, Jing'an* ☎*021/6247–2964.*

★ **Madame Mao's Dowry.** This covetable collection of mostly revolutionary-propaganda items from the '50s, '60s, and '70s is sourced from the countryside and areas in Sichuan province and around Beijing and Tianjin. Mixed in are hip designs from local and international designers. Although this could be your one-stop shopping experience, remember this is communism at capitalist prices: expect to pay Y800 for a small Revolution-era teapot and around Y1,800 for a Revolution-era mirror. ⊠*207 Fumin Lu, Luwan* ☎*021/65403–3551* ⊕ *www.madame-maos-dowry.com* ⊠*Gallery: 50 Moganshan Lu, Building 6, 5th fl., Putuo* ☎*021/6276–9932.*

CARPETS

Torana House. Two stories here are filled with carpets handmade by Tibetan artisans in rural areas using top-quality wool and featuring auspicious symbols. This is also a good place to pick up an antique piece from Tibet or Xinjiang. ⊠*164 Anfu Lu, Xuhui* ☎*021/5404–4886* ⊕*www.toranahouse.com.*

CLOTHING & SHOES

Boutique Cashmere Lover. The small collection of wickedly soft cashmere and blends is contemporary in design; some have Chinese details. Made-to-order is available. ⊠*248 Taikang Lu, No. 31, Luwan* ☎*021/6473–7829.*

Feel. The *qipao* may be a traditional Chinese dress, but Feel makes it a style for modern times as well with daring cutouts and thigh skimming designs. ⊠*La. 210, No. 3, Room 110, Taikang Lu, Luwan* ☎*021/5465–4519 or 021/6466–8065* ⊠*Shop 305, The Loft, 508 Jiashan Lu, Luwan* ☎*021/5465–9319.*

Qipao Aplenty

You'll find dozens of *qipao* (traditional Chinese dress) shops on **Changle Lu** between Maoming Nan Lu and Shaanxi Nan Lu. These two streets are also home to many tiny boutiques in the blocks just north and south of Huaihai Lu. They sell ready-to-wear and many offer a tailoring service. However, the prices will probably be lower at the **South Bund Soft Spinning Material Market** (⇨ *Markets below)*, where costs for a qipao start around Y500 (including fabric).

Other places that create tailor-made qipao: **Feel** (⇨ *above)*, which charges from around Y1,000 for a silk qipao; and **Hanyi** (⇨ *Tailor-Made for You box, below)*.

In general, it takes around seven days for a qipao to be made at any of these shops.

insh and Helen Li *(In Shanghai)*. A local designer sells cheeky clothes that are not for the fainthearted at these two locations. Skirts barely cover bottoms, but there are cute takes on traditional qipao, as well as a more lifestyle-oriented range in the street-side store. It's a good place for T-shirts featuring stylish Chinese-inspired designs. ✉ *200 Taikang Lu, Luwan* ☎ *021/6466–5249* ⊕ *www.insh.com.cn* ✉ *11A, La. 210, Taikang Lu* ☎ *021/6415–7877.*

La Vie. Asian-style and more eclectic pieces—some quite unusual—are sold here. There is a lot of attention to detail and collections reflect essentials of Chinese imagery such as kites and phoenixes. ✉ *Courtyard 7, La. 210, Taikang Lu, Luwan* ☎ *021/6445–3585* ✉ *Bund 18, 18 Zhongshan Yi Lu, 2nd fl., Huangpu* ⊕ *www.lavie.com.cn.*

L'Atelier Mandarine. Clothing and accessories focus on children and lounging. The French designer uses natural fabrics such as silk, cotton, and cashmere for her own designs as well as stocking other local labels. The simple and chic designs let the quality of the fabric speak for itself. ✉ *Studio No. 318, No. 3, La. 210, Taikang Lu, Luwan* ☎ *021/6473–5381.*

QiongZi. The Hubei-born designer personally sources fabrics from different parts of the world for her feminine designs, which have strong Chinese and Japanese influences. Ready-to-wear and haute couture are both available. ✉ *620 Julu Lu, Xuhui* ☎ *021/6289–2372.*

Rouge Baiser Elise. Yet another French designer in Shanghai, Rouge Baiser Elise has beautiful linen and cotton housewares and clothing, including children's clothes. Items can be made to order in your choice of color, and children's names can be sewn onto clothing for no extra cost. Handmade pieces have subtle embroidery, and everything looks distinctly French. Go just to check out the beautiful building. ✉ *299-2 Fuxing Xi Lu, Xuhui* ☎ *021/6431–8019* ⊕ *www.rougebaiser-elise.com.*

★ **Shanghai Tang.** This is one of China's leading fashion brands with distinctive acid-bright silks, soft-as-a-baby's-bottom cashmere, and funky housewares. Sigh at the beautiful fabrics and designs and gasp at the inflated prices. ⊠ *Xintiandi 15, North Block 181, Taicang Lu, Luwan* ☎ *021/6384–1601* ⊠ *Jin-Jiang Hotel, Shop E, 59 Maoming Nan Lu, Luwan* ☎ *021/5466–3006* ⊠ *Shangri-La Hotel, Lobby Level, 33 Fucheng Lu, Pudong* ☎ *021/5877–6632* ⊕ *www.shanghaitang.com.*

★ **Shanghai Trio.** Chinese fabrics mixed with French flair, irresistible children's clothes in bright colors and sweet little kimonos, great utilitarian satchels that scream

urban chic, and crafty necklaces are the stars of this range. The shop has expanded recently to accommodate a housewares collection, with items such as blankets at Y800. ⊠ *Xintiandi, 181 Taicang Lu, Luwan* ☎ *021/6355–2974* ⊕ *www.shanghaitrio.com.cn.*

Shirtflag. A hipper-than-thou collection of witty and slickly designed T-shirts, accessories, and notebooks at this fun shop takes on propaganda art with a humorous and funky edge. Check out unusual takes on brand icons and crazed-looking pandas. ⊠ *Room 8, No. 7, La. 210, Taikang Lu, Luwan* ☎ *021/6466–7009* ⊠ *330 Nanchang Lu, Luwan* ☎ *021/5465–3011* ⊠ *Bldg. 17, 50 Moganshan Lu, Putuo* ☎ *021/6298–6483* ⊠ *336 Changle Lu, 1st fl., Xuhui* ☎ *021/6255–7699* ⊕ *www.shirtflag.com*

The Thing. Find strange yet compelling graphics with a 1970s art feel or a Chinese twist printed on bags, sneakers, tees, and sweats. The designs are increasingly popular with Shanghai fashionistas. ⊠ *276 Changle Lu, Luwan* ☎ *021/6384–9229* ⊕ *www.thething.cn* ⊠ *60 Xinle Lu, Luwan* ☎ *021/5404–3607* ⊠ *No. 22, 1st fl., Metrotown, 890 Changning Lu, Changning* ☎ *021/5241–0007.*

Village Girl. Hand-selected by the owner, the clothing, shoes, embroidery pieces, and other items—vintage and new—sold here are made by people (mostly women) of China's ethnic minorities who live in small villages in Guizhou, Guangxi, and Hunan. The most interesting is a reasonable selection of fabrics. If you're going on to southwest China, wait to buy there. Fabric starts at Y60 per meter. ⊠ *155 Anfu Lu, Xuhui* ☎ *021/5403–5754* ⊠ *Shop 5, Taikang Lu, Luwan* ☎ *021/6473–7787.*

FURNITURE

Asian View. A longtime favorite among expats for Chinese furniture, this store is now devoted to furnishings from throughout Asia. Reasonably priced and beautifully made tables, beds, and accessories from Indonesia, India, Malaysia, and Thailand fill the 4,000-square-

Tailor-Made for You

Tailors usually charge a flat fee per type of garment and may require a deposit, with the balance paid upon satisfactory completion of the garment. If you can, bring in a picture of what you want made or an existing garment for them to copy. Usually, copying is the most successful. Try to allow enough time for an initial and follow-up fitting as tailors are accustomed to working with Chinese bodies and may need to adjust the garment a bit more to achieve a proper fit on Western frames.

Dave's Custom Tailoring. Now in its 40th year of operation, Dave's has an English-speaking staff and skilled

tailoring, making it a favorite among expats and visiting businesspeople. The shop specializes in men's dress shirts and wool suits, which require around 10 days and two fittings to complete. ⊠ *No. 6, 288 Wuyuan Lu, Xuhui* ☎ *021/5404–0001* ⊕ *www. tailordave.com.*

Hanyi. A well-respected qipao shop, Hanyi has a book of styles that its tailors can make in a week, at the fastest, or more complex, finely embroidered patterns that require a month for proper fitting. Prices start from Y1,000. ⊠ *221 Changle Lu, Luwan* ☎ *021/5404–4727* ⊕ *www. shanghai1888.com.*

---

foot showroom. ⊠ *233 Shaanxi Nan Lu, Luwan* ☎ *021/6474–1051* ⊕ *www.asianview.com.cn.*

Paddy Field. Ready-made and made-to-order furniture feature a blend of Southeast Asian and Chinese influences. The modern and the ancient are also combined in designs, and quality materials such as teak and elm are used. Custom-made furniture takes around three weeks. ⊠ *30 Hunan Lu, Xuhui* ☎ *021/6437–5567* ⊕ *www.paddy-field.com.cn.*

GIFTS & HOUSEWARES

Harvest Studio. Drop in to watch the Miao women with their distinctive hair knots embroidering, and sometimes singing. This studio sells Miao-embroidered pillows, purses, and clothing as well as the silver jewelry that traditionally adorns the Miao ceremonial costume. It also has a funky range of contemporary cotton and jersey pieces. ⊠ *3 La. 210, Room 118, Taikang Lu, Luwan* ☎ *021/6473–4566.*

Jooi. This Danish-owned design studio focuses on bags and accessories in fabrics ranging from industrial felt to shiny patent. Now, it also incorporates Nest, devoted to eco-friendly products. ⊠ *Studio 201, International Artist Factory, La. 210, Taikang Lu, Luwan* ☎ *021/6473–6193* ⊕ *www.jooi.com.*

Simply Life. Popular buys include chunky, shiny, red-glazed pottery and delicate bone porcelain painted with Chinese iconic items such as Ming vases and ancient clothing. Better values can be found elsewhere, but it's a good place for lazy shoppers. The flagship store is at the Xintiandi location. ⊠ *Unit 101, Xintiandi, 159 Madang Lu, Luwan* ☎ *021/6387–5100* ⊠ *9 Dongping Lu, Xuhui* ☎ *021/3406–0509* ⊕ *www.simplylife-sh.com.*

JEWELRY

Skylight. Beautiful Tibetan jewelry is on display at Skylight. Although you could probably get it cheaper at the Yu Gardens or even from street vendors, at least you know it's real. You can also buy breathtaking photos of Tibet and her people taken by the owner. Mounted images start from Y25. ✉28 Fuxing Xi Lu, Xuhui ☎021/6473–5610.

SOUVENIRS

Arts and Crafts Research Institute. Shanghai artisans create pieces of traditional Chinese arts and crafts such as embroidery and paper-cutting right before your eyes at this institute. You can purchase everything from paper-cuts to snuff bottles, although at prices higher than you'll pay at the stalls around Yu Garden. ✉79 Fenyang Lu, Xuhui ☎021/6437–2509 ✍Y8.

TEA

Shanghai Huangshan Tea Company. The nine Shanghai locations of this teashop sell traditional Yixing teapots as well as a huge selection of China's best teas by weight. The higher the price the better the tea. ✉605 Huaihai Zhonglu, Luwan, ☎021/5306–2974.

PUDONG

MALLS

Next Age. This veritable behemoth of a department store–meets-mall has loads of foreign brands, especially in the beauty department. ✉501 Zhangyang Lu, Pudong ☎021/5830–1111.

Super Brand Mall. At 10 stories, this is one of Asia's largest malls. It has a massive Lotus supermarket along with a mind-boggling array of international shops and food stops and a movie complex. It can be overwhelming if you don't love to shop. ✉168 Lujiazui Lu, Pudong ☎021/6887–7888 ⊕www.superbrandmall.com.

Times Square. The high-end products—and prices—at Times Square result in fewer customers than at most malls. Brand names such as Escada and Loewe have stores here. ✉500 Zhangyang Lu, Pudong ☎021/5836–7777.

Xinmei Union Square. Smaller, newer, and funkier than Pudong's other malls, Xinmei focuses on hip foreign brands such as Miss Sixty, G-Star Raw, Fornarina, and Swatch. ✉999 Pudong Nan Lu, Pudong ☎021/5134–1888.

PEARLS & JEWELRY

Lilli's. Here you'll find pearls, dainty silver bracelets with Chinese characters, and mah-jongg–tile bracelets. There's a pricey selection of swank silk photo albums and purses. Jewelry can also be designed and made to order ✉Level 3, River Wing, Pudong Shangri-La, 33 Fucheng Lu, Pudong ☎021/5887–6577 ⊕ www.lillishanghai. com ✉Maosheng Mansion, Suite 1D, 1051 Xinzha Lu, Jing'an ☎021/6215–5031 ✉Shanghai Center, Suite 605, 1376 Nanjing Xi

Lu, Jing'an ☎021/6279–8987 ✉*The Gatehouse, Dong Hu Villas, 1985 Hongqiao Lu, Changning* ☎021/6270–1585.

NORTH SHANGHAI

ANTIQUES

Henry Antique Warehouse. This company is the antique Chinese–furniture research, teaching, and training institute for Tongji University. Part of the showroom sometimes serves as an exhibition hall for the modern designs created jointly by students and the warehouse's 50 craftsmen. Wandering through the pieces on display is a trek through Chinese history, from intricately carved traditional altar tables to 1920s art deco furniture. ✉*796 Suining Lu, Changning* ☎*021/5219–4871* ⊕*www.antique-designer.com.*

ART

1918 Artspace. Excellent up-and-coming artists such as Jin Shan are showcased at this independent gallery's warehouse space. ✉*78 Changping Lu, Putuo* ☎*021/5228–6776* ⊕*www.1918artspace.com.*

Art Scene Warehouse. A comprehensive collection of mostly local works—from installations to photography to sculpture—fills this spacious gallery. ✉*50 Moganshan Lu, Bldg. 4, 2nd fl., Putuo* ☎*021/6277–2499* ⊕*www.artscenewarehouse.com.*

★ **M50.** This complex on Moganshan Lu is one of the hippest places in Shanghai. Get down to these old warehouses and hang out with the crowds. It's a great place to spend time wandering around the smaller galleries, chatting with the artists and dealers, and seeing China's more established artists' work as well. ✉*50 Moganshan Lu, Putuo* ☎*021/6266–0963* ⊕*www.m50.com.cn.*

ShanghART. The city's first modern-art gallery, ShanghART is *the* place to check out the work of art-world movers and shakers such as Ding Yi, Xue Song, and Shen Fan. Here you can familiarize yourself with Shanghai's young, contemporary, avant-garde artists, who are garnering increasing international attention. The gallery represents around 30 local artists as well as putting on great shows and openings in its adjacent H Space. It sells some catalogs of artists it represents and of past shows. ✉*50 Moganshan Lu, Putuo* ☎*021/6359–3923* ⊕*www.shanghartgallery.com* ✉*F-Space 315–317, 800 Guoshu Dong Lu, Yangpu* ☎*021/5506–5989.*

Shine. This stylish gallery usually showcases one or two artists at a time, and places an emphasis on painting. ✉*50 Moganshan Lu, Block 9, Putuo* ☎*021/6266–0605* ⊕*www.shineartspace.com* ✉*Shine W800, 309–313, 800 Guoshu Dong Lu, Yangpu* ☎*021/5506–9086.*

SOUVENIRS

Friendship Store. This state-owned chain for foreigners started in major Chinese cities as a sign of friendship when China first opened to the outside world. The prices, however, are not very friendly. Still, it's a good, quick source of Chinese silk clothes, snuff bottles, carpets, cal-

Continued on page 112

MARKETS
A GUIDE TO BUYING SILK, PEARLS & POTTERY

Chinese markets are hectic and crowded, but great fun for the savvy shopper. The intensity of the bargaining and the sheer number of goods available are pretty much unsurpassed anywhere else in the world.

Nowadays wealthier Chinese may prefer to flash their cash in department stores and designer boutiques, but generally, markets are still the best places to shop. Teens spend their pocket money at cheap clothing markets. Grandparents, often toting their grandchildren, go to their local neighborhood food market almost daily to pick up fresh items such as tofu, fish, meat, fruit, and vegetables. Markets are also great places to mix with the lo-cals, see the drama of bargaining take place, and watch as the Chinese banter, play with

their children, challenge each other to cards, debate, or just lounge.

Some markets have a mish-mash of items, whereas others are more specialized, dealing in one particular ware. Markets play an essential part in the everyday life of the Chinese and prices paid are always a great topic of conversation. A compliment on a choice article will often elicit the price paid in reply and a discussion may ensue on where to get the same thing at an even lower cost.

GREAT FINDS

The prices we list below are meant to give you an idea of what you can pay for certain items. Actual post-bargaining prices will of course depend on how well you haggle, while pre-bargaining prices are often based on how much the vendor thinks he or she can get out of you.

PEARLS

Many freshwater pearls are grown in Taihu; seawater pearls come from Japan or the South Seas. Some have been dyed and others mixed with semiprecious stones. Designs can be pretty wild and the clasps are not of very high quality, but necklaces and bracelets are cheap. Post-bargaining, a plain, short strand of pearls should cost around Y40.

ETHNIC-MINORITY HANDICRAFTS

Brightly colored skirts from the Miao minority and embroidered jackets from the Yunnan area are great boho souvenirs. The heavy, elaborate jewelry could decorate a side table or hang on a wall. Colorful children's shoes are embellished with animal faces and bells. After bargaining, a skirt in the markets should go for between Y220 to Y300, and a pair of children's shoes for Y40 to Y60.

RETRO

Odd items from the hedonistic '20s to the revolutionary '60s and '70s include treasures like old light fixtures and tin advertising signs. A rare sign such as one banning foreigners from entry may cost as much as Y10,000, but small items such as teapots can be bought for around Y250. Retro items are harder to bargain down for than mass-produced items.

毛泽东思想永放光芒

"MAOMORABILIA"

The Chairman's image is readily available on badges, bags, lighters, watches, ad infinitum. Pop-art–like figurines of Mao and his Red Guards clutching red books are kitschy but iconic. For soundbites and quotes from the Great Helmsman, buy the Little Red Book itself. Pre-bargaining, a badge costs Y25, a bag Y50, and a ceramic figurine Y380. Just keep in mind that many posters are fakes.

CERAMICS

Most ceramics you'll find in markets are factory-made, so you probably won't stumble upon a bargain Ming Dynasty vase, but ceramics in a variety of colors can be picked up at reasonable prices. Opt for pretty pieces decorated with butterflies, or for the more risqué, copulating couples. A bowl-and-plate set goes for around Y25, a larger serving plate Y50.

BIRDCAGES

Wooden birdcages with domed roofs make charming decorations, with or without occupants. They are often seen being carried by old men as they promenade their feathered friends. A pre-bargaining price for a medium-sized wooden cage is around Y180.

PROPAGANDA AND COMIC BOOKS

Follow the actions of Chinese revolutionary hero, Lei Feng, or look for scenes from Chinese history and lots of *gongfu* (Chinese martial arts) stories. Most titles are in Chinese and often in black and white, but look out for titles like *Tintin and the Blue Lotus,* set in Shanghai and translated into Chinese. You can bargain down to around Y15 for less popular titles.

SILK

Bolts and bolts of silk brocade with blossoms, butterflies, bamboo, and other patterns dazzle the eye. An enormous range of items made from silk, from purses to slippers to traditional dresses, are available at most markets. Silk brocade costs around Y35 per meter, a price that is generally only negotiable if you buy large quantities.

JADE

A symbol of purity and beauty for the Chinese, jade comes in a range of colors. Subtle and simple bangles vie for attention with large sculptures on market stalls. A lavender jade Guanyin (Goddess of Mercy) pendant runs at Y260 and a green jade bangle about Y280 before bargaining.

MAH-JONGG SETS

The clack-clack of mah-jongg tiles can be heard late into the night on the streets of most cities in summer. Cheap plastic sets go for about Y50. Far more aesthetically pleasing are ceramic sets in slender drawers of painted cases. These run about Y250 after bargaining, from a starting price of Y450. Some sets come with instructions, but if not, instructions for the "game of four winds" can be downloaded in English at www.mahjongg.com.

SHOPPING KNOW-HOW

When to Go

Avoid weekends if you can and try to go early in the morning, from 8 AM to 10 AM, or at the end of the day just before 6 PM. Rainy days are also good bets for avoiding the crowds and getting better prices.

Bringin' Home the Goods

Although that faux-Gucci handbag is tempting, remember that some countries have heavy penalties for the import of counterfeit goods. Likewise, that animal fur may be cheap, but you may get fined a lot more at your home airport than what you paid for it. Counterfeit goods are generally prohibited in the United States, but there's some gray area regarding goods with a "confusingly similar" trademark. Each person is allowed to bring in one such item, as long as it's for personal use and not for resale. For more details, go to the travel section of www.cbp.gov. The HM and Revenue Customs Web site, www.hmrc.gov.uk, has a list of banned and prohibited goods for the United Kingdom.

⚠ The Chinese government has regular and very public crackdowns on fake goods, so that store you went to today may have different items tomorrow. In Shanghai, for example, pressure from the Chinese government and other countries to protect intellectual property rights led to the demise of one of the city's largest and most popular markets, Xiangyang.

BEFORE YOU GO

■ Be prepared to be grabbed, pushed, followed, stared at, and even to have people whispering offers of items to buy in your ear. In China, personal space and privacy are not valued in the same way as in the West, so the invasion of it is common. Move away but remain calm and polite. No one will understand if you get upset anyway.

■ Many Chinese love to touch foreign children, so if you have kids, make sure they're aware of and prepared for this.

■ Keep money and valuables in a safe place. Pickpockets and bag-slashers are becoming common.

■ Pick up a cheap infrared laser pointer to detect counterfeit bills. The light illuminates the hidden anti-counterfeit ultraviolet mark in the real notes.

■ Check for fake items, e.g. silk and pearls.

■ Learn some basic greetings and numbers in Chinese. The local people will really appreciate it.

HOW TO BARGAIN

Successful bargaining requires the dramatic skills of a Hollywood actor. Here's a step-by-step guide to getting the price you want and having fun at the same time.

DO'S

Browsing in a silk shop

■ Start by deciding what you're willing to pay for an item.

■ Look at the vendor and point to the item to indicate your interest.

■ The vendor will quote you a price, usually by punching numbers into a calculator and showing it to you.

■ Here, expressions of shock are required from you, which will never be as great as those of the vendor, who will put in an Oscar-worthy performance at your prices.

■ Next it's up to you to punch in a number that's around 25% of the original price—or lower if you feel daring.

■ Pass the calculator back and forth until you meet somewhere in the middle, probably at up to (and sometimes less than) 50% of the original quote.

DONT'S

Chinese slippers at a ladies' market

■ Don't enter into negotiations if you aren't seriously considering the purchase.

■ Don't haggle over small sums of money.

■ If the vendor isn't budging, walk away; he'll likely call you back.

■ It's better to bargain if the vendor is alone. He's unlikely to come down on the price if there's an audience.

■ Saving face is everything in China. Don't belittle or make the vendor angry, and don't get angry yourself.

■ Remain pleasant and smile often.

■ Buying more than one of something gets you a better deal.

■ Dress down and leave your jewelry and watches in the hotel safe on the day you go marketing. You'll get a lower starting price if you don't flash your wealth.

SHANGHAI MARKETS

Antiques Market of Shanghai Old Town God Temple. (Huabao Building). Prices are high due to the prime location of this basement market in the main Yu Garden shopping complex. Shop No. 22 has revolution-era materials, including an original Little Red Book. No. 200 has textiles and embroidery. ⊠ *Yu Garden, 265 Fangbang Zhonglu, Huangpu* ✛ *On the corner of Fangbang Lu* ☎ *021/6355–9999* ⊙ *Daily 10 AM–6 PM.*

Cang Bao Antiques Building (Cang Bao Lou). During the week, you can browse four floors of booths that sell everything from Mao paraphernalia to real and fake antique porcelain. There are pearls in a wide range of colors and styles, starting from Y10 for a simple bracelet. Curios and other jewelry are on the ground floor, and check out the third floor for old photos, clothing, books, and obscure household kitsch. On Sunday the action starts long before sunrise when, according to a local saying, only ghosts should be awake, hence the market's nickname: *guishi* or "ghost market." Hawkers from the provinces arrive early to lay out their goods on the sidewalk or inside on the fourth floor. Ivory, jade,

and wood carvings are among the many goods sold here, all at negotiable prices. ⊠ *457 Fangbang Zhonglu, Huangpu* ✛ *End of Fangbang Lu near the gate to Henan Zhong Lu* ⊙ *Weekdays 9–5:30, weekends 5 AM–5:30 PM.*

★ **Fodor's Choice** Dongtai Lu Market. Mao statues, tiny shoes for women with bound feet (though foot-binding is rarely practiced in China anymore), ethnic minority-crafted clothing and embroidery, ceramic bracelets, gramophones —it's all here. This is one of the best places in town to buy gifts and souvenirs, and it's within walking distance of the shops at Xintiandi. Most of the stalls sell similar items, so your bargaining power is high as you can just walk to another store if you don't like the price. Real antiques are rare. Squeeze behind the stalls to check out the shops in the back. ⊠ *Dongtai Lu (near Xizang Lu)* ☎ *021/ 5306–8888* ✛ *Just west of Xizang Lu* ⊙ *Daily 10–6.*

Fuyou Gate Market. This department-store-meets-market with a wild variety of items spreads over three floors. On the ground floor, , No. 128 sells brightly colored Chinese folk textiles, including children's shoes, and on the second floor, shop No. 1 sells Korean stationery. ⊠ *427 Fuyou Lu, Huangpu* ✛ *Take bus No. 66 from Xizang Nan Lu* ⊙ *Daily 7 AM–5:30 PM.*

Fuyuan Market. The first floor of this market, also in the Yu Garden area, specializes in Chinese medicine. You can get jujube seeds for insomnia and kudzu vine flower for hangovers, or just wander around and marvel at the weird-looking ginseng. ⊠ *338 Fuyou Lu, Huangpu* ✛ *Across the street and just east of Fuyou Gate Market* ⊙ *Daily 7 AM–5:30 PM.*

Pu'an Lu Children's Market. A mecca for parents, children, and doting relatives, this underground market sells toys, accessories, shoes, and clothing for kids. Hunt out French and Swedish clothing brands, and big-name toy manufacturers such as Lego and Barbie, as well as some beautiful Japanese wooden toys. You might find a pretty dress for Y29 or a small wooden Noah's ark for Y35. ⊠ 10 Pu'an Lu Lu, Luwan ⊹ Take metro line 1 to Huangpi Nan Lu and walk east down Huaihai Lu a few blocks, then turn left ⊙ Daily 9:30 AM–6:30 PM.

Qi Pu Clothing Wholesale Market. Three large buildings (and counting) are stuffed to the rafters with cheap clothing here. It's good for children's clothes, but women's clothing tends to be very petite, and shoe lovers with big feet will be heartbroken. You're most likely to come away with fake designer sneakers and a T-shirt printed with misspelled or vaguely obscene English. ⊠ 168 and 183 Qipu Lu, by Henan Bei Lu, Zhabei ⊹ Take bus No. 66 from Xizang Nan Lu to Qipu Lu, or take the long walk north from the Henan Zhong Lu metro stop ⊙ Daily 6 AM–6 PM.

★ Fodor's Choice South Bund Soft-Spinning Material Market. The unusual name alludes to the veritable treasure chest of fabrics, from lurid synthetics to silk brocades, spread over three floors. Shop No. 313 can produce embroidery based on a digital image for Y40, while Nos. 231, 399, 353, 161 are Aladdin's caves of buttons and braids. No. 189 has masses of silk brocade from a negotiable Y35 per meter. Most stores have a tailoring service with prices starting at Y40 for a shirt and Y50 for a pair of pants. Be warned: the tailoring is very hit or miss. Opt for a tailor whose display clothes are similar to those you want to have made. ⊠ 399 Lujiabang Lu, Huangpu ⊹ Near the Zhongshan Er Lu end of Lujiabang Lu ⊙ Daily 8:30 AM–6 PM.

Shanghai Tan Shangsha. If craft and sewing is your bag, then heaven truly awaits at this first floor haberdashery market. With feathers, zippers, and every imaginable decoration imaginable, you will find an Aladdin's Cave of sewing and craft supplies. In general, it's a wholesale market, so the sellers are downright unfriendly when it comes to small purchases but they will sell to you eventually. If you've had enough of their attitude tip out into the surrounding side streets for more creative treats. ⊠ 388 Renmin Lu, ground floor ⊙ 7:30 AM–5:30 PM. ☎ 021/6323–0833

Wenmiao Book Market. The Sunday book market at Shanghai's only Confucian temple is worth a look for old propaganda material, comic books, and other cheap paperbacks mainly in Chinese. Look about under the tables for the cheapest items or flip through someone else's photo album. You can pick up a propaganda magazine for Y15 and then head out to the street to eat or have sticker photos made. ⊠ Wenmiao Lu, off Huaihai Lu, Huangpu ⊙ Sun. 10 AM–4 PM 🎫 Y1.

WHERE TO EAT

Street vendors selling snacks and meals surround most markets. Wenmiao market has a particularly good selection of street food, including cold noodles served from carts, fried meat on sticks, and in summer, fresh coconut milk. At the South Bund Soft-Spinning Market, on Nancang Jie, you'll find similar offerings. Rumor has it that you can even eat snake there; look for the baskets outside the small food vendors' stores. Dongtai Lu is close to Xintiandi, where you can choose from a wide selection of cafés, bars, and restaurants.

■TIP→ Avoid tap water, ice, and uncooked food. Cooked food from street vendors is generally safe unless it looks like it has been sitting around for a while.

ligraphy, jade, porcelain, and other traditional items that are certified as authentic. There's no bargaining, but there are occasional sales. ✉*1188 Changshou Lu, Changning* ☎*021/6252–5252* ⊕*www. bund-sfs.com.*

TEA

Tianshan Tea City. This place stocks all the tea in China and then some. More than 300 vendors occupy the three floors. You can buy such famous teas as West Lake dragon well tea and Wuyi red-robe tea, and the tea set to serve it in. ✉*520 Zhongshan Xi Lu, Changning* ☎*021/6259–9999* ⊕*www.dabutong.com.*

> ### BUDDHIST PARAPHERNALIA
>
> Around the **Jade Buddha Temple** (✉*Yufo Si, corner of Anyuan Lu and Jiangning Lu, Putuo*) is a cluster of stores selling Buddhist items including monks' clothing, prayer beads, lotus lamps, and candles and incense for the temple. Get an embroidered monk's bag for Y15.

XUJIAHUI & SOUTH SHANGHAI

ANTIQUES

★ **Hu & Hu Antiques.** Co-owner Marybelle Hu worked at Taipei's National Palace Museum as well as Sotheby's in Los Angeles before opening this shop with sister-in-law Lin in 1998. Their bright, airy showroom contains Tibetan chests and other rich furniture as well as a large selection of accessories, from lanterns to mooncake molds. Their prices are a bit higher than their competitors, but so is their standard of service. ✉*Alley 1885, 8 Caobao Lu, Minhang* ☎*021/3431–1212* ⊕*www. hu-hu.com.*

MALLS

Grand Gateway. Look for the dome; beneath you'll find more than 1.4 million square feet of shopping and entertainment, including a movie complex, restaurants, and floor after floor of clothing stores, plus a large number of Shanghai's shoppers. ✉*1 Hongqiao Lu, Xuhui* ☎*021/6407–0111* ⊕*www.grandgateway.com.*

HONGQIAO & GUBEI

GIFTS

Lee's Decor. Photo albums, bags, and other gifts are made using a range of Chinese brocades. Lee's is a cut above the rest due to the unusual patterns of the fabric and its range of gorgeous lamps, such as ones made from a birdcage and another shaped like a giant lotus. It's a good place for small mementoes such as business card files and ponytail bands. ✉*1038 Guyang Lu, Changning* ☎*021/6219–9230* ✉*633 Biyun Lu, Suite C3, Jinqiao, Pudong* ☎*021/5030–5733.*

NAME	PINYIN	CHINESE
Amy Lin's Pearls and Jewelry	àimǐnlínshì zhūbǎo	艾敏林氏珠宝
Art Scene	Yìshùjǐng	艺术景
Arts and Crafts Research Institute	Shànghǎi gōngyì měishù yánjiū suǒ	上海工艺美术研究所
Asian View	Yìyùchédǎo jiājù	异城岛家俱
Blue Shanghai White	Hǎishàngqīnghuā	海上青花
Brilliance Shimao International Plaza	Bǎiliánshìmào guójì guángchǎng	百联世茂国际广场
Brocade Country	Jǐnxiufǎng	锦绣纺
Bund 18	Wàitān shíbā hào	外滩十八号
Chaterhouse Books	Sānlián shūdiàn	三联书店
Commune	Gōngshè	公社
Dongtai Antique Shop	Dōngtái gǔwāndiàn	东台古玩店
Feel	Jīnfěnshìjiā	金粉世家
Foreign Languages Bookstore	Wàiwén shūdiàn	外文书店
Friendship Store	Yǒuyì shāngdiàn	友谊商店
Grand Gateway	Gǎnghuì guángchǎng	港汇广场
Hanyi	Hànyì	瀚艺
Harvest Studio	Shànghǎi yǐngjiāfǎng gōngzuòshǐ	上海盈稼坊工作室
Henry Antique Warehouse	Hànruì gǔdiǎn jiājù	汉瑞古典家俱
Hu & Hu Antiques	ǔyuè jiājù	古悦家俱
Insh	Yīngshàng gōngmào	莺裳工贸
Jade Buddha Temple	Yùfósì	玉佛寺
Jin	Jīnfěnshìjiā	金粉饰家
Jooi	Ruìyì	瑞逸
La Vie	Shēngzhífǎng	生织纺
Lee's Decor	Lìshì	力饰
Ling Ling Pearls & Jewelry	ínglíng zhūbǎo	玲玲珠宝
Madame Mao's Dowry	LMáotài shèjì	毛太设计
Mr. Yang's Calligraphy Store (no actual English name)	Yángzhènhuá bǐzhuāng	杨振华笔庄
Next Age	Dìyībābǎiban	第一八佰伴
Old Street of Yu Gardens	Lǎojiē	老街
Paddy Field	Dào	稻
Pearl City	Shànghǎi lǚyóupǐn shāngshà	上海旅游品商厦
Qiong Zi	Qíongzǐ	琼子
Raffles City	Láifúshì guángchǎng	来福士广场

NAME	PINYIN	CHINESE
Shanghai Antique and Curio Store	Shànghǎi wénwù shāngdiàn	上海文物商店
Shanghai Hongqiao Friendship Shopping Centre	Shànghǎi hongqiao yǒuyì shāngchéng	上海友谊商城
Shanghai Huangshan Tea Company	Shànghǎi huángshān cháyè yǒuxiàn gōngsī	上海黄山茶叶有限公司
Shanghai Museum Shop	Shànghǎi bǓowˇugǔan shāngdiàn	上海博物馆商店
Shanghai No. 1 Department Store	Dìyī bǎihuˇo	第一百货
Shanghai No. 1 Dispensary	Yīyào yī diàn	医药一店
Shanghai Tang	Shànghǎitān	上海滩
Shanghai Trio	Shànghǎi zǔhé	上海组合
ShanghArt	Xiánggénà huàláng	香格纳画廊
Shine	Shēng yìshù kōngjiān	升艺术空间
Shirtflag	Zédóngshíshàng	泽东时尚
Simply Life	Yìjū shēnghuóguǎn	逸居生活馆
Skylight	Tiānlài	天籁
Studio Rouge	Hóngzhài dāngdài yìshù huàláng	红寨当代艺术画廊
Super Brand Mall	Zhèngdà guǎngchǎng	正大广场
Three on the Bund	Wàitān sān hào	外滩三号
Tianshan Tea City	Dàbùtóng Tiānshān chāchéng	大不同天山茶城
Times Square	Shídài guǎngchǎng	时代广场
Tom's Gallery	Hénggǔtáng	恒古堂
Torana House	Túlánnà	图兰纳
Village Girl	Cūngū xiùwū	村姑绣屋
Xinmei Union Square	Xīnméi liánhé guǎngchǎng	新梅联合广场
Yu Gardens	Yùyuān	豫园
1918 Artspace	Yījiǔyībā yìshù kōngjiān	一九一八 艺术空间
Markets		
Antiques Market of Shanghai Old Town	Huábǎolóu	华宝楼
Cangbao Antiques building	Cángbǎolóu	藏宝楼
Dongtai Road Antiques Street	Dōngtái lù	东台路
Fuyou Gate Market	Fúyòumén shāngshà	福佑门商厦
Fuyuan Building	Fúyuán shāngshà	福源商厦
Pu'an Road Children's Market	Níhóng értóng guángchǎng	霓虹儿童广场

Arts & Nightlife

WORD OF MOUTH

"In the evening we attended a touristy attraction, but worth going to! Our seats were outstanding. The Chinese Acrobats was a non-stop show!"

—teacup123456

ARTS & NIGHTLIFE PLANNER

What's Happening Now

Nightlife is a difficult business in Shanghai, and, aside from a few stalwarts, venues can open and close faster than the speed of apartment block construction, and even places that retain the same name and location can rapidly change owners, concepts, and clientele.

For up-to-date information, check out *That's Shanghai, City Weekend,* and *SH* monthly, biweekly, and weekly expatriate magazines available at Western bars, restaurants, and hotels throughout town; or *Shanghai Daily,* the English-language newspaper.

Safety After Dark

Overall, Shanghai is very safe, but the more foreign-targeted bar districts are full of beggars and flower sellers who may grab for an unguarded wallet. Take the same precautions you would take anywhere, and refrain from overindulging unless you have a trusted companion to tuck you safely into bed. Also, be wary of the too-friendly girls at the bar streets, since odds are they are more interested in your purse strings than your handsome mug.

Top After-Dark Spots

Cotton's. A cozy, friendly, unassuming little bar in an old house with a garden, Cotton's is one of the most popular hangout spots in town.

Shanghai Dramatic Arts Center. Experience the latest in Chinese drama at the city's only professional theater.

Shelter. House goes basement in this cavernous underground dive.

Glamour Bar. This retro Bund venue is a requisite stop during any Shanghai visit.

JZ. Top-notch live jazz keeps Shanghai grooving.

Yuyintang. This unassuming concert space showcases Shanghai rock at its edgiest.

Getting Around

Although downtown Shanghai is fairly compact, suburban sprawl is creeping in nefariously. Most nightlife destinations are downtown, but pockets of activity are creeping up in farther-flung areas. Go by taxi: it's fairly safe and fairly affordable. Prices are rising, and some drivers will take advantage of drunk or ignorant passengers and go the "scenic" route, so be sure to keep your wits about you and your eyes on the route. Also, many taxi drivers are new and from out of town, so they simply do not know where they are going.

What to Wear

The Shanghai dress code is fairly laid-back, and even nicer establishments are unlikely to turn away the casually dressed. Women in Shanghai like to doll it up, and are very brand-conscious, but one need not feel obliged to follow suit; men usually head out in jeans and a tee or polo shirt. Smoking is universal in China's bars and clubs, so wear clothing that washes well or that you don't mind carrying a souvenir fragrance of smoke and stale beer.

Updated by
Lisa Movius

4

Fueled equally by expatriates and an increasingly adventurous population of locals, Shanghai boasts an active and diverse nightlife. It's hardly the *buyecheng* (city that never sleeps) of the 1930s—most places peter out after 1 or 2 AM—but until then there's a bit of something for everyone.

When it comes to the arts, Shanghai lacks the sort of performing-arts scene one would expect from a city its size, but it's getting there. The city has two world-class, state-of-the-art spaces in the Shanghai Grand Theater and the Oriental Art Center, but stodgy government management means their offerings are spotty at best. Recent years have witnessed an enthusiasm for importing popular Broadway shows, such as *Mamma Mia!* and *Hairspray,* and international music acts like Linkin Park and Avril Lavigne descend with erratic frequency. Things like acrobatics are solely of interest to tourists, and unrelated to this modern city's cultural life; however, traditional forms of Chinese opera remain popular with older citizens and are even enjoying a resurgence among young people. The city also has several competent symphonies. The Shanghai Ballet and the Shanghai Folk Dance Troupe are excellent, although forced by official directive to restrain their creativity; both perform at the various theaters around town.

THE ARTS

For modern culture more in tune with Shanghai's vibe, head to the Shanghai Dramatic Arts Center. Despite being a state-owned institution, it manages to offset sumptuous historical epics with small, provocative plays that examine burning social issues like infidelity, divorce, finances, and AIDS. The center also does projects in conjunction with the city's handful of struggling but plucky modern-dance pioneers, who also perform at private venues like Zhijiang Dream Factory and Downstream Warehouse and, occasionally, on larger stages.

ACROBATICS

Shanghai Acrobatics Troupe. The Shanghai Acrobatics Troupe performs remarkable gravity-defying stunts at both the Shanghai Center Theater and Shanghai Circus World, a glittering gold and green dome located in the center of Jing'an that seats more than 1,600 people. ✉ *Shanghai Center Theater, 1376 Nanjing Xi Lu, Jing'an* ☎ *021/6279–8945* ✉ *Shanghai Circus World, 2266 Gong He Xin Lu, Zhabei* ☎ *021/6652–7750* 💰 *Y50–Y150* ⏰ *Shows daily at 7:30* PM.

CHINESE OPERA

Kunju Opera Troupe. Kun opera, or Kunju, originated in Jiangsu Province more than 400 years ago. Because of the profound influence it exerted on other Chinese opera styles, it's often called the mother of Chinese opera. Its troupe and theater are located in the lower part of the Former French Concession. ✉ *9 Shaoxing Lu, Luwan* ☎ *021/6437–1012* 💰 *Y20–Y50* ⏰ *Performances Sat. at 1:30.*

Yifu Theatre. Not only Beijing Opera, but also China's other regional operas, such as Huju, Kunju, and Yueju, are performed regularly at this theater in the heart of the city center. Considered the marquee theater for opera in Shanghai, it's just a block off People's Square. Call the box office for schedule and ticket information. ✉ *701 Fuzhou Lu, Huangpu* ☎ *021/6351–4668.*

DANCE & CLASSICAL MUSIC

XINTIANDI & CITY CENTER

Shanghai Concert Hall. City officials spent $6 million in 2003 to move this 73-year-old hall two blocks to avoid the rumble from the nearby highway. Only then did they discover that they had moved it to sit over an even more rumbly subway line. Oops. It's the home of the Shanghai Symphony Orchestra and also hosts top-level classical musicians from around China and the world. ✉ *523 Yanan Dong Lu, Jing'an* ☎ *021/6386–9153.*

Shanghai Grand Theatre. The premier venue in town, this spectacular stage hosts top-billed domestic and international music and dance performances. In 2003 the theater hosted *Riverdance* and the Vienna Boys' Choir. ✉ *300 Renmin Dadao, Huangpu* ☎ *021/6372–8701, 021/6372–8702, or 021/6372–3833.*

FORMER FRENCH CONCESSION

Jing An Hotel. Every Sunday, the Shanghai Symphony Orchestra performs chamber music in the lobby of the Jing An Hotel. Past concerts have included pieces by Bach, Ravel, and Chinese composer Huang Yongxi. ✉ *San Diego Hall, Jing An Hotel, 370 Huashan Lu, Jing'an* ☎ *021/6248–1888 Ext. 687* 💰 *Y20.*

Shanghai Conservatory of Music. This 780-seat hall is considered a top venue for acoustic performances where the conservatory's talented students—and visiting Asian and Western musicians—perform. ⊠*20 Fenyang Lu, Xuhui* ☏*021/6431–8756.*

NANJING XI LU & JING'AM

Shanghai Center Theater. This stage serves as a home to tourist favorites the **Shanghai Acrobatic Troupe** and has hosted performers such as the Israel Contemporary Dance Group and Wynton Marsalis. The building's distinct bowed front was designed to resemble the Marriott Marquis Theater in New York's Times Square. ⊠*Shanghai Center, 1376 Nanjing Xi Lu, Jing'an* ☏*021/6279–8663.*

PUDONG

Shanghai Oriental Art Center. Designed to resemble a white magnolia in full bloom, the glass-shrouded Shanghai Oriental Art Center is an attempt to kick-start Pudong's performing-arts scene, although thus far it has featured mostly unimpressive acts. This $94-million center hopes to eventually rival the Shanghai Grand Theater and includes a 2,000-seat symphony hall, 1,100-seat theater, and 300-seat auditorium. ⊠*425 Dingxiang Lu, Pudong* ☏*021/3842–4800.*

XUJIAHUI & SOUTH SHANGHAI

★ **Downstream Warehouse.** Experimental-dance troupe Niao and other avant-garde dance and theater performers use this small, underground space for rehearsals and occasional performances. ⊠*Longcao Lu, La. 200, No. 100, 3rd fl., Xujiahui* ☏*021/5448–3368.*

Shanghai Grand Stage. Built in 1975, this 12,000-seat arena usually hosts sports events and rock and pop concerts. In 2004 the venue got a multimillion-dollar face-lift thanks to the return of favorite son Yao Ming in an NBA exhibition match. ⊠*1111 Caoxi Bei Lu, inside Shanghai Stadium Xuhui* ☏*021/6473–0940.*

THEATER

XINTIANDI & CITY CENTER

Shanghai Grand Theater. As the premier stage in town, the Shanghai Grand Theater hosts top national and international performances. When Broadway shows come to Shanghai they play here. ⊠*300 Renmin Dadao, Huangpu* ☏*021/6372–8701, 021/6372–8702, or 021/6372–3833.*

FORMER FRENCH CONCESSION

Lyceum Theatre. Although the renovation of Shanghai's oldest theater sadly replaced the dark wood with glaring marble and glass, the design of the space makes for an intimate theater experience. The Lyceum regularly hosts drama and music from around China as well as smaller local plays and Chinese opera performances. ⊠*57 Maoming Nan Lu, Luwan* ☏*021/6217–8539.*

Fodor'sChoice **Shanghai Dramatic Arts Center.** Shanghai's premier theater venue and
★ troupe, with several busy stages, the Dramatic Arts Center presents an award-winning lineup of its own original pieces, plus those of other cutting-edge groups around China. It also stages Chinese-language

adaptations, sometimes very inventive, of Western works, such as a festival of Samuel Beckett works reinterpreted through Chinese opera. It also invites a steady lineup of renowned international performers, such as the Royal Shakespeare Company. Despite being a state-owned institution, the Shanghai Dramatic Arts Center manages to offset sumptuous historical epics with small, provocative plays that examine burning social issues like infidelity, divorce, finances, and AIDS. ✉ *288 Anfu Lu, Xuhui* ☎ *021/6473–4567* ⊕ *www.china-drama.com.*

NAJING XI LU & JING'AN

★ **Majestic Theatre.** Once Asia's largest movie theater, this elegantly restored, beautiful 1930s art-deco gem regularly presents top-ticket theater from China's major troupes, as well as novelty acts and some Western performances. The venue does not have an affiliated drama troupe, so the space is open to all and sundry comers. ✉ *66 Jiangning Lu, Jing'an* ☎ *021/6217–4409.*

Shanghai Theatre Academy. The academy's performance hall presents a full schedule of student and professional works. ✉ *630 Huashan Lu, Jing'an* ☎ *021/6248–2920 Ext. 3040* ⊕ *www.sta.edu.cn.*

Zhijiang Dream Factory. A small, private, commercial theater in the trendy Tonglefang New Factories, Zhijiang stages a mixture of its own, visiting international, and collaborative theater and dance productions, as well as frequent rock concerts. It primarily targets young, white-collar Shanghainese. ✉ *28B Yuyao Lu, New Factories Bldg. 10, 4F, Jing'an* ☎ *021/6255–4062.*

NIGHTLIFE

Offerings range from world-class swank to dark and dingy dens or from young Shanghainese kids screaming experimental punk to Filipino cover bands singing "Hotel California" in a hotel basement. Prices, scenes, crowds, and ambience can range just as wildly.

Once the exclusive province of downtown, bars and clubs now dot all parts of Shanghai. There are, however, a few concentrations for those hoping to hop conveniently.

Maoming Nan Lu has long been Shanghai's nightlife hub, with the slightly seedy offerings of the main drag contrasting with the classy, upscale venues—most notably, **Face**—in the adjacent Ruijin Guest House, a hotel complex that takes up an entire city block. It has mostly closed down, with the action migrating to the newer **Tongren Lu** bar street.

Tongren Lu does have some good clubs for those who like their nightlife on the wild side. The infamous **Julu Lu** bar street is still going strong. All three of these are crowded with "fishing girls," who ask gents to give them money to buy drinks in exchange for their company (or something more)—and then they either pocket the money or take a cut from the bar.

Those looking for less-blatant sexual commerce should head to the bar, restaurant, and shopping complex of **Xintiandi**, an old Shanghai pastiche and tourist favorite with an array of clean and pleasant but pricey bars. **The Bund** is gradually emerging as a center for upscale dining and drinking, and every year sees new, swank destinations debuting in its historic halls. **Hengshan Lu** and **Fuxing Park** also offer concentrations of bars and clubs.

BARS

XINTIANDI & CITY CENTER

Barbarossa. Above the lily pond in People's Park and next to the MoCA, this beautiful Moroccan restaurant switches into a bar at night. Usually quiet and classy, it switches to hot, hip, and hopping on weekend nights, especially in summertime. ⊠*231 Nanjing Xi Lu, Huangpu* ☎*021/6318–0220.*

TMSK. Short for Tou Ming Si Kao, this exquisitely designed little bar is an aesthete's dream. Glisteningly modern, TMSK is stunning—as are the prices of its drinks. ⊠*Xintiandi North Block, Unit 2, House 11, 181 Taicang Lu, Luwan* ☎*021/6326–2227.*

THE BUND & NANJING DONG LU

Bar Rouge. The gem in the crown of the trendy, upscale Bund 18 complex, Bar Rouge is the destination du jour of Shanghai's beautiful people. It has retained that distinction for a surprisingly long time, considering the fickle nature of Shanghai's denizens of the dark. Pouting models and visiting celebrities are among the regular clientele. ⊠*Bund 18 7F, 18 Zhongshan Dong Lu, Huangpu* ☎*021/6339–1199.*

Glamour Bar. The lounge of the perennial favorite **M on the Bund**, Glamour Bar offers beautiful decor in a classy, low-key setting. ■TIP➔**However, bar patrons are forbidden from visiting the restaurant's balcony and enjoying the view that made the place famous, so visitors not planning to eat should head to other Bund locations instead.** ⊠*7F, 20 Guangdong Lu, Huangpu* ☎*021/6350–9988.*

Number Five. One of the few unpretentious bars on the Bund, Five wears its position in the basement of the Glamour Bar with pride. Affordable drinks, generously proportioned pub food, Wednesday swing-dancing nights, and sports broadcasts attract a crowd of dedicated regulars. ⊠*20 Guangdong Lu, BF, the Bund, Huangpu* ☎*021/6289–9108.*

★ **Three on the Bund.** The sophisticated Three complex, suitably enough, encloses three different bars: the swanky, dark-wood-paneled **Bar JG** on the fourth floor; the sleek white **Laris** on the sixth floor; and the more casual **New Heights/Third Degree** on the seventh floor. ⊠*3 Zhongshan Dong Lu, Huangpu* ☎*021/6321–0909.*

FORMER FRENCH CONCESSION

★ **Arch Bar and Café.** For an artsy expatriate circle, head to Arch. Its location in Shanghai's copy of the Flatiron building and in a popular residential district attracts architects and design professionals. ⊠ *439 Wukang Lu, Xuhui* ☎ *021/6466–0807.*

The Blarney Stone. The friendly Irish bartenders and lively chatter make the Blarney Stone one of the best places for drinking alone in Shanghai. ⊠ *5A Dongping Lu, Xuhui* ☎ *021/6415–7496.*

Fodor's Choice **Cotton's.** This friendly, laid-back favorite moved many times before set-
★ tling into the current old garden house. Busy without being loud, Cotton's is a rare place where you can have a conversation with friends—or make some new ones. ⊠ *132 Anting Lu, Xuhui* ☎ *021/6433–7995.*

Face. Once the see-and-be-seen place in Shanghai, Face's hipster clientele has mostly moved to Manifesto with former owner Charlie, leaving it mostly a tourist destination. But it's still beautiful: candlelit tables outside and a four-poster bed inside are the most vied-for spots in this colonial villa with Indonesian furnishings. ⊠ *Bldg. 4, Ruijin Hotel, 118 Ruijin Er Lu, Luwan* ☎ *021/6466–4328.*

Guandii. Opened by several Hong Kong celebrities, Guandii's minimalist low-slung bar attracts terminally hip Overseas Chinese who flash their wealth by ordering bottles of one of the 30 champagnes on the drink menu. ⊠ *Fuxing Park, 2 Gaolan Lu, Luwan* ☎ *021/5383–6020.*

O'Malley's. The most beloved of Shanghai's Irish pubs—not that there's much competition—O'Malley's has the requisite Guinness on tap and live Irish music. Its outdoor beer garden packs in crowds in the summer and during broadcasts of European soccer and rugby matches. Popularity with expatriate professionals makes the place expensive even by Shanghai standards. ⊠ *42 Taojiang Lu, Xuhui* ☎ *021/6474*

Sasha's. A favorite with longtime expatriates, Sasha's promises dependable drinks and food in a sumptuous villa that was once Song Meiling's home. Its rolling garden is one of the nicest places to cool off on a hot summer's night. ⊠ *9 Dongping Lu, House 11, Xuhui* ☎ *021/6247–2400.*

★ **Time Passage.** Shanghai has always been a place more inclined toward slick nightclubs and posh wine bars than mellow, conversation dives, but Time Passage has always been the exception. Cheap beers, friendly service, and a cool, if grungy, atmosphere makes it the best way to start—or end—a night on the town. ⊠ *Huashan Lu, La. 1038, No. 183, Xuhui, by Fuxing Lu* ☎ *021/6240–2588.*

Windows. Shanghai's budget-drinking chain, Windows lures patrons with Y10 drinks. Packed solid on weekends, relaxed on weekdays, it's the place to meet foreign students and hard-core booze hounds. ⊠ *Windows Roadside: 186 Maoming Nan Lu, Luwan* ☎ *021/6445–7863* ⊠ *Windows Scorecard: 681 Huaihai Zhong Lu 3F, Xuhui* ☎ *021/5382–7757* ⊠ *Windows Tembo: 66 Shaanxi Bei Lu, Jing'an* ☎ *021/5116–8857*

✉ *Windows Too: J104, Jingan Si Plaza J104, 1669 Nanjing Xi Lu, Jing'an.*

Zapata's. This Mexican restaurant and cantina thumps all night with ample margaritas and go-go dancers on the bars. Popular with the young party crowd, its ladies' nights and other specials are well attended. ✉ *5 Hengshan Lu, Xuhui* ☎ *021/6433–4104.*

NANJING XI LU & JING'AN

Blue Frog. The multiple locations of Blue Frog are popular among Westerners primarily for their hearty pub food. The chummy chill-out pads serve up more than 100 shots and well-mixed cocktails. ✉ *86 Tongren Lu, near Yanan Xilu, Jing'an* ☎ *021/6445–6634* ✉ *206-7 Maoming Nan Lu, Luwan* ☎ *021/6445–6634* ✉ *Green Sports & Leisure Center, R3-633 Biyun Lu, Pudong* ☎ *021/5030–6426* ✉ *Hongmei Entertainment St. #30, 3888 Hongmei Lu, Gubei* ☎ *021/6445–6634.*

Long Bar. In the Shanghai Center, the narrow, horseshoe-shaped Long Bar has a loyal expat-businessman clientele. Rousing rounds of liar's dice, a big-screen TV, and chest-thumping conversations among executives provide the entertainment, but the real attraction is the nightly "model show." ✉ *1376 Nanjing Xi Lu, Jing'an* ☎ *021/6279–8268.*

Malone's American Café. A magnet for Western expats and travelers, Malone's is always packed. A cover band belts out pitch-perfect versions of Van Morrison and No Doubt. TVs broadcast sporting events, and pool tables draw people upstairs to the second floor. The Shanghai Comedy Club brings in English-speaking comedians one weekend each month to the makeshift third-floor stage. ✉ *255 Tongren Lu, Jing'an* ☎ *021/6247–2400.*

★ **Manifesto.** The mastermind behind Face opened this coolly minimalist yet warmly welcoming space and took most of his clientele with him. Popular with foreigners and local white-collars alike, it serves up standard cocktails plus excellent tapas from its sister restaurant Mesa. ✉ *748 Julu Lu, Jing'an* ☎ *021/6289–9108.*

PUDONG

Dublin Exchange. Dublin Exchange is a great place for a Pudong pint. Its upmarket Irish banker's-club ambience caters to the growing wannabe Wall Street that is Lujiazui. ✉ *HSBC Bldg., 2nd fl., 101 Yincheng Dong Lu, Pudong* ☎ *021/6841–2052.*

HONGQIAO & GUBEI

Fodor'sChoice **The Door.** The stunningly extravagant interior of the Door distracts from
★ the bar's overpriced drinks. Take in the soaring wood-beam ceilings, sliding doors, and the museum's worth of antiques as you listen to the eclectic house band, which plays modern, funky riffs on Chinese music on the *erhu, pipa,* and other traditional instruments. ✉ *4F, 1468 Hongqiao Lu, Changning* ☎ *021/6295–3737.*

HOTEL BARS

XINTIANDI & CITY CENTER

JW Lounge. At the top of the JW Marriott, this lounge has a panoramic view of downtown Shanghai. ⊠ *JW Marriott, 40F, 399 Nanjing Xi Lu, Huangpu* ☎ *021/5359–4969.*

THE BUND & NANJING DONG LU

Jazz Bar. Within the historic and romantic Peace Hotel, this German-style pub has earned its fame due to the nightly performances (tickets, Y80) of the Peace Hotel Old Jazz Band. The musicians, whose average age is above 70, played jazz in dance halls in pre-1949 Shanghai. However, they're not quite as swingin' as in their prime, and a sense of tradition, rather than the quality of the music, has sustained these performances. ⊠ *Peace Hotel, 20 Nanjing Dong Lu, Huangpu* ☎ *021/6321–6888.*

FORMER FRENCH CONCESSION

Ye Lai Xiang (The Garden Hotel Bar). Few people know the real name of the Garden Hotel's terrace bar. Considered one of the most romantic spots in town for a drink when the weather is nice, this third-floor terrace overlooks the fountain and hotel's namesake 2-acre garden. ⊠ *Okura Garden Hotel, 58 Maoming Nan Lu, Luwan* ☎ *021/6415–1111.*

NANJING XI LU & JING'AN

★ **Jazz 37.** The Four Seasons' jazz bar matches its penthouse view with a stylish interior. Grab a canary-yellow leather chair by the white grand piano for some top-quality live jazz. ⊠ *The Four Seasons, 37F, 500 Weihai Lu, Jing'an* ☎ *021/6256–8888.*

Ritz-Carlton Bar. Like an airline's first-class lounge, the Ritz-Carlton Bar is the domain of a high-flying executive clientele. Cigar smoke, specialty scotches, and some of the best jazz in town cap the elite atmosphere. ⊠ *The Portman Ritz-Carlton, 1376 Nanjing Xi Lu, Jing'an* ☎ *021/6279–8888.*

PUDONG

B.A.T.S. *(Bar at the Shangri-La).* Tucked away in the basement of the Shangri-La, B.A.T.S.'s crowd ebbs and flows depending on the quality of the band. The cavelike brick-walled space has diner-style booths arranged around a large central bar. ⊠ *Pudong Shangri-La, 33 Fucheng Lu, Pudong* ☎ *021/6882–8888.*

★ **Cloud 9.** Perched on the 87th floor of the Grand Hyatt, Cloud 9 is the highest bar in the world. It has unparalleled views of Shanghai from among—and often above—the clouds. The sky-high views come with sky-high prices. ■ TIP➜ **There's a two-drink minimum in the evening, so go in the late afternoon to avoid this.** The class is offset with kitsch, as Chinese fortune-tellers and various artisans ply their skills to customers. ⊠ *Grand Hyatt, 88 Shiji Dadao, Pudong* ☎ *021/5049–1234.*

★ **Jade on 36.** This gorgeous, swanky spot in the new tower of the Pudong Shangri-La has swish drinks in a swish setting. Exquisite design and corresponding views (when Shanghai's pollution levels cooperate) have made Jade popular with the in set. ✉*Pudong Shangri-La, Tower 2, 36F 33 Fucheng, Pudong* ☎*021/6882–3636.*

Patio Bar. No skyline views here, just a dazzling, dizzying view of the Grand Hyatt's soaring 33-story atrium. It's an expensive, but impressive, stop for a pre- or postdinner drink. ✉*Grand Hyatt, 88 Shiji Dadao, Pudong* ☎*021/5049–1234.*

Pu-J's. In the Grand Hyatt, Pu-J's offers a variety of musical styles on various dance floors, plus a quiet bar area, sometimes with live jazz, and rentable karaoke rooms upstairs. ✉*Grand Hyatt, 3rd fl., 88 Shiji Dadao, Pudong* ☎*021/5049–1234 Ext. 8732.*

GAY–LESBIAN BARS & CLUBS

The gay and lesbian scene in Shanghai is low-profile, staying under the gaydar of China's still-conservative social norms. Bars and clubs usually list under the euphemism of "alternative," and some of the more popular spots have been forced to move repeatedly. Contrary to the usual clichés, the pick-up scene in Shanghai's gay bars—and there are a lot more gays than lesbians at them—is much more laid-back and low-key than the supercharged sexuality at most "mainstream" clubs. Be aware that the more aggressive pick-up scenes play out at public toilets, parks, and some bathhouses. The following are all in the Former French Concession.

Eddy's. Flamboyant, occasional drag queen Eddy has had to move his male-friendly bar all over the city over the years, but has found an apparently permanent home on this quiet stretch of Huaihai. ✉*1877 Huaihai Zhong Lu, Luwan* ☎*021/6282–0521.*

Pink Home. Pretty boys are always welcome at this happening home of the men's pick-up scene. ✉*18 Gaolan Lu, Xuhui* ☎*021/5383–2208.*

Vogue in Kevin's. At the heart of Shanghai's "alternative"—that is, gay—scene, Vogue in Kevin's is a popular party and pick-up spot. The circular bar is a good perch for people-watching and scoping out prospective partners. ✉*House 4, 946 Changle Lu, Xuhui* ☎*021/6248–8985.*

DANCE CLUBS

XIANTIANDI & CITY CENTER

Babyface. An outpost of the popular Guangzhou nightclub chain, Babyface draws a well-dressed crowd of wannabes and already-ares who don't mind waiting outside along the velvet rope before dancing to progressive house and hard trance. ✉*Shanghai Square, Unit 101, 138 Huaihai Zhong Lu, Luwan* ☎*021/6375–6667.*

Moments. The former Pegasus has never quite taken wing as well as its prior incarnation, but its convenient location keeps it on the party circuit. ✉*Golden Bell Plaza 2F, 98 Huaihai Zhong Lu, Luwan* ☎*021/5385–8187.*

Rojam. A three-level techno behemoth, Rojam is like a never-ending rave that bulges with boogiers and underground lounge lizards from the under-30 set. ✉*4/F, Hong Kong Plaza, 283 Huaihai Zhong Lu, Luwan* ☎*021/6390–7181.*

FORMER FRENCH CONCESSION

California Club. Celebrity guest DJs play everything from tribal to disco for the bold and beautiful crowd at this hip establishment. The club is part of the Lan Kwai Fong complex at Park 97, which also includes Baci and Tokio Joe's restaurants. ✉*Park 97, 2A Gaolan Lu, Luwan* ☎*021/5383–2328.*

The Shelter. Opened by a collective of Shanghai's leading DJs, the former bomb shelter basement is not for the claustrophobic, but is a favorite of Shanghai scenesters, with cheap drinks and low or no cover. ✉*5 Yongfu Lu, by Fuxing Lu, Luwan* ☎*021/6437–0400.*

YY's. The small, mellow YY's is long past its glory days, but remains a favorite for some, especially come the wee hours, and sometimes revives for big all-out parties. Named for the ancient Chinese yin-and-yang symbol, the club balances a quiet lounge with a techno dance floor that's popular with members of both sexes. ✉*125 Nanchang, Luwan* ☎*021/6466–4098.*

NANJING XI LU &JING'AN

Judy's Too. A veteran on the club scene, Judy's Too is infamous for its hard-partying, meat-market crowd. The den of iniquity was memorialized in Wei Hui's racy novel *Shanghai Baby,* among others, but in its new location it's just one more fly on the Tongren strip. ✉*78–80 Tongren Lu, Jing'an* ☎*021/6289–3715.*

The Lab. A conceptual space for Shanghai's DJs to practice their craft, the Lab also has special events and occasional barbecues on its rooftop terrace. ■TIP➔**Patrons should bring their own booze, as no alcohol is served here.** The trade-off is that most events are free. Enjoy the music while lolling on the terrace, or take a turn at showing off your spinning prowess. ✉*343 Jiaozhou Lu, Jing'an* ☎*021/5213–0877.*

Fodor's Choice
★ **Muse.** Picturesque warehouse grunge in the artsy Tonglefang New Factories makes Muse a hip-hop favorite. ✉*68 Yuyao Lu, New Factories, Jing'an* ☎*021/6218–8166.*

KARAOKE

Karaoke is ubiquitous in Shanghai; most nights, the private rooms at KTV (Karaoke TV) establishments are packed with Shanghainese crooning away with their friends. Many KTV bars employ "KTV girls" who sing along with (male) guests and serve cognac and expensive snacks. (At most establishments, KTV girls are also prostitutes.) That said, karaoke is a popular—and sometimes legitimate—pastime among locals. Many bars also have KTV rooms, but these places are dedicated karaoke establishments.

Haoledi. Crowded at all hours with locals of all ages crooning pop favorites, the popular Haoledi chain has branches virtually every-where. These listed are just a few of the outlets downtown. ✉*1111 Zhaojiabang Lu, Xuhui* ☎*021/6311–5858* ✉*180 Xizang Zhong Lu, Luwan* ☎*021/6311–5858* ✉*438 Huaihai Zhong Lu, Luwan* ☎*021/6311–5858.*

Party World. This giant establishment is one of Shanghai's most popular KTV bars, and among the few that's dedicated to the KTV instead of the KTV girls. Its warren of rooms is packed nightly. ✉*459 Wulu-muqi Bei Lu, Jing'an* ☎*021/6374–1111* ✉*109 Yandan Lu, inside Fuxing Park, Luwan* ☎*021/5306–3888* ✉*68 Zhejiang, Huangpu* ☎*021/6374–1111.*

LIVE MUSIC

Shanghai has a burgeoning alternative-music scene. Several bars have good live music nightly, and far more put on interesting concerts over the weekend. Any given Saturday, Shanghai has at least five worthy gigs to choose between. Although the alternative-recording industry remains stagnant, Shanghai has scores of active original bands giving voice to the city's evolution, and stylistically there is a bit of something for everyone.

XINTIANDI & CITY CENTER

CJW. The acronym says it all: cigars, jazz, and wine are what this swank lounge is all about. Its second location atop the Bund Center throws in a breathtaking view of the river. ✉*Xintiandi, House 2, 123 Xingye Lu, Luwan* ☎*021/6385–6677* ✉*Bund Center 50F, 222 Yanan Dong Lu, Huangpu* ☎*021/6329–9932.*

FORMER FRENCH CONCESSION

★ **Club JZ.** JZ continues its role as the king of Shanghai's jazz offerings. Various house bands and stellar guest performers from around the world mix it up nightly. ✉*46 Fuxing Xi Lu, Xuhui* ☎*021/6431–0269.*

Cotton Club. A dark and smoky jazz and blues club, the Cotton Club is an institution in Shanghai and still one of the best places to catch live jazz. The house band is a mix of Chinese and foreign musicians with a sound akin to Blues Traveler. ✉*8 Fuxing Xi Lu, Xuhui* ☎*021/6437–7110.*

★ **House of Blues and Jazz.** Decked out in memorabilia from Shanghai's jazz era of the 1930s, Blues and Jazz would be a great bar even without the music. But the several nightly sets make it a must visit. Owner Lin Dongfu, a local television personality, ensures a steady stream of minor celebrities, if the band isn't entertainment enough. ✉*60 Fuzhou Lu, Huangpu* ☎*021/6437–5280.*

NORTH SHANGHAI

Bandu Music. An unpretentious café and bar in the M50 art compound, Bandu sells hard-to-find CDs and holds concerts of traditional Chinese folk music every Saturday night. ✉*50 Moganshan Lu, Unit 11, 1F, Zhabei* ☎*021/6431–0269.*

LOCAL BREWS

Northern Chinese swear by their Baijiu, a strong, usually sweet, clear liquor, but Shanghainese opt for milder poison. Most beloved is Huangjiu, a brown brew from Shaoxing with a mild taste that resembles whiskey, which may explain why the latter is the most popular foreign liquor among locals. Huangjiu's quality is determined by whether it was brewed two, five, or 10 years ago. It is usually served warm, sometimes with ginger or dried plum added for kick.

Beer is also widely consumed; although there is a Shanghai Beer brand, it is cheap, very bitter, and mostly found in the suburbs. More common are Suntory, or Sandeli, a local brewery opened by the Japanese brand, and Reeb (yes, it's meant to be "beer" spelled backward), or Li Bo. Most bars, however, serve Qingdao and imports like Tiger, Heineken, and Budweiser, which are more expensive. More premium imported beers can also be had, but the markup is steep. For example, expect to pay at least Y60 for a pint of Guinness.

021 Live House. Take-no-prisoners grunge is the motif of this dingy, proudly underground-music dive. The clientele is mostly drawn from the nearby student population, as are most of the acts, but occasionally it attracts better-known Chinese rock bands. Relocated in 2008, the vibe persists. ⊠*1436 Jinguang Lu, Yangpu* ☎*139/1801–5880.*

Live Bar. Another grungy rock dive catering to students and serving up cheap beer and loud music, Live Bar features heavy punk, metal, and hardcore sounds as well as some pop and folk rock. ⊠*721 Kunming Lu, Yangpu* ☎*021/2833–6764.*

XUJIAHUI & SOUTH SHANGHAI

★ **288/The Melting Pot.** With live music of varying styles nightly, and up-and-coming rockers on weekends, this laid-back bar is a favorite with a range of rockers and office fodder, Chinese and foreigners alike. ⊠*288 Taikang Lu, Xuhui* ☎*021/ 6467–9900.*

Fodor'sChoice **Yuyintang.** No one or thing has done as much to bring Shanghai rock
★ out from the underground and into the open than the Yuyintang collective. Headed by sound engineer and former musician Zhang Haisheng, the group started organizing regular concerts around town and eventually opened its own space. Regular concerts, usually on Friday and Saturday nights or Sunday afternoons, spotlight the best and latest in Chinese music. Visit the Web site for a schedule. ⊠*1731 Yanan Xi Lu, but entered on Kaixuan Lu, Little White Building in Tianshan Park, Xuhui* ☎*021/5237–8662* ⊕*www.yuyintang.org.*

ARTS AND NIGHTLIFE	PINYIN	CHINESE
021 Live House	021 jiǔ bā	021酒吧
Arch Bar and Cafe	Jiǔjiān jiǔbā	玖间酒吧
B.A.T.S. (in Pudon Shangri-La)	Biānfú jiǔbā (Pǔdōng Xiānggélǐlā Diàn)	蝙蝠酒吧（浦东香格里拉店）
Bandu Music	Bàndù yīnyuè	半度音乐
Barbarossa	Bābālùshā jiǔbā	巴巴路莎酒吧
The Blarney Stone	Bùlà'nísīdòng cāntīng	布拉尼斯栋餐厅
Blue Frog	Lánwá xīcāntīng	蓝娃西餐厅
The Bund	Wàitān	外滩
California Club	Jiālìfúníyà jiǔbā	加利福尼亚酒吧
CJW	CJW juéshìyuè jiǔbā	CJW爵士乐酒吧
Cloud 9 (in Grand Hyatt)	Jiǔxiāo jiǔbā (jūnyuèjiǔdiàn nèi)	九霄酒吧（君悦酒店内）
Club JZ	Chúncuì juéshìyuè jiǔbā	纯粹爵士乐酒吧
Cotton Club	Miánhuā jùlèbù	棉花俱乐部
Cotton's	Miánhuā jiǔbā	棉花酒吧
The Door	Qiánmén jiǔbā	乾门酒吧
Downstream Warehouse	Xiàhémǐcāng	下河米仓
Dublin Exchange	Dōubólín kāfēiguǎn	都柏林咖啡馆
Fuxing Park	Fùxīng gōngyuán	复兴公园
Glamour Bar (in M on the Bund)	Mèilì jiǔbā (waitān wu hao)	魅力酒吧（外滩5号）
Guandii	Guāndǐ jiǔbā	官邸酒吧
Haoledi	Hǎolèdī KTV	好乐迪KTV
Hengshan Road	Héngshān lù	衡山路
House of Blues and Jazz	Bùlǔsī yǔ juéshì zhīwū	布鲁斯与爵士之屋
Jade on 36 (in Pudon Shangri-La)	Fěicuì 36 jiǔbā (Pǔdōng Xiānggélǐlā diàn)	翡翠36酒吧（浦东香格里拉店）
Jazz 37 (in Four Seasons)	Juéshì 37 jiǔbā (sìjì jiǔdiàn nèi)	爵士37酒吧四季酒店内）
Jazz Bar (in Peace Hotel)	Juéshì bā (hépíng fàndiàn nèi)	爵士吧（和平饭店内）
Jing An Hotel	Jìng'ān bīnguǎn	静安宾馆
Julu Road Bar Street	Jùlùlù jiǔbājiē	巨鹿路酒吧街
JW Lounge (in JW Marriott)	JW (wànháo jiǔdiàn nèi)	JW（万豪酒店内）
Kunju Opera Troupe	Shànghǎi kūnjùtuán	上海昆剧团
The Lab	Shíyànshì	实验室
Live Bar	Xiànchǎng jiǔbā	现场酒吧
Long Bar	Chángláng jiǔbā	长廊酒吧
Lyceum Theatre	Lánxīn dàxìyuàn	兰馨大戏院

ARTS AND NIGHTLIFE	PINYIN	CHINESE
Majestic Theatre	Měiqí dàxìyuàn	美琪大戏院
Malone's American Café	Mǎlóng měishì cāntīng	马龙美式餐厅
Maoming Nan Road Bar Street	Màomíngnánlù jiǔbājiē	茂名南路酒吧街
Number Five Bar On the Burn	Waitān wǔhào jiǔbā	外滩五号酒吧
Number Three on the Bund	Wàitān sānhào	外滩三号
O'Malley's	Oumǎlì jiǔbā	欧玛莉酒吧
Party World	Qiánguì KTV	钱柜KTV
Patio Bar (in Grand Hyatt)	Tiāntíng jiǔbā (jūnyuè jiǔdiàn nèi)	天庭酒吧（君悦酒店内）
Ritz-Carlton Bar	Lìjiā jiǔbā	丽嘉酒吧
Rojam	Luójié jiǔbā	罗杰酒吧
Sasha's	Sàshā	萨莎
Shanghai Acrobatics Troupe	Shànghǎi aájìtuán	上海杂技团
Shanghai Center Theater	Shànghǎi shāngchéng jùyuàn	上海商城剧院
Shanghai Concert Hall	Shànghǎi yīnyuètīng	上海音乐厅
Shanghai Conservatory of Music	Shànghǎi yīnyuè xuéyuàn	上海音乐学院
Shanghai Dramatic Arts Center	Shànghǎi huàjù yìshù zhōngxīn	上海话剧艺术中心
Shanghai Grand Stage	Shànghǎi dàwǔtái	上海大舞台
Shanghai Grand Theater	Shànghǎi dàjùyuàn	上海大剧院
Shanghai Oriental Art Center	Shànghǎi dōngfāng yìshù zhōngxīn	上海东方艺术中心
Shanghai Theatre Academy	Shànghǎi xìjù xuéyuàn	上海戏剧学院
Time Passage	Zuotianjintianmingtian jiǔbā	昨天今天明天酒吧
TMSK (short for Tou Ming Si Kao)	Tòumíngsīkǎo jiǔbā	透明思考酒吧
Tongren Road	Tóngrén lù jiǔbājiē	同仁路酒吧街
Xintiandi	Xīntiāndì	新天地
Ye Lai Xiang (The Garden Hotel Bar) (in Okura Garden Hotel)	Yèláixiāng jiǔbā (huāyuán fàndiàn nèi)	夜来香酒吧（花园饭店内）
Yifu Theatre	Yìfū wǔtái	逸夫舞台
Yuyintang	Yùyīntáng	育音堂
Zapata's	Zapata's jiǔbā	Zapata's 酒吧

Where to Eat

Tea ceremony in Whampoa Club at Three on the Bund

WORD OF MOUTH

"We passed the Naxiang Dumpling Restaurant and I actually passed up the chance to get on line and buy some . . . I just couldn't get another dumpling into my mouth . . . a miracle . . . Previously unbeknownst to me, I had a dumpling limit, and I had reached it. We ended up eating there later on in the week, and the lunch was so fabulous that I'm glad I waited until I was actually hungry."

—wiselindag

WHERE TO EAT PLANNER

Dining Hours

Dining in Shanghai can be a protracted affair. Dinner hours in restaurants begin at around 5 PM, but often carry on late into the night. Many of the classic, local restaurants popular with the Shanghainese only close after the last diners have left, which sometimes keeps them open until the wee hours of the morning. Generally, though, dinner is eaten between 6 and 11 PM, with fine dining generally happening later than casual meals.

Reservations & Dress

Reservations are always a good idea: we mention them only when they're essential or not accepted. Book as far ahead as you can, and reconfirm as soon as you arrive. Generally, we mention dress only when men are required to wear a jacket or a jacket and tie. Many upmarket restaurants don't require a jacket or tie, but have a no-shorts or -sandals policy. This can be a problem in the extreme summer heat, so call ahead to confirm the dress code.

Top 5 Restaurants

Meilongzhen. Shanghai's most famous restaurant is known for its extensive seafood menu.

T8. Innovative, elegant, and classy T8 is the star performer in the very competitive Xintiandi restaurant market. It has excellent food, impeccable service, and beautiful surroundings.

Roosevelt Steakhouse. Located in the historic Marshall Mansions in the French Concession, Roosevelt offers the best steak in the city (and quite possibly the country) in a relaxed ambience.

Jade on 36. This opulent restaurant is an experience second to none, and has a spectacular 36th-floor view across the Huangpu to the historical sights of the Bund.

Whampoa Club. Offering excellent interpretations of Shanghainese cuisine, this Bund showpiece combines the classic and contemporary in an exquisite location.

Street Snacks

Shanghai's street snacks are the city's main culinary claim to fame. You'll see countless sidewalk stands selling the famed *xiaolongbao* (the city's signature steamed dumplings, filled with pork or crab and soup broth), as well as various types of *bing* (Chinese pancakes), and *baozi* (filled or unfilled steamed buns).

On the Menu

Shanghainese food is fairly typical Chinese, with dark, sweet, and oily dishes served in great abundance. The dish sizes can be quite small, so be careful when ordering—it's not unusual for two diners to polish off six dishes plus rice. The drink of choice with Shanghainese food is *huangjiu*, or yellow wine. It's a mild-tasting sweetish rice wine, which pairs well with the local cuisine.

Shanghai is full of fine restaurants from around the world, but sometimes, the finest dining experience in the city can be had with a steamer tray of xiaolongbao (Shanghai's signature dumplings—small steamed buns filled with pork and crab meat in broth) matched with a cold beer. River fish is often the highlight (and most expensive part) of the meal, and hairy crab is a seasonal delicacy. It may not be the finest dining, but it's an enjoyable and genuine taste of the city.

Prices

From an American or European point of view, fine dining in Shanghai can be very economical. Even in the fanciest restaurants, main courses are unlikely to cost more than US$35. However, in Shanghai, like everywhere else, fame is on par with price. The famous restaurants charge as much as the international market will bear—prices that often don't reflect the quality of the dining experience.

If you're looking for an excellent meal and you don't care about the restaurateur's name, then exceptional dining experiences can be had for half the price, without sacrificing quality or ambience. Sadly, the difference between $$$$ and $$$ is often just fame and face rather than quality.

For the adventuresome, great local food can be found everywhere for laughably cheap prices, even in fairly nice restaurants. The food is good and inexpensive ($1 to $5 per dish), and the experience of eating at a small, unknown restaurant is pure China. We recommend you try it at least once.

What It Costs in Yuan

¢	$	$$	$$$	$$$$
Restaurants				
under Y40	Y40–Y80	Y81–Y150	Y151–Y300	over Y300
Prices are for a main course at dinner.				

Paying & Tipping

Credit cards are becoming more widely accepted, but this is still a cash economy. Hotels and upmarket international restaurants will take plastic. Be aware, though, that there are occasional lapses in international banking services, so when in doubt, bring cash. Ask your hotel for more information about international ATMs.

China is not a tipping nation, so tip carefully! Most hotels add a service charge (usually 15%) onto the bill—check the fine print on the menu. If the service has been very good, tipping 5% to 15% is a welcome gesture. Bear in mind that some restaurants will not allow the staff to accept tips, whereas in others the tips are seized by management.

5

Updated by
David Taylor

When eating out, you'll notice most Chinese restaurants in Shanghai have large, round tables. The reason will become clear the first time you eat a late dinner at a local restaurant and are surrounded by jovial, laughing groups of people toasting and topping off from communal bottles of beer, sharing cigarettes, and spinning the lazy Susan loaded with food.

Dining out with friends and family isn't just a favorite social activity; it's a ritual. Whether feting guests or demonstrating their growing wealth, hosts will order massive, showy spreads. Although take-away boxes for leftovers are starting to become popular, proud hosts wouldn't deign to use them. Shanghai's standing as China's most international city is reflected in its dining scene. You can enjoy *jiaozi* (dumplings) for breakfast, foie gras for lunch, and Kobe beef teppanyaki for dinner.

It's traditional to order several dishes, plus rice, to share among your party. Tipping is not expected, but sophistication still comes at a price. Although you can easily eat as the locals do at Chinese restaurants for less than Y40, even simple Western meals will cost you a more Western price.

Most restaurants in Shanghai offer set lunches—multicourse feasts—at a fraction of the usual price. It's the best dining deal going, allowing you to eat at local Chinese restaurants for Y25 or less and at such places as M on the Bund without completely blowing your budget. Also, check out the "Restaurant Events" section of *That's Shanghai*, or *Smartshanghai.com*, which list dining discounts and promotions around town.

OLD CITY

Narrow and crowded, the Old City is all that's left of old China in Shanghai. The area is home to the spectacular Yuyuan Gardens, and can be a good location to find some traditional-style food in an authentic environment. We recommend that the adventurous go out into the side streets around Fangbang Lu in search of authentic Chinese snacks.

■TIP→ When dining in these small local restaurants always ask the price first—with no English menu, many sellers in this area aren't above raising the price after your first bite.

$$ ✕**Lv Bo Lang.** A popular stop for visiting dignitaries, Lv Bo Lang (pro-
CHINESE nounced "Lü Bo Lang") is a perfect photo op of a restaurant. The traditional three-story Chinese pavilion with upturned eaves sits next to the Bridge of Nine Turnings in the Yu Garden complex. The food is good but not great, with many expensive fish choices on the menu. Among the best dishes are the crab meat with bean curd, the braised eggplant with chili sauce, and the sweet *osmanthus* cake, made with the sweetly fragrant flower of the same name. ⊠*115 Yuyuan Lu, Huangpu* ☎*021/6328–0602* ⚑*Reservations essential* ▤*AE, DC, MC, V.*

XINTIANDI & CITY CENTER

5

The center of the gastronomic city, the City Center and Xintiandi contain some of the finest restaurants in the city, like T8, the JW Marriott's restaurants, and the trendy Barbarossa.

$$ ✕**Barbarossa.** Modern Middle Eastern food in a setting taken from
MIDDLE EASTERN the *Arabian Nights,* Barbarossa is a popular evening destination. The decoration is amazing, albeit possibly flammable, with billowing draperies swathing the space, and the food and service are reasonable. At around 10 PM, Barbarossa becomes a club, so don't aim for a late dinner unless you like mingling with the party people. ⊠*People's Square, 231 Nanjing Xi Rd., next to the Shanghai Art Museum, Luwan* ☎*021/6318–0220* ▤*AE, DC, MC, V.*

$–$$ ✕**Kabb.** Serving burgers, salads, and other standards of American
AMERICAN food, this café in Xintiandi is distinguished for its superb location. The food is good, but without distinction, though the portions are massive. Service is slightly indifferent, and the pricing is rather high for such pedestrian fare. However, it does fill the bill for a quick lunch on the sidewalk tables. ⊠*Xintiandi, 181 Taicang Lu, 5 Xintiandi Bei Li, Luwan* ☎*021/3307–0798* ▤*AE, DC, MC, V.*

$$$ ✕**T8.** A veteran of the Shanghai fine dining scene, T8 has garnered
INTERNATIONAL its share of headlines for its stunning interior and inspired contem-
Fodor'sChoice porary cuisine. The restaurant occupies a traditional shikumen house
★ within Xintiandi and has modernized the space with raw stone floors, carved-wood screens, and imaginative lighting that transforms shelves full of glasses into a modern-art sculpture. The show kitchen turns out exciting fusion dishes from fresh seasonal ingredients. Like the clientele, the wine list is exclusive, with many labels unavailable elsewhere in Shanghai. ⊠*No. 8, North Block, Xintiandi, La. 181 Taicang Lu, Luwan* ☎*021/6355–8999* ⚑*Reservations essential* ▤*AE, DC, MC, V* ☽*No lunch Mon.*

$$ ✕**Tairyo.** Teppanyaki has invaded Shanghai. More down-to-earth than a
JAPANESE sophisticated sushi bar, teppanyaki (Japanese barbecue) includes sushi, sashimi, barbecued meats, and a wide variety of Western and Eastern dishes. It does serve à la carte, but at Y150 for all you can eat and drink, Tairyo's main attraction is obvious. Just walk in, take a seat

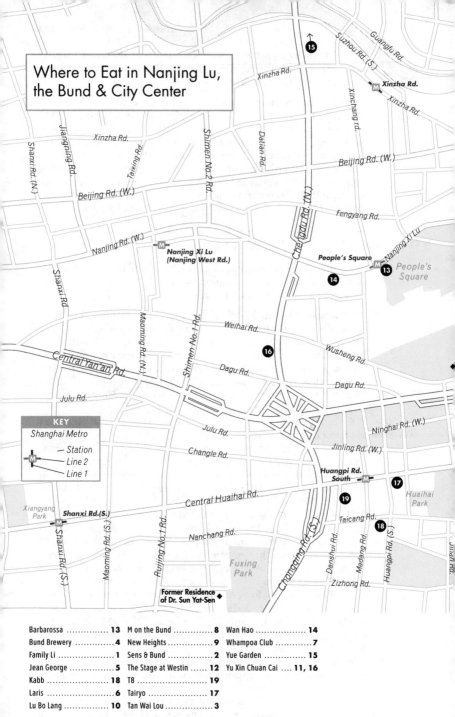

Where to Eat in Nanjing Lu, the Bund & City Center

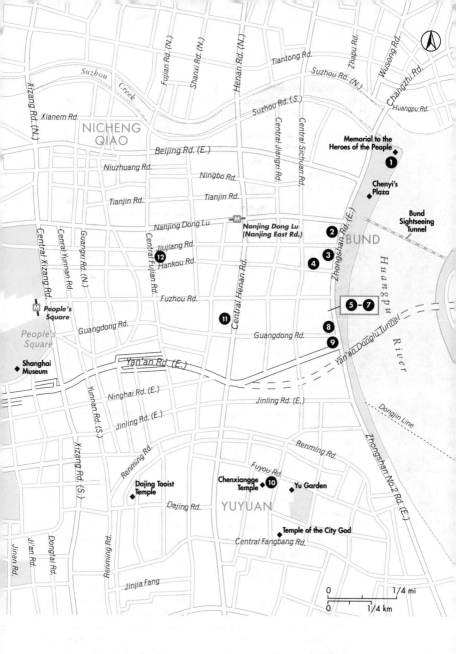

CHINESE CUISINE

To help you navigate China's cuisines we have used the following terms in our restaurant reviews.

Cantonese: A diverse cuisine that roasts and fries, braises and steams. Spices are used in moderation. Dishes include fried rice, sweet-and-sour pork, and roasted goose.

Chinese: Catch-all term used for restaurants that serve cuisine from multiple regions of China.

Chinese fusion: Any Chinese cuisine with international influences.

Chiu chow: Known for its vegetarian and seafood cuisine, which are mostly poached, steamed, or braised. Dishes include *popiah* (non-fried spring rolls), baby oyster congee, and fish ball noodle soup.

Hunan: Cooking methods feature stewing, frying, braising, and smoking. Flavors are spicy, with chili peppers, shallots, garlic, and dried and preserved condiments. Signature dishes are Mao's braised pork, steamed fish head with shredded chilies, and spicy eggplant in garlic sauce.

Macanese: An eclectic blend of southern Chinese and Portuguese cooking, featuring the use of salted dried fish, coconut milk, turmeric, and other spices. Common dishes are "African" barbecued chicken with spicy piri piri sauce, pork buns, and curried baked chicken.

Mandarin (Beijing): Dishes from Beijing typically are snack sized, featuring ingredients like dark soy paste, sesame paste, and sesame oil. Regional specialties include Peking duck, moo shu pork, and quick-fried tripe.

Northern Chinese (inner Mongolia and environs): Staples are lamb and mutton, preserved vegetables, and noodles, steamed breads, pancakes, stuffed buns, and dumplings. Common dishes are cumin-scented lamb, congee porridge with pickles, and Mongolian hotpot.

Shanghainese: Cuisine characterized by rich flavors produced by braising and stewing, and the use of alcohol in cooking. Dumplings, noodles, and bread are served more than rice. Signature dishes are baby hairy crabs stir-fried with rice cake slices, steamed buns and dumplings, and "drunken chicken."

Sichuan (central province): Famed for bold flavors and spiciness from chilies and Sichuan peppercorns. Dishes include "dan dan" spicy rice noodles, twice-cooked pork, and tea-smoked duck.

Taiwanese: Diverse cuisine centers on seafood, pork, rice, soy, and fruit. Specialties include "three cups chicken" with a sauce made of soya, rice wine, and sugar; oyster omelets; cuttlefish soup; and dried tofu.

Tibetan: Cuisine reliant on foodstuffs grown at high altitudes, including barley flour; yak meat, milk, butter, and cheese; and mustard seed. Salted black tea with yak butter is a staple beverage.

Yunnan (southernmost province): This region's cuisine is noted for its use of vegetables, fruit, bamboo shoots, and flowers in its spicy preparations. Dishes include rice noodle soup with chicken, pork, and fish; steamed chicken with ginseng and herbs; and the cured Yunnan ham.

at the grill, and indulge while the chef prepares your dinner as you watch. We recommend the Mongolian King Steak, but the menu has English and pictures, so pick and choose. This is a perfect no-effort dinner destination. Private rooms are available for groups larger than seven (reservations essential). ⊠*Hong Kong New World Plaza, South Building, 283 Huaihai Rd., 3rd fl., Luwan* ☎*021/6390–7244* ▭*AE, DC, MC, V.*

$$$–$$$$
CANTONESE
✕**Wan Hao.** On the 38th floor of the JW Marriott overlooking People's Square, Wan Hao is an elegant and relatively inexpensive Chinese restaurant. It specializes in Cantonese dishes, though the menu contains other popular options like Peking Duck and spicy chicken. The food is good without being exceptional, and the ambience is pleasant. Look to the seasonal dishes for the freshest options; the kitchen team is always updating the menu. Servings tend to be on the small side—Chinese-style—despite the Western place settings, so expect to order several dishes per person. If you're unsure about your order, the staff is happy to help. ⊠*JW Marriott at Tomorrow Square, 38th fl., 399 Nanjing Xi Lu, Luwan* ☎*021/5359–4969* ▭*AE, DC, MC, V.*

> **WORD OF MOUTH**
>
> "The best xiaolongbao soup dumplings in the world [are at] Jia Jia Tangbao! It is a hole in the wall: sit on stools at crowded tables (I shared with 3 young and pleasant office guys who wanted to practice English), no napkins, no tea. I ordered the seaweed egg flower soup. The soup dumplings with crab meat in Shanghai are sweet water crab meat——they taste special." —Shanghainese

NANJING DONG LU & THE BUND

The Bund is the heart of modern Shanghai, with the colonial history of Puxi facing the towering steel and glass of Pudong. The stellar view of the river and Pudong has attracted some of the finest restaurant development in town, including Bund18, Sens & Bund, and Three on the Bund. However, many visitors complain that the Bund restaurants are more style than substance. We find that it's well worth your effort to experience what this area has to offer.

$$
AMERICAN
★
✕**Bund Brewery.** The Bund Brewery is ostensibly a brew pub but is more popular as an off-Bund dinner alternative. The food is modern, well-portioned pub fare, and the service reasonably attentive. It's a good choice for an unpretentious meal after a day's Bund sightseeing, or before heading out to the clubs for the evening. ⊠ *11 Hankou Lu, Huangpu* ☎*021/6321–8447* ▭*AE, DC, MC, V.*

$$$$
MANDARIN
✕**Family Li Imperial Cuisine.** This spectacular restaurant, a newer branch of the famous Beijing Imperial restaurant, deserves a visit despite high prices (set menus begin at Y600). Using family recipes smuggled from the Forbidden City a century ago, Family Li gives the closest thing to a taste of imperial food. There are only nine rooms, and only set menus are served. Reservations more than 24 hours in advance are a must. ⊠*Huangpu Park, 500 East Zhongshan Yi Rd., Huangpu* ☎*021/5308–1919* ⌔*Reservations essential* ▭*AE, DC, MC, V.*

$$$$ ✕ **Jean Georges.** One of the fine-dining warhorses of the Bund, Jean
FRENCH   Georges is the Shanghai project of celebrity-chef Jean Georges Vongerichten. The dark, intimate dining room in the historic Three on the Bund brings the right note of class to the experience, though the service can occasionally be lacking. The contemporary French cuisine is well executed but expensive. This is a showcase restaurant and at its best, Jean Georges is on the top of the scene; however, too often it falls just a little short of perfection. ⊠ *Three on the Bund, 4th fl., 3 Zhong Shan Dong Yi Rd., Huangpu* ☎ *021/6321–7733* ▤ *AE, DC, MC, V.*

$$$$ ✕ **Laris.** The signature restaurant of star Australian chef David Laris,
INTERNATIONAL   this is one of the few Bund restaurants with the owner/chef in residence. The innovative Continental-inspired cuisine is good and well presented, though service can sometimes slip. Any trip to Laris, or its adjoining Vault Bar, is best crowned with a visit to the Chocolate Room, where some of Shanghai's finest chocolate creations will assault your waistline. ⊠ *Three on the Bund, 6th fl., 3 Zhongshan Dong Yi Lu, Huangpu* ☎ *021/6321–9922* ⚑ *Reservations essential* ▤ *AE, DC, MC, V.*

$$$$ ✕ **M on the Bund.** The original international restaurant on the Bund,
INTERNATIONAL   M has long had a reputation as a place to see and be seen. Its brunch is a landmark affair, business lunches are good, and the food can still occasionally reach dizzying heights. Come for a drink in the downstairs Glamour bar before your meal. ⊠ *20 Guangdong Lu, 7th fl., Huangpu* ☎ *021/6350–9988* ▤ *AE, DC, MC, V.*

$$$ ✕ **New Heights.** Perched atop prestigious Three on the Bund, New
AMERICAN   Heights is a surprisingly unpretentious restaurant. With a gorgeous
★   terrace overlooking the river and a solid menu of generally North American standard fare, this is an excellent destination for the weary Bund tourist. We recommend having a late lunch while basking in the afternoon sun on the terrace. Try the hamburger with a cold beer. ⊠ *Three on the Bund, 7th fl., 3 Zhong Shan Dong Yi Rd., Huangpu* ☎ *021/6321–0909* ▤ *AE, DC, MC, V.*

$$$$ ✕ **Sens & Bund.** The Shanghai branch of the France-based Jardin du Sens
FRENCH   Group, Sens & Bund serves contemporary Mediterranean cuisine overlooking the Huangpu. The food is good, the service well-trained, and the ambience relaxing. The prices are quite high, but the overall quality and consistency makes this a better choice than many of its neighbors. Ask for a river-view table. ⊠ *Bund 18, 1 Zhongshan Dong Yi Rd., 6th fl., Huangpu* ☎ *021/6323–9898* ▤ *AE, DC, MC, V.*

$$–$$$ ✕ **The Stage at Westin.** While The Stage is usually a fairly standard five-
ECLECTIC   star buffet, it is also home to Shanghai's most popular Sunday Cham-
★   pagne brunch. Costing almost Y500 and booked two–three weeks in advance, the brunch at the Westin has become an institution. Check it out if you feel the need for some decadent indulgence. ⊠ *Level 1, The Westin Shanghai Bund Center, 88 Henan Zhong Rd., Huangpu* ☎ *021/6335–0577* ⚑ *Reservations essential* ▤ *AE, DC, MC, V.*

$$ ✕ **Tan Wai Lou.** Bund18's Chinese restaurant, Tan Wai Lou serves up
CHINESE   nouveau-Cantonese cuisine in a refined setting. The food is good and
FUSION   well presented, though the non-Chinese service can be a little jarring for a diner expecting a classic Chinese meal. Still, the seafood is very fresh and the view of the Huangpu spectacular. ⊠ *Bund18, 5th fl., 18*

Continued on page 147

A CULINARY TOUR OF CHINA

For centuries, the collective culinary fragrances of China have drifted far beyond its borders and tantalized the entire world. In the decades following the revolution, most Westerners couldn't get anything close to genuine Chinese cuisine. But with China's arms now open to the world, a vast variety of Chinese flavors are more widely accessible than ever.

Four corners of the Middle Kingdom

In dynasties gone by, a visitor to China might have to undertake a journey of a thousand li just to feel the burn of an authentic Sichuanese hotpot, and another to savor the crispy skin and juicy flesh of a genuine Beijing roast duck. Luckily for us, the vast majority of regional Chinese cuisines have made successful internal migrations. As a result, Sichuanese cuisine can be found in Guangzhou, Cantonese dim sum in Urumuqi, and the cumin-spiced lamb-on-a-stick, for which the Uigher people of Xinjiang are famous, is now grilled all over China.

Before you begin your journey, remember, a true scholar of Middle Kingdom cuisine should first eliminate the very term "Chinese food" from their vocabulary. It hardly encompasses the variety of provincial cuisines and regional dishes that China has to offer, from succulent Shanghainese dumplings to fiery Sichuanese hotpots.

To guide you on your gastronomic journey, we've divided the country's gourmet map along the points of the compass—North, South, East, and West. Bon voyage and *bon appétit!*

NORTH

THE BASICS

Cuisine from China's Northeast is called *dongbei cai*, and it's more wheat than rice based. Vegetables like kale, cabbage, and potatoes are combined with robust, thick soy sauces, garlic (often raw), and scallions.

Even though many Han Chinese from southern climates find mutton too gamey, up north it's a regular staple. In many northern cities, you can't walk more than a block without coming across a small sidewalk grill with *yang rou chua'r*, or lamb-on-a-stick.

NOT TO BE MISSED

The most famous of all the northern dishes is Peking duck, and if you've ever had it well prepared, you'll know why Beijingers are proud of the dish named for their city.

The fowl is cleaned, stuffed with burning millet stalks and other aromatic combustibles, and then slow-cooked in an oven heated by a fire made of fragrant wood. Properly cooked, Peking duck should have crispy skin, juicy meat, and none of the grease. Peking duck is served with pancakes, scallions, and a delicious soy-based sauce with just a hint of sweetness.

The ultimate window dressing.

LEGEND HAS IT

Looking for the best roast duck in Beijing? You won't find it in a luxury hotel. But if you happen to find yourself wandering through the Qianmendong hutong just south of Tiananmen Square, you may stumble upon a little courtyard home with a sign in English reading LI QUN ROAST DUCK. This small and unassuming restaurant is widely considered as having the best Peking roast duck in the capital. Rumor has it that the late leader Deng Xiaoping used to send his driver out to bring him back Li Qun's amazing ducks.

THE CAPITAL CITY'S NAMESAKE DISH

Soy-based hoisin sauce

A perfectly prepared duck

Pancakes

Scallions

SOUTH

(left) Preparing for the feast. (top right) Dim sum as art. (bottom right) Meat-filled Beijing dumplings.

THE BASICS

The dish most associated with Southern Chinese cuisine is dim sum, which is found in great variety and abundance in Guangdong province, as well as Hong Kong and Macau. Bite-size dim sum is usually eaten early in the day. Any good dim sum place should have dozens of varieties. Some of the most popular dishes are *har gao*, a shrimp dumpling with a rice-flour skin, *siu maai*, a pork dumpling with a wrapping made of wheat flour, and *chaahabao*, a steamed or baked bun filled with sweetened pork and onions. Adventerous eaters should order the chicken claws. Trust us, they taste better than they look.

> The Cantonese saying *"fei qin zou shou"* roughly translates to "if it flies, swims or runs, it's food."

For our money, the best southern food comes from Chaozhou (Chiuchow), a coastal city only a few hours' drive north of its larger neighbors. Unlike dim sum, Chaozuo cuisine is extremely light and understated. Deep-fried bean curd is also a remarkably fresh Chaozuo dish.

NOT TO BE MISSED

One Chaozuo dish that appeals equally to the eye and the palate is the plain-sounding mashed vegetable with minced chicken soup. The dish is served in a large bowl, and resembles a green-and-white yin-yang. As befitting a dish resembling a Buddhist symbol, a vegetarian version substituting rice gruel for chicken broth is usually offered.

SOUTHWEST AND FAR WEST

Southwest

THE BASICS

When a person from the Southwest asks you if you like spicy food, consider your answer well. Natives of Sichuan and Hunan take the use of chilies, wild pepper, and garlic to blistering new heights. These two areas have been competing for the "spiciest province in China" title for centuries. The penchant for fiery food is likely due to the weather—hot and humid in the summer and harshly cold in the winter. But no matter what the temperature, if you're eating Sichuan or Hunan dishes, be prepared to sweat.

Southwest China shares some culinary traits with both Southeast Asia and India. This is likely due to the influences of travelers from both regions in centuries past. Traditional Chinese medicine also makes itself felt in the regional cuisine. Theory has it that sweating expels toxins and equalizes body temperature.

As Chairman Mao's hometown province, Hunan has a number of dishes with revolutionary names. The most popular are red-cooked Hunan fish *(hongshao wuchangyu)* and red-cooked pork *(hongshao rou)*, which was said to have been a personal favorite of the Great Helmsman.

The hotter the better.

NOT TO BE MISSED

One dish you won't want to miss out on in Sichuan is *mala zigi*, or "peppery and hot chicken." It's one part chicken meat and three parts fried chilies and a Sichuanese wild pepper called *huajiao* that's so spicy it effectively numbs the tongue. At first it feels like eating Tiger Balm, but the hot-cool-numb sensation produced by crunching on the pepper is oddly addictive.

KUNG PAO CHICKEN

One of the most famous Chinese dishes, Kung Pao chicken (or gongbao jiding), enjoys a legend of its own.

Though shrouded in myth, its origin exemplifies the improvisational skills found in any good Chinese chef. The story of Kung Pao chicken has to do with a certain Qing Dynasty–era (1644-1911) provincial governor named Ding Baozhen, who arrived home unexpectedly one day with a group of friends in tow. His cook, caught in between shopping trips, had only the chicken breast and a few vegetables he was planning to cook for his own dinner. The crafty chef diced the chicken into tiny bits and fried it up with everything he could find in the cupboard—some peanuts, sugar, onion, garlic, bits of ginger, and a few handfuls of dried red peppers—and hoped for the best.

(top left) Chowing down at Kashgar's Sunday Market. (center left) Eat, drink, and be merry! (bottom left) Monk stirring tsampa barley. (right) Juggling hot noodles in the Xinjiang province.

Far West

THE BASICS

Religion is the primary shaper of culinary tradition in China's Far West. Being a primarily Muslim province, chefs in Xinjiang don't use pork products of any kind. Instead, meals are likely to be heavy on spiced lamb. Baked flat breads coated in sesame seeds are a specialty. Whole lamb roasted on a spit, fine spicy tomato salads, and lightly spiced mutton and vegetable soups are also favorites.

NOT TO BE MISSED

In Tibet, climate is the major factor dictating cuisine. High and dry, the Tibetan plateau is hardly suited for rice cultivation. Whereas a Han meal might include rice, Tibetan cuisine tends to include tsampa, a ground barley usually cooked into a porridge. Another staple that's definitely an acquired taste is yak butter tea. Dumplings, known as *momo*, are wholesome and filling. Of course, if you want to go all out, order the yak penis with caterpillar fungus.

EAST

(top left) Flash cooking with the wok. (top right) Juicy steamer dumplings. (bottom right) Harvesting China's staple. (bottom left) Shanghai's sublime hairy crab.

THE BASICS

The rice, seafood, and fresh vegetable-based cooking of the southern coastal provinces of Zhejiang and Jiangsu are known collectively as *huiyang cai*. As the area's biggest city, Shanghai has become a major center of the culinary arts. Some popular dishes in Shanghai are stir-fried freshwater eels and finely ground white pepper, and red-stewed fish—a boiled carp in sweet and sour sauce. Another Shanghai favorite are *xiaolong bao*, or little steamer dumplings. Similar to Cantonese dim sum, xiaolong bao tend to be more moist. The perfect steamed dumpling is meant to explode in your mouth in a juicy burst of meat.

NOT TO BE MISSED

Drunken anything! Shanghai chefs are known for their love of cooking with wine. Dishes like drunken chicken, drunken pigeon, and drunken crab are all delectable meals cooked with prodigious amounts of Shaoxing wine. People with an aversion to alcohol should definitely avoid these. Another meal not to be missed is hairy freshwater crabs, which only come into season in October. One enthusiast of the dish was 15th-century poet and essayist Li Yu, who wrote of the dish in near-erotic terms. "Meat as white as jade, golden roe . . . to use seasoning to improve its taste is like holding up a torch to brighten the sunshine."

Zhongshan Dong Yi Rd., Huangpu ☎*021/6339–1188* ✍*Reservations essential* ☰*AE, DC, MC, V.*

$$$ ✕**Whampoa Club.** A popular member of the Bund scene, Whampoa
CHINESE Club is nouveau Chinese at its best. With a focus on fresh seafood
FUSION and interesting interpretations of Shanghai classics, this is a destina-
tion worth checking out. As befits a celebrity venue, prices are steep,
but generally worth the expense. ⊠*Three on the Bund, 4th fl., 17
Guangdong Lu, Huangpu* ☎ *021/6321–3737* ✍*Reservations essen-
tial* ☰*AE, DC, MC, V.*

$$ ✕**Yu Xin Chuan Cai.** Yu Xin offers fantastic Sichuan food and is extremely
SICHUAN popular with the locals. Each of the two locations seats hundreds and
is always full. Book ahead, or be prepared to wait around 30–60 minutes for a table. Try the tea-smoked duck. ⊠ *3F, 333 South Cheng
Du Lu and 5F, No. 399, Jiu Jiang Lu, Huangpu* ☎*021/5298–0438,
021/5298–0439 (Cheng Du Lu), 021/6361–1777 (Jiu Jiang Lu)* ✍*Reservations essential* ☰*No credit cards.*

FORMER FRENCH CONCESSION

Brimming with fine-dining options and small bistros in a maze of tree-
lined streets, the Old French Concession is the place to go for diverse
cuisine, from traditional French to local Shanghainese.

$$ ✕**A Future Perfect.** Hidden away down a little lane off Huashan Road,
INTERNATIONAL AFP has the kind of terrace space that most Shanghai-restaurant own-
Fodor'sChoice ers can only dream of: spacious, tranquil, yet intimate. It is a must
★ for those hot afternoons and evenings in Shanghai when you need a
break from shopping and sightseeing and deserve some good food and
good drinks. We recommend being adventurous; the menu is fresh
and there is plenty to satisfy any taste. AFP has an on-site bakery and
serves breakfast every morning. ⊠*16, La. 351, Huashan Lu, Xuhui*
☎*021/6248–8020* ☰*AE, DC, MC, V.*

$$ ✕**Azul and Viva.** In creating his continent-hopping New World cuisine,
INTERNATIONAL owner Eduardo Vargas drew upon his globe-trotting childhood and
Fodor'sChoice seven years as a restaurant consultant in Asia. As a result, the menus
★ in Azul, the tapas bar downstairs, and Viva, the restaurant upstairs,
feature a delicious, delicate balance of flavors that should please any
palate. Classics like beef carpaccio contrast cutting-edge dishes like
coffee-glazed pork. Lunch and weekend brunch specials are lower
priced. The relaxed, romantic interior—dim lighting, plush pillows,
and splashes of color against muted backdrops—invites you to take
your time on your culinary world tour. ⊠*18 Dongping Lu, Xuhui*
☎*021/6433–1172* ☰*AE, DC, MC, V.*

$$–$$$ ✕**Baci.** Good Italian food can be difficult to find in Shanghai, but one
ITALIAN such place is Baci at Park 97 in Fuxing Park, the Shanghai entertainment complex of Hong Kong's famous Lan Kwai Fong Group. The
restaurant itself is elegant and subdued, with intimate booths lining
the walls. The only complaint would be the clubs next door in the Lan
Kwai Fong complex: after 10 PM, it can get noisy, so be aware that a

CLOSE UP

Where to Refuel Around Town

When all you want is a quick, inexpensive bite, look for these local chains. They all have English menus and branches in Shanghai's tourist areas.

Ajisen Noodles: This Japanese-style noodle joint has an English menu with photos, and fast service.

Babela's Kitchen: Western food, Chinese style. Babela's offers acceptable pizza, wings, pasta, and some Chinese dishes for prices below Y40. It's a useful option for families with younger children who want something familiar.

Bi Feng Tang: Dim sum is the sum of the menu, from chickens' feet to less exotic items such as shrimp wontons and barbecue pork pastries.

Blue Frog: A popular destination for after-work dinner and drinks, Blue

Frog offers American fare, good drinks, and weekly specials. Blue Frog now has locations in Shanghai's most popular districts: Hongmei, Xujiahui, Jing'an, and the Concession.

Sumo Sushi: Sit along the carousel and watch the chefs slice and dice fresh made-to-order sushi. You can order set lunches, à la carte, or all you can eat.

Gino Café: The inexpensive Italian fare at this café chain includes pizza, pasta, sandwiches, and good desserts.

Manabe: This Japanese coffeehouse chain serves Western fast food, such as club sandwiches and breakfast fare, as well as Japanese snacks and a long list of teas.

---

late dinner mightn't be so tranquil. ⊠*Fuxing Park, 2A Gaolan Rd., Xuhui* ☎*021/5383–2328 or 021/5383–2208* ⊟*AE, DC, MC, V.*

¢–$
SHANGHAINESE
✕**Bao Luo.** Although its English menu caters to tourists, Bao Luo is Chinese dining as the Chinese enjoy it, a fact confirmed by the usual long wait for a table. The freshness of the ingredients comes through in every dish, from perfectly steamed broccoli to tender stewed crab and pork meatballs. Tables are packed tightly in this small, two-story restaurant, and the light-wood interior merely serves as backdrop to the can't-miss cuisine. However, look closely for the red-scroll neon sign with a tiny BL, or you may miss the restaurant altogether. ⊠*271 Fumin Lu, by Changle Lu, Jing'an* ☎*021/5403–7239* ⚑*Reservations essential* ⊟*No credit cards.*

$$–$$$
ITALIAN
✕**Da Marco.** Its reasonably priced authentic Italian fare makes Da Marco a universal favorite in Shanghai. The original location, on Dong Zhu An Bang Lu, is a magnet for Italian expats in search of a late dinner, whereas the Yandang Lu location attracts a mix of locals, expats, and tourists. Lasagna, ravioli, Caprese salad, and pizza (11 types) are among the classic dishes on the menu. The wine list includes many selections under Y200. Three-course set lunches are a popular option. You can choose alfresco dining under the bright orange awning or a comfy seat on the banquette in the sunshine-yellow dining room. ⊠*62 Yandang Lu, Luwan* ☎*021/6385–5998* ⚑*Reservations essential* ⊟*No credit cards.*

¢
KOREAN
✕**Gao Li Korean Restaurant.** Hidden on a small lane, Gao Li is a bit of a hole-in-the-wall, but its eight tables are packed with patrons until 2 AM.

It serves great, cheap food and specializes in tender and delicious grilled meats. You do the cooking, placing thin cuts of meat on a small gas grill and then wrapping them in a lettuce leaf and adding chili sauce. The noodle dishes are some of the best in town: try the cold Korean noodles for dessert. ⊠*No. 1, 181 Wuyuan Lu, Xuhui* ☎*021/6431–5236* ⊟*AE, DC, MC, V.*

$–$$ ✕ **Ginger.** Tucked away in the avenues of the French Concession, Ginger
CAFÉ is a European-flavored café. Small and intimate, Ginger is a place for conversations over lunch, or a relaxing afternoon coffee. We recommend having your drinks in the tiny enclosed terrace, for a rare tranquil Shanghai moment. ⊠ *299 Fuxing Xi Lu, near Huashan Lu, Xuhui* ☎*021/6433–9437* ⊟*AE, DC, MC, V.*

$–$$ ✕ **Gokohai.** Possibly the best shabu-shabu restaurant in Shanghai, Goko-
JAPANESE hai is a hidden gem. Shabu-shabu is Japanese hotpot—each diner gets a pot and chooses a selection of meats (served in enormous, sombrero-shaped piles) and vegetables to cook in the broth. You'll need to ask for the all-you-can-eat deal for Y88 (drinks not included), because it is not mentioned on the menu. ⊠ *1720 Huaihai Lu, near Wuxing Lu, Xuihui* ☎*021/6471–7657* ⊟*Local only.*

¢–$ ✕ **Grape.** Entry-level Chinese food at inexpensive prices has been Grape's
CHINESE calling card since the mid-1980s. This cheerful two-story restaurant
★ remains a favorite among expatriates and travelers wandering the Former French Concession. The English menu, with photos, includes such recognizable fare as sweet-and-sour pork and lemon chicken as well as delicious dishes like garlic shrimp and *jiachang doufu* (home-style bean curd), all of which are served with a smile. ⊠*55 Xinle Lu, Luwan* ☎*021/5404–0486* ⊟*No credit cards.*

¢–$ ✕ **Hot Pot King.** *Huo guo,* or hotpot, is a popular Chinese ritual of at-
CHINESE the-table cooking, in which you simmer fresh ingredients in a broth. Hot Pot King reigns over the hotpot scene in Shanghai because of its extensive menu as well as its refined setting. The most popular of the 17 broths is the yin-yang, half spicy red, half basic white pork-bone broth. Add in a mixture of veggies, seafood, meat, and dumplings for a well-rounded pot, then dip each morsel in the sauces mixed tableside by your waiter. The minimalist white-and-gray interior has glass-enclosed booths and well-spaced tables, a nice change from the usual crowded, noisy, hotpot joints. ⊠*1416 Huaihai Rd., 2nd fl., Xuhui* ☎*021/6473–6380* ⊟*AE, DC, MC, V.*

¢–$ ✕ **Indian Kitchen.** The Indian chefs working their magic in the show
INDIAN kitchen provide the entertainment while you wait for a table at this tremendously popular restaurant. Delicious butter chicken marsala and tandoor-cooked chicken tikka taste as good as they look in the picture menu, which is packed with classic Indian dishes. The many bread selections include melt-in-your-mouth spring onion *parotas* (fried flat bread). Two blocks from the Hengshan Lu metro station and bar neighborhood, Indian Kitchen is a convenient dining spot and the perfect start to an evening out on the town. ⊠*572 Yongjia Lu, Xuhui* ☎*021/6473–1517* ⌂*Reservations essential* ⊟*AE, DC, MC, V.*

$$–$$$ ✕ **Leonardo's.** The Hilton's Italian restaurant, Leonardo's is unusually
ITALIAN good, with solid interpretations of Italian classics. The service is five-

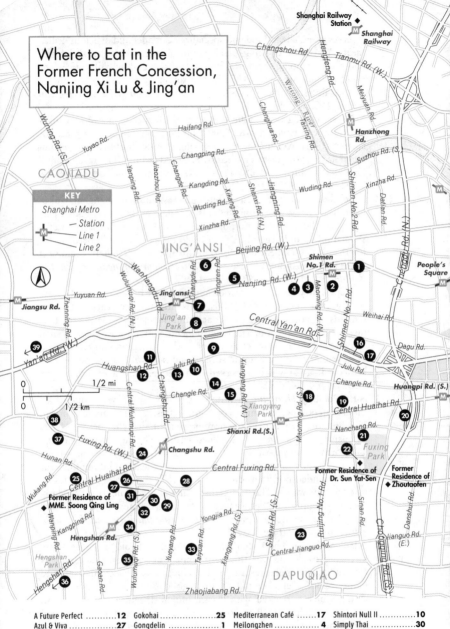

Where to Eat in the Former French Concession, Nanjing Xi Lu & Jing'an

KEY

Shanghai Metro
- Station
Ⓜ — Line 1
— Line 2

star standard, though the location, at the rear of the Hilton's lobby, is slightly inconvenient. The menu is seasonal, and matched with an adequate wine list, though wines are on the expensive side. The easy chairs in the Leonardo da Vinci–themed dining room are a little too comfortable, making it slightly difficult to sit at a table. ⊠ *Hilton Shanghai, 250 Huashan Rd., Luwan* ☏ *021/6248–0000* ▤ *AE, DC, MC, V.*

$-$$ ✕ **Lost Heaven.** Lost Heaven serves Yunnan cuisine—Southern Chinese
YUNNAN from the borders of Myanmar and Cambodia. The food is reminiscent
★ of Thai cuisine, and well-prepared, while the dining room evokes Yunnan architecture despite its location in the middle of the French Concession. Service is acceptable without being polished. Certainly worth a look. ⊠ *38 Gao You Lu, near Fuxing Xi Lu, Luwan* ☏ *021/6433–5126* ▤ *AE, DC, MC, V.*

$$-$$$ ✕ **Mesa.** Nestled on the quiet residential street Julu Lu, Mesa is a little
INTERNATIONAL hard to find. The unassuming facade is backed with a stark minimalist
☾ decor, which belies the sophistication of the seasonal menu. The cuisine is contemporary, meaning the chef has been allowed to experiment, and the results are impeccable. The wine list is comprehensive, with an excellent by-the-glass selection, and not overpriced. ⊠ *748 Julu Lu, Luwan* ☏ *021/6289–9108* ▤ *AE, DC, MC, V* ⊘ *No lunch Mon. Brunch Saturday and Sunday, 9:30-4. Babysitting available for brunch.*

¢ ✕ **Nepali Kitchen.** An intimate space with low tables and cushions
NEPALESE upstairs, and paper-lamp-lit small tables downstairs, Nepali Kitchen is a cozy spot to sample the subtleties of Nepalese fare. In addition to the curries and naan found at most Indian restaurants, there are tasty starters like fried cheese balls and potato chili. ⊠ *La. 819, 4 Julu Rd., Xuhui* ☏ *021/5404–6281* ⌕ *Reservations essential* ▤ *No credit cards* ⊘ *Closed Mon.*

$$$-$$$$ ✕ **Paulaner Brauhaus.** There's a shortage of good German food in Shang-
GERMAN hai. Paulaner Brauhaus does its best to fill the void with a menu of classic German dishes like Wiener schnitzel, bratwurst, and apple strudel, accompanied by the house-brewed lager. The food isn't inspiring, and seems pricy, but the beer is excellent. The Fenyang Lu location is more laid-back, with a courtyard beer garden in the summer. The Xintiandi branch, open for lunch, is great for people-watching. ⊠ *150 Fenyang Lu, Xuhui* ☏ *021/6474–5700* ⊘ *No lunch* ⊠ *House 19–20, North Block Xintiandi, 181 Taicang Lu, Luwan* ☏ *021/6320–3935* ▤ *AE, DC, MC, V.*

$-$$ ✕ **Quan Ju De.** The original Beijing branch of this restaurant has been
MANDARIN *the* place to get Peking duck since 1864. This Shanghai branch opened in 1998, but the Peking duck is just as popular here. Few dishes are more definitively Chinese than Peking duck, the succulent, slow-roasted bird that is never quite prepared properly overseas. The ambience here is "old Chinese" to the point of absurdity, complete with hostesses dressed in traditional imperial outfits including platform tasseled shoes and flashy headpieces, and with lattice screens scattered throughout the dining room. The menu has both pictures and English text to explain the different types of duck available. One minor drawback is the size of the portions. There are no half ducks on the menu, and a full duck is rather a lot for two people. ⊠ *786 Huaihai Zhonglu, 4th fl., Luwan* ☏ *021/5404–5799* ⌕ *Reservations essential* ▤ *AE, DC, MC, V.*

$$$–$$$$
AMERICAN
Fodor'sChoice
★

✕ **Roosevelt Prime Steakhouse.** Located in the historic Marshall Mansions of the French Concession, Roosevelt offers the best steak in the city (and quite possibly the country) in a relaxed steak-house ambience. The meat is USDA Prime, cooked to your specification in an imported stone oven. These steaks are not cheap, ranging in price from Y300 to Y1,200 for the porterhouse, though regular mains are considerably more reasonable. Try the mac and cheese with black truffle, and the excellent Caesar salad. ✉ *160 Taiyuan Lu, Xuhui* ☎*021/6433–8240* ▤*AE, DC, MC, V.*

¢
CHINESE

✕ **Shen Yue Xuan.** Dim sum is the big draw at Shen Yue Xuan. It's the featured fare at breakfast and lunch and has its own separate menu. The restaurant's Cantonese–Shanghainese dinner menu features good-for-you foods, though the amount of grease often counteracts other ingredients. The two-story restaurant is nestled in Dingxiang Garden, a verdant 35-acre playground the late Qing Dynasty–mandarin Li Hongzhang gave to his concubine Ding Xiang. There's outdoor seating on a large terrace, and the second floor overlooks the garden. Book early if you want a table by the window. ✉*849 Huashan Lu, Xuhui* ☎*021/6251–1166* ⌕*Reservations essential* ▤*AE, DC, MC, V.*

$$$
JAPANESE

✕ **Shintori Null II.** The restaurant's plain gray wall facing Julu Lu belies the futuristic design masterpiece that lies behind it. With its magic sliding doors, etched glass, and concrete airplane hangar of a dining room, the restaurant is often compared to a set from *Blade Runner*. The French-influenced Japanese cuisine uses curry and foie gras to dress up the sushi, sashimi, tempura, and noodle dishes. ✉*803 Julu Lu, Jing'an* ☎*021/5404–5252* ⌕*Reservations essential* ▤*AE, DC, MC, V* ⊘*No lunch weekdays.*

$–$$
THAI
Fodor'sChoice
★

✕ **Simply Thai.** Unpretentious Thai fare at moderate prices has earned this restaurant a loyal expat clientele. Customers flock to the tree-shaded patio to savor such favorites as green and red curries (on the spicy side) and stir-fried rice noodles with chicken (on the tame side). The appetizers are all first-rate, especially the crispy spring rolls and samosas. The wine list includes a half-dozen bottles under Y200, a rarity in Shanghai. The branch in Xintiandi is a bit noisier but features the same great food and prices. ✉*5C Dongping Rd., Xuhui* ☎*021/6445–9551* ⌕*Reservations essential* ▤*AE, DC, MC, V.*

$–$$
SICHUAN
★

✕ **South Beauty.** The elegant interior and spicy fare are both worth beholding at South Beauty. As the sliding-glass front door opens—revealing a walkway between two cascading walls of water—it splits the restaurant's trademark, red, Chinese-opera mask in two. Likewise, the menu is split down the middle between cooler Cantonese cuisine and sizzling-hot Sichuan fare. Don't be fooled: even dishes with a one-pepper rating, like sautéed baby lobster, will singe your sinuses. ✉*28 Taojiang Lu, Xuhui* ☎*021/6445–2581* ⌕*Reservations essential* ▤*AE, DC, MC, V.*

$$–$$$
INDIAN

✕ **The Tandoor.** Don't miss the unbelievable *murgh malei kebab* (tandoori chicken marinated in cheese and yogurt), or try some vegetable curries—*palak aloo* (spinach with peas) or *dal makhani* (lentil). Decorated with mirrors, Indian artwork, and Chinese characters dangling from the ceiling, the restaurant is ingeniously designed to show the route of Buddhism from India to China. The management and staff, all from India, remain close at hand throughout the meal to answer questions and attend to your needs. ✉*Jinjiang Hotel, South Building, 59 Maoming Nan Lu, Luwan* ☎*021/6472–5494* ⚲*Reservations essential* ▤*AE, DC, MC, V.*

$–$$
ITALIAN

✕**Trattoria Isabelle.** Inexpensive, slightly run-down, and quirkily romantic, Trattoria Isabelle offers simple Italian food in an old Concession row house. The food is very well prepared for the price, and the wine list has a selection of bottles under Y200, a rarity for Western restaurants. ✉ *139 Xing'an Lu, near Yandang Lu, Luwan* ☎*021/5386–0827* ▤*No credit cards.*

$
INDIAN
★

✕**Vedas.** In the heart of the Old French Concession, Vedas is a popular destination for quality Indian food at affordable prices. Decor is dark and comfortable. The menu focuses on northern Indian cuisine, and the hand-pulled naan bread, thick and succulent curries, fiery vindaloos, and house-made chutneys are excellent. Vedas is extremely popular, and always bustling. Don't expect an intimate, tranquil dining experience, but do expect spectacular food and great service in a pleasant if busy environment. ✉*550 Jianguo Xi Lu, Xuhui* ☎*021/6445–8100* ⚲*Reservations essential* ▤*AE, DC, MC, V.*

$–$$
CAFÉ
Fodor's Choice
★

Vienna Café. With coffee, cakes, and excellent breakfasts, Vienna is a Shanghai institution, for those in the know. This is not a trendy café, nor is it trying to be anything other than an Austrian coffeehouse. With wood-paneled main room and a tiny solarium, this is a perfect place for a Sunday breakfast. Try an Einspanner with the Sachertorte, and never mind the effects to your waistline. ✉ *25 Shaoxing Lu, near Ruijin Er Lu, Xuhui* ☎*021/6445–2131* ▤*No credit cards.*

$–$$
SHANGHAINESE

✕**Yang's Kitchen.** Traditional Shanghainese food without the usual *renao* (hot and noisy atmosphere) draws customers down the narrow laneway to the restored villa that's now home to Yang's Kitchen. The 19-page menu includes familiar dishes like mandarin fish, the obligatory *xiaolongbao*, as well as 22 soups. An apricot-and-white side dining room, with small tables spaced widely for privacy, is popular among couples and solo diners seeking a quiet and inexpensive meal. ✉*No. 3, 9 Hengshan Lu, Xuhui* ☎*021/6445–8418* ▤*AE, DC, MC, V.*

NANJING XI LU & JING'AN

A business hub, the Jing'an area is understandably heavy on Western dining options. Familiar American franchises like Tony Roma's rub shoulders with Buddhist restaurants and popular expat destinations like Element Fresh and Malone's, making this a vibrant dining destination.

$–$$
SHANGHAINESE
★

✕**1221.** This stylish but casual eatery is a favorite of hip Chinese and expatriate regulars. The dining room is streamlined chic, its crisp white tablecloths contrasting the warm golden walls. Shanghainese food is the mainstay, with a few Sichuan dishes. From the extensive 26-page menu (in English, pinyin, and Chinese), you can order dishes like sliced *you tiao* (fried bread sticks) with shredded beef, a whole chicken in a green-onion soy sauce, and *shaguo shizi tou* (pork meatballs). ⊠*1221 Yanan Xi Lu, Changning* ☎*021/6213–6585 or 021/6213–2441* ⚑*Reservations essential* ▤*AE, DC, MC, V.*

$$–$$$
KOREAN
✕**Arirang.** One of Shanghai's oldest Korean eateries, Arirang serves meat and seafood barbecued on smoky coals right before your eyes, along with *kimchi* (pickled cabbage), noodles, and cold appetizers. The meat dishes are a good choice here, as is the always delicious *congyoubing*, or onion pancake. ⊠*28 Jiangsu Bei Lu, 2nd fl., Changning* ☎*021/6252-7146* ▤*AE, DC, MC, V.*

$–$$
SICHUAN
✕**Ba Guo Bu Yi.** Its name translates as "Sichuan Common People," which describes both the restaurant's style of food and the local clientele it attracts. The menu is a greatest hits of Sichuan cuisine, including *mapo tofu,* braised tofu with chili and brown pepper, and *lazi ji,* chicken smothered in chili peppers. The two-story dining room is arranged like a traditional Chinese house, around a central courtyard. ⊠*1018 Dingxi Lu, Changning* ☎*021/5239-7779* ⚑*Reservations essential* ▤ *AE, DC, MC, V.*

$–$$
INDONESIAN
✕**Bali Laguna.** Overlooking the lily pond in Jing'an Park and with interior and alfresco dining, Bali Laguna is a popular choice for couples. Balinese music piped along the statue- and palm-lined walkway sets the mood even before the sarong-clad hostess welcomes you inside the traditional, three-story, Indonesian-style house or to a pond-side table. The menu is heavy on seafood, such as grilled fish cakes and chili crab, which captures the fire of Indonesian cuisine. Quench it with a Nusa Dua Sunset or other Bali-inspired cocktail. ⊠*Jing'an Park, 189 Huashan Lu, Jing'an* ☎*021/6248–6970* ⚑*Reservations essential* ▤*AE, DC, MC, V.*

$
BRAZILIAN
✕**Brasil Steak House.** Shanghai has developed a taste for *churrascarias,* Brazilian-style barbecue restaurants. Brasil Steak House is perhaps the best, due in large part to the percentage of South Americans on staff. The all-you-can-eat lunches and dinners pair a salad bar with an unending rotation of waiters brandishing skewers of juicy chunks of meat for your consideration; just nod your approval and they'll slice off a piece for your plate. The large picture windows brighten up the room and let you observe the parade of people passing through Jing'an Park. ⊠*1649 Nanjing Xi Lu, Jing'an* ☎*021/6255–9898* ▤*AE, DC, MC, V.*

$–$$
AMERICAN
✕**Element Fresh.** Freshly made and generously portioned salads and sandwiches draw crowds of people to this bright lunch spot in the Shanghai Center. The creative menu of innovative sandwiches, light pasta dishes, and excellent salads has made Element Fresh one of the most popular lunch destinations in the city. For the health-conscious, an equally creative drink menu has long lists of fresh fruit juices and smoothies. ⊠*Shanghai Center, 1376 Nanjing Xi Lu, Jing'an* ☎*021/6279–8682* ▤*AE, DC, MC, V.*

¢–$
VEGETARIAN
FodorsChoice
★
✕ **Gongdelin.** A two-story gold engraving of Buddha pays tribute to the origins of the inventive vegetarian dishes this restaurant has served for 80 years. Chefs transform tofu into such surprising and tasty creations as mock duck, eel, and pork. The interior is just as inspired, with Mingstyle, wood-and-marble tables; metal latticework; and a soothing fountain. Tables fill up quickly after 6 PM, so either arrive early or buy some

goodies to go at the take-out counter. ⊠ *445 Nanjing Xi Lu, Huangpu* ☎ *021/6327–0218* ▭ *AE, DC, MC, V.*

$$$–$$$$
ITALIAN
★
✕**Issimo.** Located in JIA hotel and run by Salvatore Cuomo, Issimo is a great (albeit upmarket) Italian restaurant. The food is well-prepared and plentiful (all pastas are for two), and the ambience is as exquisite as a designer boutique venue should be. The menu is small and focused on seasonal offerings and the wine list excellent. Reservations are recommended. ⊠ *JIA Hotel, 2nd fl., 931 West Nanjing Lu, entrance on Taixing Lu, Jingan* ☎ *021/6287–9009* ▭ *AE, DC, MC, V.*

$$–$$$
FRENCH
✕**Le Bouchon.** This charming French wine bar and bistro serves up tasty traditional French fare in a cozy 12-table hideaway. The Y350 degustation menu is a greatest hits of French cuisine: escargot, foie gras, and duck breast. The baked Alaska (ice cream over a sponge cake topped with meringue), a rare treat in Shanghai, must be ordered separately, but it's worth it. The wine list includes two dozen reasonably priced French selections. ⊠ *1455 Wuding Xi Lu, Changning* ☎ *021/6225–7088* ⌲ *Reservations essential* ▭ *AE, DC, MC, V* ⊘ *No lunch. Closed Sun.*

$–$$
AMERICAN
✕**Malone's American Café.** An attempt at a classic American sports bar in Shanghai, Malone's is very popular with the expat crowd. Its substantial menu includes American favorites like buffalo wings, burgers, and pizza, as well as Asian dishes. The food isn't superb but it's satisfying as a casual meal in a cheerful bar setting. ⊠ *255 Tongren Lu, Jing'an* ☎ *021/6247–2400* ▭ *AE, DC, MC, V.*

$
INDIAN
✕**Masala Art.** A rising star of the Indian dining scene, Masala Art is a little hard to find but worth the effort. Serving excellent breads and sublime curries in an understated dining area, Masala Art wins praise for fine food at very reasonable prices. ⊠ *397 Dagu Lu, Jing'an* ☎ *021/6327–3571* ⌲ *Reservations essential* ▭ *AE, DC, MC, V.*

$
MEDITERRA-
NEAN
✕**Mediterranean Café.** Buried in the east end of town, the Med is a hidden gem. Small and unpretentious, it is one of the few places in town serving authentic Mediterranean food. With highlights of genuine bagels (you'll be hard-pressed to find them elsewhere in the city), kosher-deli foods, feta, and falafel, this is a perfect lunch destination. We recommend the pita falafel—hot, green, and crunchy, served with an Israeli salad—and the latkes, which are perfectly fried potato pancakes served with sour cream. ⊠ *415 DaGu Rd., Jing'an* ☎ *021/6327–0897 or 021/6295–9511* ▭ *No credit cards.*

$$$
SHANGHAINESE
Fodor's Choice
★
✕**Meilongzhen.** Probably Shanghai's most famous restaurant, Meilongzhen is one of the oldest dining establishments in town, dating from 1938. The building served as the Communist Party headquarters in the 1930s, and the traditional Chinese dining rooms still have their intricate woodwork, and mahogany and marble furniture. The exhaustive menu has more than 80 seafood options, including such traditional Shanghainese fare as Mandarin fish, and dishes with a more Sichuan flair, like shredded spicy eel and prawns in chili sauce. Since this is a stop for most tour buses, expect a wait if you haven't booked ahead. ⊠ *No. 22, 1081 Nanjing Xi Lu, Jing'an* ☎ *021/6253–5353* ⌲ *Reservations essential* ▭ *AE, DC, MC, V.*

$–$$
CANTONESE
✕**The Onion.** On the high-traffic sector of Nanjing Xi Lu, Onion is a simple concept Cantonese restaurant, serving quality Cantonese dishes

at reasonable prices. The decor is light and airy, with well-spaced tables and efficient service. The menu is extensive and bilingual, with lunch specials and dim sum. This is a very low-stress restaurant, and a great destination for a simple and satisfying meal. ⊠*881 Nanjing Xi Lu, 3rd fl., Jing'an* ☎*021/6267–5477* ▭*No credit cards.*

$$–$$$ ✕**Palladio.** As befits the showcase Italian restaurant at the Ritz, the
ITALIAN award-winning Palladio is simply excellent. With a seasonal menu and positively obsequious service, this restaurant will always satisfy your senses—though it might also deplete your wallet. Set lunches begin at Y198, and dinners soar into the heady heights. ⊠*Portman Ritz-Carlton, 1376 Nanjing Xi Lu, Jing'an* ☎*021/6279–7188* ⚑*Reservations essential* ▭*AE, DC, MC, V.*

$$–$$$ ✕ **roomtwentyeight.** Roomtwentyeight is the signature restaurant of the
FUSION URBN boutique hotel, but is remarkably unpretentious. With an open, airy dining space and a menu of fresh Australian contemporary cuisine, roomtwentyeight is a great place to have a relaxing meal and drink away from the Shanghai hustle. ⊠*URBN Hotel, 183 Jiao Zhou Lu, near Beijing Lu, Jingan* ☎*021/5172–1300* ▭*AE, DC, MC, V.*

$$$–$$$$ ✕**Summer Pavilion.** Helmed by Ho Wing, the former chef of Hong
CANTONESE Kong's famed Jockey Club, Summer Pavilion serves delicious Cantonese specialties ranging from simple dim sum to delicacies such as shark fin, bird's-nest soup, and abalone. As befits the Portman Ritz-Carlton, the restaurant's dining room is elegant, with black and gold accents and a raised platform that makes you feel as though you're center stage—a sense heightened by the attentive servers, who stand close at hand, but not too close, anticipating your needs. ⊠*Portman Ritz-Carlton, 2nd fl., 1376 Nanjing Xi Lu, Jing'an* ☎*021/6279–8888* ⚑*Reservations essential* ▭*AE, DC, MC, V.*

NORTH SHANGHAI

Often neglected, North Shanghai is a historic neighborhood, with a selection of good Chinese restaurants.

¢–$ ✕**Yue Garden.** In the Great Wall Wing of the Holiday Inn Downtown,
CHINESE Yue Garden serves Cantonese and Shanghainese classics. The dishes are well prepared and presented, and the service is always good. Close to the train station and reasonably priced, Yue Garden is a good option for travelers coming through. ⊠*Holiday Inn Downtown, 585 Heng Feng Rd., 2nd fl., Zhabei* ☎*021/6353–8008* ▭*AE, DC, MC, V.*

PUDONG

Steep and shining, the skyscraper-rich financial district of Pudong is home to a surprising number of high-class eateries, including the Shangri-La's Yi Café and the Hyatt's towering Cloud 9.

$$–$$$ ✕**Cloud 9.** Pudong can be an intimidating concrete jungle, with lit-
CONTEMPORARY tle respite in sight. If you're looking for refreshment on your Pudong safari, try Cloud 9 on the 87th floor of the Hyatt. Be aware, this is not

FODOR'S FIRST PERSON

David Taylor
Fodor's Writer

"Chi le ma?" ("Have you eaten yet?") When old friends meet, this is what they ask. There's time later to inquire about health, families, and gossip, but first, the food! Food and eating are the cornerstones of Chinese society, and I for one love it. Don't think that means "fine dining" is common or even fully understood, but when it comes to enjoying their food, the Chinese are past masters and I have devoted myself to their lessons. Here, every meal is a chance to savor and indulge in a break from an otherwise frantic city.

My favorite places for a genuine Chinese meal aren't famous, though they are very popular with the locals. My local Xinjiang (Western Chinese Muslim) place has half-hour waits for tables from 5 to 8 pm, probably because of its superb lamb and chicken dishes and somewhat liberal interpretations of the Islamic dietary laws. (No pork is ever served, but they do offer Xinjiang beer and other alcoholic beverages.) I often stop by on my way home for a few *yang rou chuan* (barbecued lamb skewers) and *nang bing* (crispy flatbread shaped like a pizza crust). While I'm waiting I chat with the barbecue man in terrible Mandarin—his native language is Uighur, so we're well matched—about food.

It's the Chinese joy of eating which creates the *rennao* (hot and noisy) atmosphere that most foreigners find so hard to accept. To the Chinese (and especially the Shanghainese), food isn't some somber sacrament but a festival. To eat without friends, without talking, without exuberance—well, that isn't eating at all!

As you're out and about on the streets of Shanghai, try a small, local restaurant at least once. Sit down at a big table with a bunch of people you don't know, order food in a language you don't speak, and let the community of eating speak for you. You may eat some improbable foods, and you'll almost definitely end up toasting the health of total strangers, but you will be part of a culinary camaraderie that can't be found in more formal venues. Ganbei!

a cheap lounge—there is a dress code, but the view is spectacular. Kick back and drink in the city laid out beneath you, while nibbling tasty Asian-inspired tapas and snacks. ⊠*Grand Hyatt, 87th fl., 88 Shiji Dadao, Pudong* ☎*021/5049–1234* ⚑*Reservations essential* ▤*AE, DC, MC, V.*

$$–$$$ ✕**Danieli's.** This is one of the finest Italian restaurants in the city, and
ITALIAN worth the commute to Pudong. The intimate dining area is spacious
★ without being overwhelming, and the staff is very well trained. Its business lunch is famed for its speed and quality, but it is at dinner that Danieli's really shines. The menu is well balanced with seasonal dishes, and boasts an excellent five-course set menu. Prices can be expensive, especially for wine, but it is worth the money. ⊠*St. Regis, 889 Dongfang Lu, Pudong* ☎*021/5050–4567* ⚑*Reservations essential* ▤*AE, DC, MC, V* ☾ *No lunch Sat.*

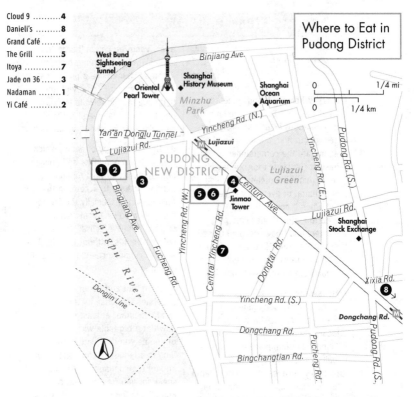

Where to Eat in
Pudong District

$$–$$$
CONTINENTAL
✗**Grand Café.** Two of the Grand Hyatt's restaurants *(the other is the Grill, below)* present Continental cuisine with absolutely spectacular views of Shanghai—unless the building is shrouded in fog. The sophisticated 24-hour restaurant touts its "show kitchen" buffet, which includes appetizers, daily specials, fresh seafood, and desserts. ⊠*Grand Hyatt, 88 Shiji Dadao, Pudong* ☎*021/5049–1234* ⌛*Reservations essential* ⊟*AE, DC, MC, V.*

$$–$$$
CONTINENTAL
✗**The Grill.** Part of the Hyatt's three-in-one, open-kitchen restaurant concept, the Grill shares the 56th floor with two other restaurants (serving Japanese and Italian cuisine). At the Grill you can feast on a great seafood platter or unbelievably tender steak. ⊠*Grand Hyatt, 88 Shiji Dadao, Pudong* ☎*021/5049–1234* ⌛*Reservations essential* ⊟*AE, DC, MC, V.*

$–$$
JAPANESE
✗**Itoya.** The waitstaff's precision teamwork makes dining at Itoya a pleasure. Servers pause to greet all guests in unison. You're handed a hot towel upon sitting down and instantly after finishing your meal. The menu sticks to traditional Japanese fare: tempura, sushi, sashimi. In line with its location directly across from the Grand Hyatt's entrance, the restaurant also has several budget-busting items such as Kobe beef and lobster sashimi. ⊠*178 Huayuan Shiqiao Lu, Pudong* ☎*021/5882–9679* ⊟*AE, DC, MC, V.*

$$$$
INTERNATIONAL
Fodor's Choice
★
✕ **Jade on 36.** This is a restaurant that must be experienced to be believed. Perched on the 36th floor of the Shangri-La tower, the Jade lounge/restaurant is simply beautiful. There is no à la carte menu; instead, diners choose from a selection of set menus named simply by colors and sizes. The cuisine is innovative and extremely fresh, the service impeccable, and the view pleasant. Menus vary from five to eight courses, with an emphasis on fresh seafood and tender meats. The jumbo shrimp in a jar is especially enjoyable, as is the signature lemon tart. It's an expensive indulgence, but worth every penny. ✉*Pudong Shangri-La, 36th fl., 33 Fu Cheng Lu, Pudong* ☎*021/6882–8888* ▤*AE, DC, MC, V.*

$$$–$$$$
JAPANESE
✕ **Nadaman.** Sleekly elegant and stylized, Nadaman is modern Japanese dining taken to its extreme. The accents of raw granite merged into a formalized designer interior reflect the restaurant's origins in the modern Tokyo, looking almost overdesigned. With a focus on freshness and presentation, Nadaman gives diners superb cuisine at a price tag to match. The sushi is some of the finest in the city. ✉*Pudong Shangri-La, 2nd fl., 33 Fu Cheng Lu, Pudong* ☎*021/6882–8888* ⚑*Reservations essential* ▤*AE, DC, MC, V.*

$$$
ECLECTIC
✕ **Yi Café.** Popular and busy, the Yi Café at the Shangri-La is open-kitchen dining at its finest, serving a world of cuisines. The Yi Café is very popular with the Lujiazui business set, as well as local diners for the quality and variety of the food. It's a great place to people-watch over a selection of the finest dishes Asia has to offer. This experience doesn't come cheap, at Y268 per person, but it's worth it. The restaurant slightly underrepresents Western cuisine, focusing more on Asian dishes. ✉*Pudong Shangri-La, 2nd fl., 33 Fu Cheng Lu, Pudong* ☎*021/6882–8888* ▤*AE, DC, MC, V.*

HONGQIAO & GUBEI

The neighborhoods of Hongqiao, with its conference centers and hotels, and Gubei, with its high-end residential properties, have a few great options. Be sure to check out the Hongmei Entertainment Street, a pedestrian street hosting a diverse selection of restaurants.

¢–$
CAFÉ
☺
✕ **Bastiaan Bakery & Konditorei.** Good bread and café fare on the Hongmei Entertainment street. Bastiaan bakes its bread fresh daily, and offers a good range of soups, sandwiches, and pastries with its excellent coffee. It's very kid-friendly, with a play area available. ✉*Hong Mei Entertainment St. La. 3338, No. 18, Hongqiao On the pedestrian-only lane, just off Hong Mei Lu* ☎*021/6465–8022* ▤ *AE, DC, MC, V.*

¢–$
TAIWANESE
✕ **Bellagio.** Taiwanese expatriates pack the bright, sunlit dining room of Bellagio for an authentic taste of home. Red fabric–covered chairs and black streamlined tables contrast the white walls and decorative moldings. Waiters, chic in black sweaters, move efficiently between the closely spaced tables. The menu includes such traditional entrées as three-cup chicken as well as 25 noodle dishes spanning all of Southeast Asia. Save room for dessert: shaved-ice snacks are obligatory Taiwanese treats and come in 14 varieties. ✉*778 Huangjin Cheng Dao, by Gubei Lu, Changning* ☎*021/6278–0722* ⚑*Reservations not accepted* ▤*AE, DC, MC, V.*

$–$$
CANTONESE ✕**The Dynasty.** Although its cuisine is mostly Cantonese, Dynasty does serve some other regional fare, such as first-rate Peking duck and Sichuan-influenced hot-and-sour soup. The Cantonese seafood dishes, especially the prawns and lobster, are particularly good, and the shrimp *jiaozi* (dumplings) are delicious. Keyhole cutouts in the subdued pewter walls showcase Chinese vases and artifacts. Thick carpets mute any hotel noise, but the prices quickly remind you this is indeed a hotel restaurant. ⊠*Renaissance Yangtze, 2099 Yanan Xi Lu, Changning* ☎*021/6275–0000* ⌂*Reservations essential* ▤*AE, DC, MC, V.*

$$–$$$
ITALIAN
★ ✕**Giovanni's.** Its Italian courtyard with a penthouse view provides a wonderful backdrop for Giovanni's traditional Italian fare. The antipasta and calamari are delicious, and the pastas are served perfectly al dente. Seasonal promotions keep the menu fresh. ⊠*Sheraton Grand Tai Ping Yang, 27th fl., 5 Zunyi Nan Lu, Changning* ☎*021/6275–8888* ⌂*Reservations essential* ▤*AE, DC, MC, V.*

$–$$
MEXICAN ✕**Mexico Lindo.** Fiery fare in a south-of-the-border setting has made Mexico Lindo Cantina & Grill the best entry on Shanghai's limited Mexican-dining scene. This Spanish-style casa is hidden off Hongmei Lu, down a tiny alley that's evolved into a well-respected restaurant row. In addition to tacos, fajitas, and quesadillas, the menu includes spicy prawns—rated three peppers—and a tasty one-pepper carnita pork burrito. A stairway mural depicts farm workers as well as fiesta revelers, whose ranks you can join with the eight margaritas and eight tequilas on the drink menu. ⊠*Villa 1, 3911 Hongmei Lu, Changning* ☎*021/6262–2797* ⌂*Reservations essential* ▤*AE, DC, MC, V.*

XUJIAHUI & SOUTH SHANGHAI

Once solely a shopping destination for locals, Xujiahui has blossomed into the center of the southwest. Good dining is a little hard to find; the majority of restaurants serve Chinese-style fast food, but there are some diamonds in the rough.

$–$$
BRAZILIAN ✕**Dagama Barbeque.** This can't be considered fine dining, but it is good, and particularly satisfying for families who are shopped out after a long day. A churrascaria done Shanghai style, Dagama serves all-you-can-eat grilled meats carved at your table, has a buffet of sides and desserts, and occasionally features a band playing Sino-pop versions of American classics. It's an excellent value for the money, especially if you've got a big appetite. ⊠*Metro City, 8th fl., by Caoxi Bei Lu, 1111 Zhaojiabang Lu, Xuhui* ☎*021/6426–7056* ▤*No credit cards.*

¢–$
AMERICAN ✕**Rendezvous Café.** With its inexpensive menu of juicy hamburgers and bacon-and-eggs breakfasts, Rendezvous Café is as close to an American diner as you'll find in Shanghai. Owner Richard Soo ran its namesake predecessor in San Francisco before pulling up stakes for Taiwan, then Shanghai. The café's coffee selections are equally satisfying, which is no surprise considering that Soo also owns a nearby coffee shop. ⊠*435 Jin Feng Lu, Minhang* ☎*021/5226–4353* ▤*MC, V.*

¢–$
CHINESE ✕**Shanghai Xinjiang Fengwei Restaurant.** You'll probably hear this restaurant before you see its blue-canopied entrance and street-side kabob stand; pounding Xinjiang (Western Chinese Muslim) music throbs from

the second-story windows. The lively singing waitstaff frequently recruits diners as dance partners; service often falters as a result. The traditional Xinjiang menu is heavy on lamb but also includes a few chicken and fish dishes. A bottle of Xinjiang black beer is a must to wash it all down. ⊠*280 Yishan Lu, Xuhui* ☎*021/6468–9198* ▭*No credit cards.*

WHERE TO EAT	PINYIN	CHINESE
1221	Yīèrèryī cāntīng	1221餐厅
Arirang	Alǐláng	阿里郎
Ba Guo Bu Yi	Bāguóbùyī	巴国布衣
Bali Laguna	dōushì táohuā yuán	都市桃花源
Bao Luo	Bǎoluó	保罗
Barbarossa	Bābālùshā	芭芭露莎
Bastiaan Bakery & Konditorei	Báshì miàn bāo fáng	跋视面包房
Bellagio	Bǎilègōng	百乐宫
Brasil Steak House	Bāxī shāokǎowū	巴犀烧烤屋
Bund Brewery	Wàitān pí jiǔ zǒng huì	外滩啤酒总汇
Cloud 9	Jiǔchòngtiān	九重天
Da Marco	Dàmǎkě	大马可
Dagama Barbeque	Dájiāmǎ	达加马
Element Fresh	Xīnyuánsù	新元素
Family Li Imperial Cuisine	Lìjiā cài	历家菜
Korean Restaurant	Gāolì cāntīng	高丽餐厅
Ginger Café	Jīngé kā fēi	金格咖啡
Giovanni's	Jífànnísī	吉范尼斯
Gokohai	Yùxiānghaǐ	钰香海
Gongdelin	Gōngdélín	功德林
Grand Café	Jīnmào Jūnyuè kāfēitīng	金茂君悦咖啡厅
Grape	Pútáoyuán	葡萄园
Hot Pot King	Láifúlóu	来福楼
Indian Kitchen	Yìndù xiǎochú	印度小厨
Itoya	Yīténgjiā	伊藤家
Jade on 36	Fěicuìsānshíliù	翡翠36
Kabb	Kāibóxī	凯博西
Laris	Lùwéixuān	陆唯轩
Le Bouchon	Bóxùn	勃逊
Lost Heaven	Huāmǎtiāntáng	花马天堂
M on the Bund	Mǐshì xīcāntīng	米氏西餐厅
Malone's American Café	Mǎlóng měishì cāntīng	马龙美式餐厅

5

WHERE TO EAT	PINYIN	CHINESE
Masala Art	Xiāngliàoyìshù	香料艺术
Mediterranean Café	Dìzhōnghǎi xīcāntīng	地中海西餐厅
Meilongzhen	Méilóngzhèn	梅龙镇
Mesa Restaurant	Méisà cāntīng	梅萨餐厅
Mexico Lindo Restaurant	Língdé Mòxīgē cāntīng	灵得墨西哥餐厅
Nadaman	Tānwàn	滩万
Nepali Kitchen	Níbóěr chúfáng	尼泊尔厨房
New Heights	Xīnshìjiǎo Cāntīng jiǔláng	新视角餐厅酒廊
Palladio	Pàlánduǒ	帕兰朵
Paulaner Brauhaus	Bǎoláinà cāntīng	宝莱纳餐厅
Quan Ju De	Quánjùdé	全聚德
Rendezvous Café	Lǎngdīmǔ	朗迪姆
Roosevelt Prime Steakhouse	Luósīfú dǐngjí níupáiguǎn	罗斯福顶级牛排馆
Sens & Bund	Yǎdé	雅德
Shanghai Xinjiang Fengwei Restaurant	Shànghǎi Xīnjiāng fēngwèi fàndiàn	上海新疆风味饭店
Shen Yue Xuan	Shēnyuèxuān	申粤轩
Shintori Null II	Xīndōulǐ wú'èrdiàn	新都里无二店
Simply Thai	Tiāntài cāntīng	天泰餐厅
South Beauty	Qiàojiāngnán	俏江南
Summer Pavilion	Xiàyuàn	夏苑
T8	T bā	T 8
Tairyo	Tailáng	太郎
Tan Wai Lou	Tānwàilóu	滩外楼
The Dynasty	Mǎnfúlóu	满福楼
The Grill	Mměishì shāokǎo	美式烧烤
The Onion Restaurant	Yángcōng cāntīng	洋葱餐厅
The Stage At Westin Restaurant	Wǔtái cān tīng	舞台餐厅
The Tandoor Restaurant	Tiāndōulǐ Yìndù cāntīng	天都里印度餐厅
Vienna Café	Weíyěnà kā fēi	维也纳咖啡
Wan Hao	Wànháo	万豪
Whampoa Club	Huángpǔhuì	黄埔会
Yang's Kitchen	Yángjiā chúfáng	杨家厨房
Yi Café	Yí kāfēi	怡咖啡
Yue Garden	Yuèyuán	粤园
Yu Xin Chuan Restaurant	Yúxìn chuāncài	渝信川菜

Where to Stay

The Westin Bund Center

WORD OF MOUTH

"When you leave your hotel, take a card with the name of your hotel—in Chinese—so if you get lost or just want to get back you can give it to a cab driver."

—gpotvin

WHERE TO STAY PLANNER

Cutting Costs

Since Shanghai's hotels target business travelers, there are often excellent deals available on weekends at upmarket establishments. Reductions on room rates are widely available (November to March), except over Chinese New Year (mid-January to mid-February).

Don't be shy to practice your bargaining skills when making reservations—the Chinese are used to negotiations. That said, you don't want to shout "Tai gui le!" (Too expensive!) when making reservations at the Four Seasons. If you stay for several nights, some three- or four-star hotels will throw in breakfast or give you a discounted rate, so always be sure to ask.

Facilities

We always list the facilities that are available, but we don't specify whether they cost extra. When pricing accommodations, always ask what's included and what costs extra. Doubles in China often come with two twin beds, though most hotels offer queens or kings, too; be sure to state your preference when making reservations. All hotels listed have private baths and air-conditioning unless otherwise noted.

Top 5 Hotels

■ **Le Royal Meridien.** Overlooking People's Park at the foot of Nanjing Lu, the Royal Meridien has set new standards for quality and service

■ **Old House Inn.** We love the Old House Inn as much for its local charm as its bargain prices.

■ **JIA Shanghai.** This beautiful boutique hotel in the center of Shanghai's shopping district was honored in 2008 by *INTERIOR DESIGN China* for its exquisite design.

■ **Ramada Plaza.** With an ace location and fabulously priced rooms, the Ramada is the number one hotel for discerning travelers seeking a moderately priced Western-style experience.

■ **Pudong Shangri-La.** The addition of a second tower means there are now twice the number of fabulous views available—if a breathtaking vista is what you're looking for, don't search any farther than this glam hotel right on the banks of the Huangpu River overlooking the Bund and the Pearl TV Tower.

Prices

Rates are generally quoted for the room alone; breakfast, whether Continental or full, usually is extra. All hotel prices listed here are based on high-season rates.

WHAT IT COSTS In Yuan

¢	$	$$	$$$	$$$$
Hotels				
under Y700	Y700– Y1,100	Y1,101– Y1,400	Y1,401– Y1,800	over Y1,800

Prices are for two people in a standard double room in high season, excluding 10%–15% service charge.

Updated by David Taylor

Although China has become a hot destination for leisure travelers, Shanghai's stature as China's business capital means that its hotels still cater primarily to business clientele and can be divided into two categories: modern Western-style hotels that are elegant and nicely appointed; or hotels built during the city's glory days, which became state-run after 1949. The latter may lack great service, modern fixtures, and convenient facilities, but they often make up for it in charm, tradition, history, and value.

Judging by the number of five-star and Western chain hotels now in Shanghai, the city has proven just how grandly it has opened to the outside world. The Grand Hyatt, JW Marriott, Westin, Portman Ritz-Carlton, and St. Regis aren't merely hotels; they're landmarks on the Shanghai skyline and standard-bearers for all lodgings in town. Even the historic properties that make up the other half of Shanghai's hotel market feel the pressure to update their rooms and facilities. And as Shanghai speeds up its preparations for the World Expo in 2010, newcomers, like the Conrad, Jumeirah, and Park Hyatt, are setting the bar even higher with their ultramodern settings and top-notch service. This increasing competition means there are bargains to be had, especially during the low season from November through March. Avoid traveling during the three national holidays—Chinese New Year (mid-January to mid-February), Labor Day (May 1), and National Day (October 1)—when rooms and prices will be at a premium.

THE OLD CITY

$$$$ ⊞ **The Westin Shanghai.** With its distinctive room layouts, glittering glass staircase, and 90-plus works of art on display, the Westin Shanghai is a masterpiece, fittingly located near the majestic Bund. Crowne Deluxe rooms are miniature suites; sliding doors divide the sitting area, bath-

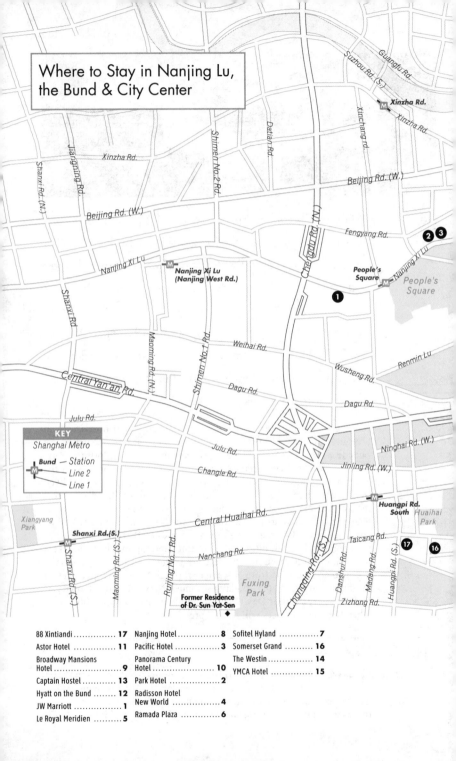

Where to Stay in Nanjing Lu, the Bund & City Center

KEY

Shanghai Metro

Bund — Station
— Line 2
— Line 1

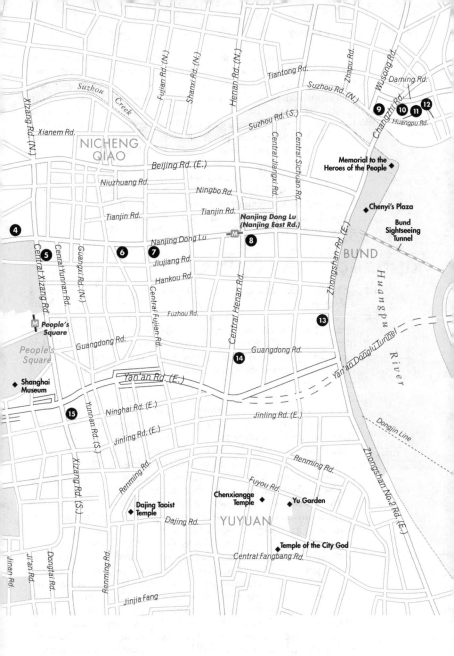

room, and bedroom (the only problem is that all these divisions make the rooms feel on the small side). Luxurious amenities include rainforest showers, extra-deep tubs, and Westin's trademark Heavenly Bed. Pampering continues at the Banyan Tree spa—China's first—and the Sunday champagne brunch at the Stage restaurant is considered the best in town by Shanghai's glitterati. **Pros:** service is so attentive that extra staff stands in front of the check-in counter to assist with luggage and information. **Cons:** expensive for what you get; located far from most shopping. ⊠ *Bund Center, 88 Henan Zhonglu, Huangpu* ☎ *021/6335–1888 or 888/625–5144* 🖷 *021/6335–2888* ⊕ *www.westin. com/shanghai* 🛏 *570 rooms, 24 suites* ♿ *In-room: safe, Wi-Fi, refrigerator. In-hotel: 3 restaurants, room service, bar, pool, gym, spa, concierge, laundry service, executive floor, parking (no fee), no-smoking rooms* 🚭 *AE, DC, MC, V.*

XINTIANDI & CITY CENTER

$$$$ 🖼 **88 Xintiandi.** Although it targets business travelers, 88 Xintiandi is a shopper's and gourmand's delight. The boutique hotel is in the heart of Xintiandi, its balconies overlooking the top-dollar shops and restaurants below. The rooms, all mini- or full-size suites with kitchens, are likewise upscale. Beds are elevated on a central, gauze-curtained platform; sitting areas have large flat-screen TVs and DVD players. Stylish wood screens accent the rooms and common areas. Deluxe rooms and the executive lounge overlook man-made Lake Taipingqiao. Guests can further indulge at the 88 Spa and Gym, with full fitness facilities and two treatment rooms. **Pros:** prime location in Xintiandi; interesting traditional Chinese decor; executive lounge **Cons:** occasionally slack service; street noise gets in. ⊠ *380 Huangpi Nan Lu, Luwan* ☎ *021/5383–8833* 🖷 *021/5353–8877* ⊕ *www.88xintiandi.com* 🛏 *12 suites, 41 rooms* ♿ *In-room: safe, kitchen, refrigerator, DVD, Wi-Fi. In-hotel: restaurant, room service, bar, pool, gym, concierge, laundry service, parking (fee), no-smoking rooms* 🚭 *AE, DC, MC, V.*

$$$$ 🖼 **JW Marriott.** For the best views in Puxi, look no further. The JW Marriott's futuristic 60-story tower on the edge of People's Square turns heads with its 90-degree twist, which divides the executive apartments below from the 22-story hotel above. The interior follows classic lines with subtle Chinese accents. Celadon vases, wedding boxes, and ornamental jades complement the soft green-and-yellow palette and warm fiddleback wood in the spacious rooms, but the real eye-catcher is the amazing cityscape vista from every room. The largely business clientele appreciates the one-touch "At Your Service" call button, and the Mandara Spa, indoor and outdoor pools, excellent restaurants, JW Lounge (with 60-plus martinis), and proximity to many of the major tourist attractions are big draws for leisure travelers. **Pros:** fantastic location; great views. **Cons:** expensive given the quality of service. ⊠ *399 Nanjing Xi Lu, Huangpu* ☎ *021/5359–4969 or 888/236–2427* 🖷 *021/6375–5988* ⊕ *www.jwmarriottshanghai.com* 🛏 *305 rooms, 37 suites* ♿ *In-room: safe, Wi-Fi, refrigerator. In-hotel: 3 restaurants,*

room service, bar, pools, gym, spa, concierge, laundry service, executive floor, parking (fee), no-smoking rooms ▤AE, DC, MC, V.

$ ▦ **Pacific Hotel.** This 1926 property has done an admirable job of preserving its charm. The marble lobby and the downstairs bar, decorated with art-deco leather chairs and archived photos of 1920s Shanghai, sweep you back to the city's glory days. In the original Italian-style front building, sixth- and seventh-floor rooms have wood floors, ornate molded ceilings, and great views of People's Park. Bathrooms, though, are rather institutional. The smaller rooms in the rear building lack the fine detail and views but are still comfortable and are a bit quieter. Amenities fall short, and soundproofing could be better, but the hotel's proud history, prime location, and prices make it an appealing choice. **Pros:** location near People's Park. **Cons:** erratic service; aging property. ⊠*108 Nanjing Xi Lu, Huangpu* ☎*021/6327–6226* 🖷*021/6372–3634* 📮*177 rooms, 5 suites* ⚒*In-room: safe (some), refrigerator, Ethernet. In-hotel: restaurant, room service, bars, spa, laundry service, parking (fee)* ▤AE, DC, MC, V.

$$ ▦ **Park Hotel** (Guoji Fandian). Once Shanghai's tallest building, the 20-story Park Hotel is now dwarfed on the Puxi skyline and eclipsed by other hotels whose glory days are present instead of past. Recently named a China Cultural Heritage Site, this 1934 art-deco structure overlooking People's Park still has great views and a musty charm, particularly in its restored marble lobby. Rooms are clean and bright, with prints of historic buildings from around the world. But bathrooms are tiny, and the hotel's limited English service and facilities have definitely slipped to second-rate. **Pros:** central location; heritage property. **Cons:** aging rooms; inadequate service. ⊠*170 Nanjing Xi Lu, Huangpu* ☎*021/6327–5225* 🖷*021/6327–6958* 📮*225 rooms, 25 suites* ⚒*In-room: safe, refrigerator, Wi-Fi. In-hotel: 3 restaurants, bars, gym, concierge, laundry service, parking (no fee), no-smoking rooms* ▤AE, DC, MC, V.

$$$$ ▦ **Radisson Hotel Shanghai New World.** A prominent figure not only on People's Square, but also on the Shanghai skyline, the flying-saucer dome-topped Radisson New World is best known for its revolving restaurant, Epicure on 45. Rooms are divided between the lower Park Tower and the higher City Tower. Park Tower rooms are more expensive but have the best views, facing People's Square. Though the hotel caters primarily to business travelers, suites—each with a huge living room, kitchen/dining room, and spacious bath—are convenient for families. In addition, most rooms have flat-screen TVs, and DVD players are available by request. Many travelers still prefer the tranquil garden setting of the Radisson's Xingguo hotel in the French Concession, but it cannot compete with the New World's central location and city views. ▮TIP→ **Be sure to ask about special weekend packages.** **Pros:** prime location. **Cons:** dark decor; taxis not readily available. ⊠*88 Nanjing Xi Lu, Xuangpu* ☎*021/6359–9999* 🖷*021/6358–9705* ⊕*www.radisson.com/shanghaicn_newworld* 📮 *429 rooms, 91 suites* ⚒*In-room: safe, Internet, refrigerator. In-hotel: 3 restaurants, room service, bar, pool, gym, spa, concierge, laundry service, parking (fee), no-smoking rooms* ▤AE, DC, MC, V.

Kid-Friendly Hotels in Shanghai

The **Somerset Grand**, in the Former French Concession, is the best option for families, with fully equipped kitchens in large apartment-like suites. The hotel has a playroom and a pool, and it's within walking distance of the shops and movie theater at Xintiandi. The **City Hotel**, also in the Former French Concession, has smallish, somewhat tired rooms but there's an indoor playroom for kids. Rooms on the executive floors are larger and more up-to-date. The **Radisson Hotel Shanghai New World**, directly on Nanjing Lu by People's Square, has large (though pricey) family suites that come with spacious living rooms and dining areas. Suites with kitchens at competitive rates are the main draw at the **Somerset Xuhui**, between the Former French Concession and Xujiahui. It's a bit far from the action on Nanjing Lu, but there's an indoor playroom and a sizeable pool.

$$$ **Somerset Grand.** Designed as serviced apartments for expats, the Somerset Grand's suites are great for families wanting extra space plus the usual hotel amenities. The twin 34-story towers have 334 one- to three-bedroom suites, ranging from 890 to 2,500 square feet. (One-bedroom suites have only one king-size bed.) The units feel homey, with blue-and-pink floral comforters and rugs, and a small kitchen. Kids can burn off steam at the pool and in the playroom. There's a great French restaurant and coffee shop on the grounds; the hotel is two blocks from the restaurants, shops, and movie theater at Xintiandi and 10 minutes to the subway. **Pros:** suites; good for kids. **Cons:** somewhat institutional decor. ⊠*8 Jinan Lu, Luwan* ☎*021/6385–6888* 🖷*021/6384–8988* ⊕*www.the-ascott.com* ⟿*334 suites* ⌂*In-room: safe, kitchen, refrigerator, Internet. In-hotel: tennis courts, pool, gym, concierge, laundry facilities, laundry service, parking (fee), no-smoking rooms* ▤*AE, DC, MC, V.*

¢–$ **YMCA Hotel.** Its central location within a 15-minute walk of People's Square, Xintiandi, and the Bund makes the YMCA Hotel a top destination for budget travelers. Built in 1929 as an actual YMCA, the 11-story brick building retains some of its original features: a temple-like exterior and painted ceiling beams on the second floor. The four dormitory rooms have single beds, rather than bunks. This is also a good chance for you to practice your bargaining skills, as discounts are almost always available. **Pros:** bargain price; close to tourist attractions. **Cons:** spartan fittings; poor service. ⊠*123 Xi Zang Nan Lu, Huangpu* ☎*021/6326–1040* 🖷*021/6320–1957* ⊕*www.ymcahotel. com* ⟿*140 rooms, 6 suites, 4 rooms with shared bath* ⌂*In-room: safe (some), dial-up. In-hotel: 2 restaurants, room service, bar, gym (fee), laundry service, airport shuttle, Internet* ▤*AE, DC, MC, V.*

THE BUND & NANJING DONG LU

¢ **⬚Captain Hostel.** Backpackers choose Captain Hostel, one of the few hostels in Shanghai, as much for its rooftop bar and restaurant as for its clean, bright rooms and convenient location a half-block west of the Bund. The dormitories accommodate five to 10 people per room in bunks resembling ships'

DRINK AND A VIEW

The hopping Noah's Bar on the sixth floor of Captain Hostel has views of the Pudong skyline that rival those from much pricier lodgings.

berths, in keeping with the nautical theme in this 1920s hotel. The 20 first-class rooms are tired but fair-sized, with TVs and private bathrooms. Bunk rooms must be paid for in cash. **Pros:** inexpensive lodging. **Cons:** worn and aging. ✉ *37 Fuzhou Lu, Huangpu* ☎*021/6323–5053* 🖶*021/6321–9331* ⊕*www.captainhostel.com.cn* 🛏*105 rooms, 85 rooms with shared bath* ⚲*In-room: no phone (some). In-hotel: 2 restaurants, laundry facilities, no-smoking rooms, Internet* ▭*MC, V.*

$$$$ **Hyatt on the Bund.** Located at the north end of the Bund near the banks
★ of the Suzhou River, the Hyatt on the Bund offers beautifully appointed rooms in an airy and modern building. This is a location which will only improve in value as the government continues its modernization of the Bund, but, for now, it is a little awkward on its own. However, the main Bund is just a short walk across the bridge, and the Hyatt on the Bund is reasonably accessible to most of the city. A major point of interest is the spectacular Vue bar, with its expansive vistas and rooftop hot tub. **Pros:** beautiful facilities; excellent restaurant. **Cons:** uninteresting neighborhood. ✉ *199 Huangpu Lu, near Wuchang Lu and the Bund, Bund* ☎*021/6393–1234* 🖶*021/6393–1313* ⊕ *www. shanghai.bund.hyatt.com* 🛏*600 rooms, 31 suites* ⚲*In-room: safe, Ethernet, refrigerator. In-hotel: 4 restaurants, room service, bars, pool, gym, spa, laundry service, executive floor, airport shuttle, no-smoking rooms* ▭*AE, DC, MC, V.*

$$$$ **Le Royal Meridien.** Dominating the foot of the Nanjing Pedestrian Street,
Fodor's Choice the Meridien has changed the face of Puxi hospitality. High ceilings,
★ massive rooms, excellent amenities, and attentive staff make this a premium destination. Ask for a park view—the "Bund" view overlooks four blocks of run-down Shanghai, while the view over People's Park is simply wonderful. However, the large banks of small elevators can make navigating the hotel's many levels a little frustrating. **Pros:** location; excellent facilities. **Cons:** service hiccups; annoying elevator structure. ✉*505 Nanjing Dong Lu, Huangpu* ☎*021/3318–9999* 🖶*021/6361–3388* ⊕*www.lemeridien.com.cn* 🛏*646 rooms, 115 suites* ⚲*In-room: safe, Internet, refrigerator. In-hotel: 4 restaurants, room service, bars, pool, gym, spa, laundry service, executive floor, airport shuttle, parking (fee), no-smoking rooms* ▭*AE, DC, MC, V.*

¢ **⬚Nanjing Hotel.** A frequent choice for budget tour groups, the Nanjing Hotel is only half a block yet a world away from the modern bustle of the Nanjing Dong Lu pedestrian walkway. Step out the front door and you'll see China as the locals do: fruit vendors balancing their loads and trash men ringing their handbells. The hotel's proximity to the metro line and the Bund compensates for the street, noise and lack of views. Built in 1931, the eight-story building is dated, yet rooms are fair-sized with Internet access and a few satellite channels. ■TIP→ **Though fifth-floor rooms were refurbished in 2006, opt for a room on the sixth floor, which is quieter. Pros:** centrally located; a good price. **Cons:** aging property; inconsistent service. ⊠ *200 Shanxi Lu, Huangpu* ☎ *021/6322–2888* 🖷 *021/6351–6520* ⟨ *In-room: safe, refrigerator, Internet. In-hotel: restaurant, room service, laundry service, Internet* ▤ *AE, DC, MC, V.*

$$$–$$$$
Fodor's Choice
★
🏨 **Ramada Plaza.** With its ornate lobby resembling a European opera house, the Ramada Plaza Shanghai brings a touch of grandeur to the Nanjing Road pedestrian walkway. Statues of Greek gods reign from atop intricate inlaid tables. Soaring marble columns direct the eye skyward to a stained-glass skylight. Although the fair-sized rooms lack any great views, they do face in toward a dramatic atrium, topped by yet another and the executive lounge. An indoor swimming pool, one of the largest in Shanghai, is housed inside an addition reminiscent of an ancient Chinese palace. Given the lush setting and ace location, the Ramada Plaza is a good value for the money. **Pros:** location; you can usually get a room for less than the rack rate if you inquire while reserving. **Cons:** no views. ⊠ *719 Nanjing Dong Lu, Huangpu* ☎ *021/6350–0000 or 800/854–7854* 🖷 *021/6350–6666* ⊕ *www.ramada international.com* ⇋ *376 rooms, 36 suites* ⟨ *In-room: safe, Wi-Fi. In-hotel: 4 restaurants, room service, bar, pool, gym, spa, concierge, laundry service, executive floor, parking (no fee), no-smoking rooms, Internet* ▤ *AE, DC, MC, V.*

$$$
🏨 **Sofitel Hyland.** Directly on the Nanjing Road pedestrian mall, the Sofitel Hyland is a convenient base for shopping and exploring the city center and the Bund. The rooms in this 30-story French-managed hotel are somewhat small but have been spruced up with prints of Chinese emperors and small replicas of terra-cotta warrior statues. The top-floor Sky Lounge serves Sunday brunch amid views of the Bund and downtown, and Le Pub 505 brews up its own beer. **Pros:** location. **Cons:** small rooms and poor frontage. ⊠ *505 Nanjing Dong Lu, Huangpu* ☎ *021/6351–5888* 🖷 *021/6351–4088* ⊕ *www.accorhotels-asia.com* ⇋ *299 rooms, 73 suites* ⟨ *In-room: safe, refrigerator, Internet. In-hotel: 3 restaurants, room service, bars, pool, gym, spa, laundry service, executive floor, airport shuttle, parking (fee), no-smoking rooms* ▤ *AE, DC, MC, V.*

FORMER FRENCH CONCESSION

$$
🏨 **Anting Villa Hotel.** Two blocks from the metro and the Hengshan Road–nightlife district, the Anting Villa Hotel is a convenient and surprisingly quiet retreat tucked away down a small side street. Superior rooms in the 10-story hotel tower have been refurbished in a "Spanish style" with garishly bright red pillowcases and leather-covered furniture; some rooms now come with flat-screen TVs. It's worth it to pay a little extra for a garden-view room with vistas of the cedar-shaded grounds and namesake 1932 Spanish-style villa. Although English

service is limited, the hotel's staff is eager and friendly. **Pros:** central location; eager-to-please service. **Cons:** a little faded; can be hard to communicate if you don't know the language. ⊠*46 Anting Lu, Xuhui* ☎*021/6433–1188* 🖷*021/6433–9726* ⊕ *antingvilla.sinohotel.com* ⇗*135 rooms, 11 suites* ⛁*In-room: safe, refrigerator, Wi-Fi. In-hotel: restaurant, room service, gym, laundry service, parking (no fee), no-smoking rooms* ▤*AE, DC, MC, V.*

$$$$ 🏨 **Crowne Plaza.** This hotel on the far western side of the Former French Concession makes up for its out-of-the-way location with service. The staff here is among the friendliest in town and makes guests, mostly business travelers, feel at home. Though the hotel's rooms are not as elegant as those of its competitors, it does have the biggest club lounge in Shanghai, with a mezzanine floor and a sleek, black-marble-topped bar. **Pros:** good service; amenity-packed. **Cons:** you'll need taxis to get to and from the hotel. ⊠*400 Panyu Lu, Xuhui* ☎*021/6280–8888 or 800/227–6963* 🖷*021/6280–3353* ⊕*www.shanghai.crowneplaza.com* ⇗*488 rooms, 12 suites* ⛁*In-room: safe, kitchen (some), refrigerator, Internet. In-hotel: 4 restaurants, room service, bars, pool, gym, executive floor, parking (no fee), no-smoking rooms* ▤*AE, DC, MC, V.*

$$$ 🏨 **Donghu Hotel.** Just off the frenzied shopping street of Huaihai Road, the Donghu Hotel remains one of Shanghai's best-preserved hotels from the city's 1920s heyday. The hotel's seven buildings have a surprising array of restaurants—Korean barbecue and Japanese, in addition to the standard Chinese and Western fare—an indoor pool, and a wide variety of room options. "Superior" rooms in Building 7 don't quite live up to their title and are simply furnished with twin beds and rather mismatched yellow wallpaper and red carpet. We suggest the Donghu deluxe rooms across the street at Building 1; with their traditional Chinese furniture and dark-wood paneling, these spacious rooms make you feel as if you've stepped back in time. **Pros:** traditional and elegant; numerous dining options available. **Cons:** poor service and upkeep. ⊠*70 Donghu Lu, Xuhui* ☎*021/6415–8158* 🖷*021/6415–7759* ⊕*www.donghuhotel.com* ⇗*240 rooms, 30 suites* ⛁*In-room: safe (some), Wi-Fi. In-hotel: 6 restaurants, room service, pool, gym, concierge, laundry service, parking (fee), Internet* ▤*AE, DC, MC, V.*

$$$ 🏨 **Hilton Shanghai.** Opened in 1988 as Shanghai's first five-star hotel, the Hilton has faded somewhat of late. Rooms are comfortable with an understated sand-tone color scheme, but not as cutting-edge as the hotel's younger competitors. But what the Hilton lacks in modern decor it makes up for with its prime location near the restaurants and nightlife of Jing'an Temple and the Former French Concession and its low-key friendly service. The delectable Gourmet Corner now occupies a large storefront in the front lobby, whereas in the rear lies the much-lauded Italian restaurant Leonardo's and the sunlit 24-hour Atrium Café, which resembles a quiet Chinese garden. On the top floors, the conference center, Penthouse Bar, and stellar Sichuan Court restaurant all have stunning views of the ever-expanding Puxi skyline. **Pros:** perfect location for food and fun. **Cons:** weary fittings; smallish rooms. ⊠*250 Huashan Lu, Xuhui* ☎*021/6248–0000 or 800/445–8667* 🖷*021/6248–3848* ⊕*www.shanghai.hilton.com* ⇗*692 rooms, 28*

6

suites △In-room: safe, refrigerator, Internet. In-hotel: 6 restaurants, room service, bars, tennis court, pool, gym, spa, concierge, laundry service, executive floor, airport shuttle, parking (fee), no-smoking rooms ▭AE, DC, MC, V.

$$$–$$$$ 🏨 **Jing An Hotel.** The weekly chamber-music concert in its lobby is just one example of how the Jing An Hotel has retained its elegance and charm after 70 years. In a 1½-acre garden, the Spanish-style main building's lobby has beautiful stained-glass windows. The ornate upstairs dining rooms often host prominent city officials. Although

> **SIZE MATTERS**
>
> Elaborately carved wooden door frames and lintels at Jing An Hotel direct the eye upward toward the 10-foot ceilings that make for some of the most spacious hotel rooms in Shanghai.

facilities are lacking compared to the newer hotels in town and the rooms in the Jing An New Building should be avoided at all costs (bathrooms are barely the size of a closet), the hotel's proximity to the subway line and its lush Former French Concession setting make this oft-overlooked property a winner. **Pros:** near public transportation; beautiful surroundings. **Cons:** poorly maintained facilities; inconsistent service. ✉370 Huashan Lu, Xuhui ☎021/6248–0088 🖷021/6249–6100 ⊕www.jinganhotel.net ⇌210 rooms, 17 suites △In-room: safe, refrigerator, Internet. In-hotel: 2 restaurants, room service, bars, gym, concierge, laundry service, airport shuttle, parking (fee), no-smoking rooms ▭AE, DC, MC, V.

$$$$ 🏨 **Jinjiang Hotel.** The former Cathay Mansions, Grosvenor Gardens, and Grosvenor House are now known collectively as the Jinjiang Hotel. It's here that President Nixon and Premier Zhou Enlai signed the Shanghai Communique in 1972 and all lobbies display photographs of the heads of state who have graced the hotel's grounds, giving the establishment a wonderful air of history. The fabulous luxury suites in the Grosvenor House start at $800 nightly. Rooms in the 1929 Cathay Building are plain but fair-sized with separate showers and tubs. Deluxe rooms are more stylish. The five-floor Cathay Garden, which reopened in 2005 after extensive renovations, now houses the hotel's best non-suite room, with guests praising the spacious modern deco furnishings and deep-soak bathtubs. For the best view, snag a room on the fourth or fifth floor. **Pros:** location; newly renovated. **Cons:** unreliable quality of service. ✉59 Maoming Nan Lu, Luwan ☎021/6258–2582 🖷021/6472–5588 ⊕jj.jinjianghotels.com/en_index.asp ⇌328 rooms, 33 suites △In-room: safe, refrigerator, Wi-Fi. In-hotel: 5 restaurants, room service, bars, pool, gym, airport shuttle, parking (no fee), no-smoking rooms ▭AE, DC, MC, V.

$$ 🏨 **Mason Hotel.** Although it caters to business travelers, the Mason Hotel is conveniently located for leisure travelers: steps from the Shaanxi Nan Lu metro station and surrounded by the shops of Huaihai Lu. Soundproofing blocks most—but not all—the street noise from the fairly large, simply furnished rooms, which face in toward a sunny, quiet, four-story courtyard. Facilities fall a bit short, but there's a Starbucks downstairs and a cozy sunroom up top in the Avenue Joffre restau-

rant. **Pros:** good location. **Cons:** spartan facilities; outside noise leaks in sometimes. ✉*935 Huaihai Zhonglu, Luwan* ☎*021/6466–2020* 🖷*021/6467–1693* ⊕*www.masonhotel.com* ❯*115 rooms, 4 suites* ⚿*In-room: safe, refrigerator, Internet. In-hotel: 2 restaurants, room service, bar, gym, concierge, laundry service, parking (no fee), no-smoking rooms* ⊟*AE, DC, MC, V.*

$$$$ 🏨**Okura Garden Hotel.** Its parklike setting in the heart of the French Concession makes this 33-story Garden Hotel a favorite Shanghai retreat, especially for Japanese travelers familiar with the Okura Group name. The first three floors, which were once old Shanghai's French Club, have been restored, with cascading chandeliers, frescoes, and art-deco details at every turn. Average-size standard rooms are simply furnished with silk wallpaper and European-style furniture and, unlike deluxe rooms and suites, lack flat-screen TVs. The romantic third-floor terrace bar overlooks the 2-acre garden, and the Japanese and French restaurants serve excellent but high-priced food. For those who want to stay connected, cell phones are available for rent at the concierge desk. **Pros:** gorgeous surroundings; central location near French Concession and Nanjing Xi Lu. **Cons:** you'll pay a hefty fee for all the beauty. ✉*58 Maoming Nan Lu, Luwan* ☎*021/6415–1111* 🖷*021/6415–8866* ⊕*www.gardenhotelshanghai.com* ❯*478 rooms, 22 suites* ⚿*In-room: safe, refrigerator, Internet. In-hotel: 5 restaurants, room service, bars, tennis courts, pool, gym, concierge, laundry service, executive floor, airport shuttle, parking (no fee), no-smoking rooms* ⊟*AE, DC, MC, V.*

$ 🏨**Old House Inn.** Hidden down a small lane, Old House Inn is one of
Fodor'sChoice Shanghai's few boutique hotels and a must if you're looking for a per-
★ sonalized experience that the larger hotels just can't offer. What this tiny gem lacks in amenities (there's no elevator, gym, concierge, or business facilities), it makes up for with its authentic Chinese style and charm. All rooms are decorated with antique dark-wood furniture and traditional porcelains, and the friendly staff is so eager to please that they'll even run down to the end of the lane and find you a taxi. Adjacent to the hotel is the swanky A Future Perfect restaurant, popular with both expats and trendy locals for its outdoor café. ■TIP➡ **Book well in advance to snag one of the moderately priced king-size rooms. Pros:** quaint and quiet; extremely helpful staff. **Cons:** small; limited services; booking at the last minute is difficult. ✉*No. 16, La. 351, Huashan Lu, Xuhui* ☎*021/6248–6118* 🖷*021/6249–6869* ⊕*www.oldhouse.cn* ❯*12 rooms* ⚿*In-room: safe, refrigerator, Internet. In-hotel: no elevator, restaurant, bar, laundry service, parking (no fee)* ⊟*AE, DC, MC, V.*

$$$$ 🏨**Radisson Plaza Xing Guo.** This quiet garden property was once the government-owned Xing Guo Hotel, a villa complex where Chairman Mao frequently stayed. The modern 16-story Radisson Plaza sprouted up in 2002, its garden-view rooms overlooking the central lawn and Mao's legendary Villa No. 1. The comfortable beige-tone rooms have ample work space, with two club chairs and a large desk. The Clark Hatch Fitness Center has top-name equipment, an aerobics room, and an elevated pool. Although the hotel's location in the consular district means it's far from the subway and most attractions, many guests still

6

prefer its tranquil setting over the hustle and bustle of downtown Puxi. **Pros:** well-equipped and well-maintained. **Cons:** poor metro access. ⊠*78 Xingguo Lu, Xuhui* ☏*021/6212–9998* 🖷*021/6212–9996 or 888/201–1718* ⊕*www.radisson.com/shanghaicn_plaza* 🛏*150 rooms, 40 suites* 🚪*In-room: safe, refrigerator, Internet. In-hotel: 2 restaurants, room service, bar, pool, gym, concierge, laundry service, executive floor, airport shuttle, parking (no fee), no-smoking rooms* ▤*AE, DC, V.*

$$$$ 🏨 **Regal International East Asia Hotel.** Its exclusive Shanghai International Tennis Center is the Regal's trump card among five-star hotels. The center has 10 tournament courts as well as one of the city's best health clubs (it's not only huge, but all cardio machines come with personal TVs). The spacious rooms were renovated in 2005 and have flat-screen TVs. Club rooms each have a curvilinear desk and ergonomic chair and a funky chaise longue; deluxe rooms have compact bathrooms with marble sinks and huge mirrors. The Hengshan Road metro station and the bar and restaurant district are just a block away, but there's plenty of entertainment downstairs at the hotel's 12-lane bowling alley and gorgeous Fragrance Chinese restaurant. **Pros:** easy access to public transportation and entertainment; lots of activities for nights you want to stay in. **Cons:** located on a high-traffic bar street. ⊠*516 Hengshan Lu, Xuhui* ☏*021/6415–5588* 🖷*021/6445–8899* ⊕*www.regal-eastasia. com* 🛏*278 rooms, 22 suites* 🚪*In-room: safe, DVD (some), Internet. In-hotel: 3 restaurants, room service, bar, tennis courts, pool, gym, concierge, executive floor, parking (no fee), no-smoking rooms, Wi-Fi* ▤*AE, DC, MC, V.*

$$$–$$$$ 🏨 **Ruijin Guest House.** Formerly the Morriss Estate, the Ruijin Hotel
★   showcases how opulently *taipans* (expatriate millionaire businessmen) lived in Shanghai's heyday of the 1930s. Rooms within the two preserved villas—No. 1 and Old No. 3—are rich with detail: high ceilings, ornate plaster molding, bamboo-etched glass. The two other buildings are significantly shorter on charm but still overlook the verdant grounds, which are shared with several top-notch restaurants (as well as the once-hip Face bar) and provide direct access to the bars on Maoming Road. New No. 3 may lack the historic cachet of the other buildings, but its standard rooms, which come with a king-size bed and hot tub, are definitely a steal. **Pros:** location. **Cons:** inconsistent facilities and service. ⊠*118 Ruijin Er Lu, Luwan* ☏*021/6472–5222* 🖷*021/6473–2277* ⊕*www.shedi.net.cn/outedi/ruijin* 🛏*62 rooms, 20 suites* 🚪*In-room: safe, refrigerator, Internet. In-hotel: restaurant, room service, bars, laundry service, parking (no fee), no-smoking rooms* ▤*AE, DC, MC, V.*

$$$ 🏨 **Shanghai Hotel.** Part of the Jinjiang-managed triumvirate that includes the Jing An Hotel and the Jing An New Building, the Shanghai Hotel has the most modern amenities of the three hotels. The executive floors are the hotel's best and executive double rooms all come with computers. Though the Shanghai Hotel is not as charming as the adjacent Jing An Hotel, its stellar location near Jing'an Temple make it a good choice among midrange hotels and very popular with Chinese and Western tour groups. **Pros:** location. **Cons:** poor service. ⊠*505 Wulumuqi Lu,*

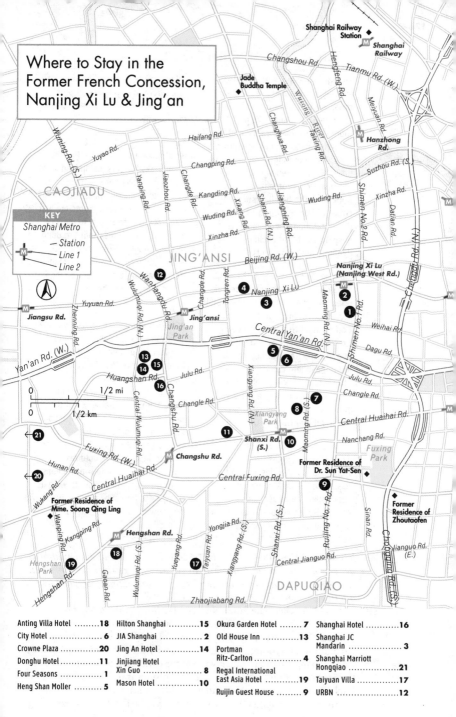

Where to Stay in the Former French Concession, Nanjing Xi Lu & Jing'an

WHICH NEIGHBORHOOD?

Shanghai may have an excellent subway system and cheap, plentiful taxis, but if you want to take full advantage of Shanghai's popular tourist sights, restaurants, and nightlife opt to stay in downtown **Puxi**, incorporating the quiet, leafy green Former French Concession, the historical promenade of the Bund, and the bustling shopping street of Nanjing Dong Lu. From these neighborhoods you'll have easy access to all of Shanghai's dynamic neighborhoods.

FORMER FRENCH CONCESSION

Sneak away from the city's frenetic energy in one of the historical hotels tucked down the Former French Concession's tree-lined streets. Excellent restaurants and shopping abound, the neighborhood's relaxing atmosphere can be a nice break after a hectic day of sightseeing. A short cab or metro ride takes you straight to any of the city's sights on the Bund and Nanjing Dong Lu.

HONGQIAO DEVELOPMENT ZONE

Hongqiao is not a destination for leisure travelers. A combination of residential complexes and business offices, Hongqiao lacks many sights or restaurants. Unless business brings you here or you have an early flight from the Hongqiao airport, there aren't many reasons to stay so far from the action.

THE BUND & NANJING DONG LU

Breathtaking views of the Pudong skyline, skyscrapers juxtaposed with Victorian architecture, and easy access to great shopping and some of the city's best restaurants are just a few reasons to stay here. Best of all, most major sites, from the Bund to the Shanghai Museum, are all within comfortable walking distance. If you want to see modern Shanghai, this is the place to be.

PUDONG

Although Pudong—with its shiny new skyscrapers and wide boulevards—can feel impersonal, and it's too far from downtown Puxi for some, it has some of the city's best hotels, all close to Pudong International Airport. Phenomenal views of the Bund are a major bonus. But if you stay here, be prepared to spend at least 30 minutes shuttling back and forth to Puxi (and it could take even longer during rush hour as millions of locals compete to flag down taxis or squeeze into subway cars almost overflowing with commuters).

Xuhui ☎021/6248–0088 🖷021/6248–1056 ⊕*www.shanghaihotel. net.cn* 🖃*540 rooms, 3 suites* ⚲*In-room: safe, refrigerator, Internet. In-hotel: 2 restaurants, room service, gym, spa, laundry service, parking (fee), no-smoking rooms* 🖃*AE, DC, MC, V.*

$$$ 🏨 **Somerset Xuhui.** The family-focused facilities of the all-suites Somerset Xuhui help compensate for its location: off the subway line, halfway between Xujiahui's shops and Former French Concession attractions. An indoor playroom, sizeable pool, and fitness center overlooking Zhaojiabang Road provide diversion for children and adults—as does the Starbucks downstairs. There are no restaurants, just small en suite kitchens. All units were renovated in 2005 and range from one to three bedrooms, the latter having a room with twin beds for kids. Cozy living

rooms and huge closets are two more reasons that this is a good spot for families in Shanghai. **Pros:** very family friendly. **Cons:** institutional-feeling decor. ⊠*888 Shaanxi Nan Lu, Luwan* ☎*021/6466–0888* 🖷*021/6466–4646* ⊕*www.the-ascott.com* 📞*167 suites* ⌂*In-room: safe, kitchen, refrigerator, DVD, Internet. In-hotel: tennis court, pool, gym, laundry facilities, laundry service* ⊟*AE, DC, MC, V.*

$$$ 🏨**Taiyuan Villa.** Nestled deep in a residential section of the Former French Concession, this offshoot of the Ruijin Hotel is a tranquil retreat from Shanghai's hustle and bustle. Once the residence of George Marshall (and the former stomping grounds of Madame Mao), the lush grounds surrounding the restored villa and the adjacent serviced apartments are planted with lush magnolia and palm trees. Rooms feel a bit worn, but are nonetheless charming, with spacious high ceilings and deco furniture. Be sure to take time to relax over a cup of tea on the porch overlooking the expansive lawn. **Pros:** quiet; beautiful location. **Cons:** poor maintenance; no easy metro access. ⊠*160 Taiyuan Lu, Luwan* ☎*021/6471–6688* 🖷*021/6471–2618* 📞*299 rooms, 73 suites* ⌂*In-room: safe, refrigerator, Internet. In-hotel: 4 restaurants, room service, bars, pool, gym, spa, executive floor, airport shuttle, parking (fee), no-smoking rooms* ⊟*AE, DC, MC, V.*

NANJING XI LU & JING'AN

$$$$ 🏨**The Four Seasons.** With palm trees, fountains, and golden-hued marble as warm as sunshine, the lobby of the Four Seasons establishes the hotel's theme as an elegant oasis in bustling downtown Puxi. Opened in 2002, this 37-story luxury hotel caters to its largely business clientele. It has impeccable service, a 24-hour business center, a gym, and butler service. The spacious rooms—just 12 to 15 per floor—include DVD/CD players, flat-screen TVs, safes big enough for a laptop, and marble showers and tubs (one of each). Nanjing Road and the Shanghai Museum are within a 10-minute walk, but there are convincing reasons to stay in: the Jazz 37 club; the exceptional Si Ji Xuan Cantonese restaurant; and ■TIP➔ **you don't want to miss one of the spa's indulgent Balinese treatments.** **Pros:** beautiful building; amenity and entertainment heavy. **Cons:** amenities may discourage you from getting out of the hotel; slack service. ⊠*500 Weihai Lu, Jing'an* ☎*021/6256–8888 or 800/819–5053* 🖷*021/6256–5678* ⊕*www.fourseasons.com* 📞*360 rooms, 79 suites* ⌂*In-room: safe, refrigerator, DVD, Internet, Wi-Fi. In-hotel: 4 restaurants, room service, bar, pool, gym, spa, concierge, laundry service, executive floor, parking (fee), no-smoking rooms, Wi-Fi* ⊟*AE, DC, MC, V.*

$$$ 🏨**Heng Shan Moller Villa.** Part gingerbread dollhouse, part castle, the Heng Shan Moller Villa was built by British businessman Eric Moller to resemble a castle his daughter envisioned in a dream. The family fled Shanghai in 1941, and after 1949 the house was the Communist Youth League's headquarters. Now a boutique hotel, the original villa has 11 deluxe rooms and has been ostentatiously restored with parquet floors, chintzy crystal chandeliers, and too much gold paint. Standard rooms in Building No. 2 are disappointingly plain, and service is merely

perfunctory. Guests have access to the neighboring Shanghai Grand Club's excellent fitness center. **Pros:** well-located; historically important; enjoyably surreal. **Cons:** mediocre service. ✉*30 Shaanxi Nan Lu, Luwan* ☎*021/6247–8881 Ext. 607* 🖷*021/6289–1020* 🌐*www. mollervilla.com* ⟿*40 rooms, 5 suites* ⌂*In-room: safe (some), refrigerator, Wi-Fi. In-hotel: 6 restaurants, laundry service, parking (no fee)* ▤*AE, DC, MC, V.*

$$$$ **JIA Shanghai.** JIA is something else—a new paradigm in Shanghai hos-

Fodor'sChoice ★ pitality. Discreetly housed in a vintage art deco building on Nanjing Xi Lu, JIA's unprepossessing exterior masks it's elegant and styled interior. The 55 rooms and suites are thoughtfully designed and just a touch over the top, making a stay in JIA an experience in itself. Every room is equipped with a kitchenette or kitchen for a pleasant, homey experience. Service is very good for China, though not quite world-class yet. Generally, the experience is smooth and unobtrusive, welcoming guests without destroying the sense of comfortable privacy. Issimo, the in-house restaurant, is genuinely extraordinary, with impeccable interiors and superb food. The service is well trained and the menu small but very well thought out. **Pros:** exquisite design and unique setting; kitchenettes; privacy. **Cons:** no pool; no business center. ✉ *931 West Nan Jing Lu, near Tai Xing Lu (entrance on Tai Xing Lu), Jing'an* ☎ *021/6217–9000* ⟿*55 rooms* ⌂ *In-room: kitchen, refrigerator, DVD, Internet, Wi-Fi. In-hotel: restaurant, room service, bar, gym, laundry facilities, laundry service, Wi-Fi, airport shuttle, no parking* ▤*AE, D, DC, MC, V.*

$$$$ 🏨 **The Portman Ritz-Carlton.** Outstanding facilities and a high-profile location in the Shanghai Center have made the Portman Ritz-Carlton one of the city's top attractions since its opening in 1998. The 50-story hotel devotes three floors solely to its fitness center and another four to its executive club rooms. The two-story lobby—a popular networking spot and the location of the best afternoon tea in town—exudes cool refinement with its ebony, marble, and chrome touches. In addition to the Shanghai Center's surrounding shops, banks, airline offices, and restaurants, the hotel has its own deli and four top-notch restaurants. Though the hotel touts its consistent rankings as one of the best employers and hotels in Asia, there have been complaints that service has slipped and there are often long lines for the concierge and taxi stand. **Pros:** renovated in 2008 with plasma TVs, DVD players, and improved decor; superb location. **Cons:** very expensive; uneven service. ✉*1376 Nanjing Xi Lu, Jing'an* ☎*021/6279–8888 or 800/241–3333* 🖷*021/6279–8887* 🌐*www.ritzcarlton.com* ⟿*510 rooms, 68 suites* ⌂*In-room: safe, refrigerator, Internet. In-hotel: 4 restaurants, room service, bars, tennis court, pool, gym, concierge, laundry service, executive floor, parking (fee), no-smoking rooms* ▤*AE, DC, MC, V.*

$$$$ 🏨 **Shanghai JC Mandarin.** At the base of the JC Mandarin's 30-story blue-glass towers lies the most memorable lobby in Shanghai. Its five-story hand-painted mural depicts the voyage of the Ming Dynasty admiral Zheng Ho. Opened in 1991, the hotel overhauled most public areas in 2004 and 2005. The Mandarin Club Lounge now occupies an inviting space on the second floor. The fitness center has added a spa. The Cuba cigar bar has carved a stylish lounge out of a former storeroom. Unfortunately, the spacious rooms are long overdue for an update. Though they are comfortable with earthy tones and natural wood, they lack the modern elegance of their five-star competitors. **Pros:** great location. **Cons:** aging rooms. ✉*1225 Nanjing Xi Lu, Jing'an* ☎*021/6279–1888 or 800/338–8355* 📠*021/6279–1822* ⊕*www.jcmandarin.com* ⬞*476 rooms, 35 suites* ⚬*In-room: safe, refrigerator, Internet. In-hotel: 4 restaurants, room service, bars, tennis court, pool, gym, spa, concierge, laundry service, executive floor, parking (fee), no-smoking rooms* ▤*AE, DC, MC, V.*

$$$$

Fodor'sChoice

★

URBN. Innovatively designed and environmentally friendly, URBN is Shanghai's first carbon-neutral hotel. Made with environmentally sensitive technology and recycled materials, URBN is a truly unique place to stay. The service is attentive and well trained, making guests feel at home from the moment they step into the hotel's tree-shaded courtyard. The design is superb, with a leather-encased reception desk, slate decor, and a quiet, private bar on the top floor. URBN provides a wide variety of alternative entertainments, including Chinese cookery, calligraphy and tai chi classes, bike tours, and yoga lessons. **Pros:** eco-friendly; luxe setting; some of the best cocktails in town; elegant design. **Cons:** not terribly suitable for mobility-impaired guests. ✉ *183 Jiaozhou Lu, near Beijing Xi Lu, Jing'an* ☎*021/5153–4600* 📠*021/5153–4610* ⊕ *www.urbnhotels.com* ⬞*24 rooms, 2 suites* ⚬*In-room: safe, refrigerator, DVD, Internet. In-hotel: restaurant, room service, bar, laundry service, executive floor, no-smoking rooms, Wi-Fi* ▤*AE, DC, MC, V.*

6

PUDONG

¢–$

🏨 **Changhang Merrylin Hotel.** The Merrylin Corporation is better known throughout China for its restaurants than its hotels, and Changhang Merrylin Hotel's exceptional Chinese restaurant overshadows its fairsize inexpensive rooms. Decor aspires to European grandeur but comes off as amusingly tacky. Reliefs and golden statues of frolicking nymphs dominate the lobby, and rooms are decked out in gold-flecked wallpaper and crackled white-painted fixtures. Service can be brusque, but the location is convenient, as it's within three blocks of the 10-story Next Age Department Store and metro Line 2 to Puxi. **Pros:** inexpensive; convenient to shopping and public transportation; delicious food in the restaurant. **Cons:** poor service. ✉*818 Zhangyang Lu, Pudong* ☎*021/5835–5555* 📠*021/5835–7799* ⬞*192 rooms, 32 suites* ⚬*In-room: refrigerator, Internet (some). In-hotel: 3 restaurants, room service, bar, concierge, laundry service, airport shuttle, parking (fee)* ▤*AE, DC, MC, V.*

$$$$

★

🏨 **Grand Hyatt.** Views, views, views are what this hotel is all about—occupying floors 53 through 87 of the spectacular Jin Mao Tower, the Grand Hyatt's interior is defined by art-deco lines juxtaposed with space-age grillwork and sleek furnishings and textures. The 33-story central atrium is a marvel in itself—a seemingly endless cylinder with an outer-space aura. Room amenities are space-age as well: CAT 5 optical lines for laptop use; Internet connections on the flat-screen TV through a cordless keyboard; and three high-pressure showerheads in the bathroom. Views from the rooms are spectacular; corner rooms have two walls of pure glass for endless panoramas of the Oriental Pearl Tower, majesty of the Bund, and expanse of the city below. ■ TIP→ **But watch out—being that high up puts you literally in the clouds and at the mercy of Shanghai's foggy weather. Pros:** beautiful rooms; high-tech amenities make you feel like you're already in the future; fantastic city views. **Cons:** extremely pricy; no guarantee of clear views. ☒ *Jin Mao Dasha, 88 Shiji Dadao, Pudong* ☎ *021/5049–1234 or 800/233–1234* 🖷 *021/5049–1111* ⊕ *www.shanghai.grand.hyatt.com* 🛏 *510 rooms, 45 suites* ♿ *In-room: safe, refrigerator, Internet, Wi-Fi. In-hotel: 5 restaurants, room service, bars, pool, gym, spa, concierge, laundry service, executive floor, parking (fee), parking (no fee)* ☰ *AE, DC, MC, V.*

$$$$ ⛨ **Hotel InterContinental Pudong.** The pièce de résistance of the 24-story InterContinental is a nearly 200-foot-high Italian Renaissance–inspired atrium decorated with red Chinese lanterns that shines natural light onto the 19 guest floors, six of which are executive floors. A vivid coat of red livens up the hallways and spacious guest rooms, which all have separate tub and shower. The restaurants cater to a wide range of tastes: Japanese, Cantonese, Shanghainese, Chaozhou, and Continental. The open kitchen of Level One restaurant turns out a great lunch buffet with samples of all those cuisines. **Pros:** well-priced for its amenities. **Cons:** difficult location for exploration on foot. ☒ *777 Zhangyang Lu, Pudong* ☎ *021/5831–8888 or 800/327–0200* 🖷 *021/5831–7777* ⊕ *www.shanghai.intercontinental.com* 🛏 *317 rooms, 78 suites* ♿ *In-room: safe, refrigerator, Internet. In-hotel: 4 restaurants, room service, bar, pool, gym, concierge, laundry service, executive floor, parking (fee), no-smoking rooms* ☰ *AE, DC, MC, V.*

$$$$
Fodor's Choice
★
⛨ **Pudong Shangri-La.** The Shangri-La occupies one of the most prized locations in Shanghai: overlooking the Huangpu River, opposite the Bund, near the Pearl Tower in Lujiazui. The hotel's breathtaking water's-edge views, white-glove service, and spacious rooms attract a mix of business and leisure travelers. The Shangri-La's two towers comprise the largest luxury hotel in Shanghai, with almost 1,000 guest rooms and numerous dining choices. Although rooms in Tower 2, behind the original hotel, come with 32-inch plasma TVs, DVD players, and fax machines, many return guests still prefer the rooms in Tower 1 for their gloriously unobstructed views of the Bund. **Pros:** altogether fantastic property; good restaurants. **Cons:** quite expensive; not ideal for nonbusiness travelers. ☒ *33 Fucheng Lu, Pudong* ☎ *021/6882–8888 or 800/942–5050* 🖷 *021/6882–6688* ⊕ *www.shangri-la.com* 🛏 *916 rooms, 65 suites* ♿ *In-room: safe, refrigerator, Internet. In-hotel: 8 restaurants, room service, bars, tennis court, pools, gym, spa, concierge, laundry service, executive floor, parking (fee), no-smoking rooms* ☰ *AE, DC, MC, V.*

$$$$
Fodor's Choice
★
⛨ **St. Regis.** Every guest is a VIP at the St. Regis. The amphitheater-like lobby sets the stage for the most indulgent hotel experience in Shanghai. The 318 rooms in this 40-story red-granite tower—its design lauded by *Architectural Digest*—spare no expense, with Bose wave radios, Herman Miller Aeron chairs, and rain-forest showers that give you the feeling of being under a waterfall. At 500 square feet, standard

rooms compare to other hotels' suites. The two women-only floors are unique in Shanghai. Butlers address all your needs 24/7 (you can even contact them by e-mail) from in-room check-in to room service, and as part of a new program, they can arrange to escort guests personally to visit local artist studios. The hotel's location—15 minutes from the riverfront—is a drawback, but the fitness center and 24-hour gym, along with the remarkable Danieli's Italian restaurant add to this pampering property's appeal. **Pros:** beautiful; service will make you feel like visiting royalty. **Cons:** far away from downtown. ⊠*889 Dong Fang Lu, Pudong* ☎*021/5050–4567 or 800/325–3589* ⎙*021/6875–6789* ⊕*www.stregis.com/shanghai* ⮡*274 rooms, 44 suites* ⌖*In-room: safe, refrigerator, Internet, Wi-Fi. In-hotel: 3 restaurants, room service, bars, tennis court, pool, gym, spa, concierge, laundry service, parking (fee), no-smoking rooms* ☰*AE, DC, MC, V.*

NORTH SHANGHAI

$$ 🏨 **Astor House Hotel.** The oldest hotel in China, the Astor House Hotel does an admirable job of capturing the feeling of Victorian Shanghai. The lobby's dark-wood columns and vaulted ceilings are accented by potted orchids and photos of famous visitors from the hotel's illustrious past (including Charlie Chaplin, Ulysses Grant, and Albert Einstein). The hotel has maintained its popularity with both budget and business travelers with its spacious, high-ceilinged rooms, often decorated with historical memorabilia, that more than compensate for the hotel's lack of views. We especially like Executive Room A, with its hardwood floors, Oriental carpet, and rain-forest shower. ■**TIP➜ Skip the renovated modern penthouse rooms—they lack the historical charm of the lower floors.** **Pros:** gorgeous building; good price. **Cons:** confused service; spartan furnishings. ⊠*15 Huangpu Lu, Hongkou* ☎*021/6324–6388* ⎙*021/6324–3179* ⊕ *www.pujianghotel.com/index.htm* ⮡*127 rooms, 3 suites* ⌖*In-room: safe (some), DVD (some), Internet. In-hotel: 2 restaurants, room service, bar, gym, concierge, laundry service, parking (no fee), no-smoking rooms* ☰*AE, DC, MC, V.*

$ 🏨 **Broadway Mansions Hotel.** One of Shanghai's revered old buildings, the Broadway Mansions Hotel has anchored the north end of the Bund since 1934. The worn wood furniture, industrial bathrooms, and steam radiators in the rooms betray their age. In contrast, business rooms are strikingly modern, with cool gray-and-tan interiors, glass-topped desks and nightstands, and separate marble showers and tubs. Riverview rooms cost Y100 extra; request a higher floor to reduce the street noise. **Pros:** location; a sense of Shanghai history. **Cons:** service irregular; rooms worn. ⊠*20 Suzhou Bei Lu, Hongkou* ☎*021/6324–6260 Ext. 2326* ⎙*021/6306–5147* ⊕*www.broadwaymansions.com* ⮡*161 rooms, 72 suites* ⌖*In-room: safe (some), Internet. In-hotel: 2 restaurants, room service, bars, gym, laundry service, executive floor, airport shuttle, parking (no fee)* ☰*AE, DC, MC, V.*

$ 🏨 **Panorama Century Court.** In a part of town dominated by historic properties, Panorama Century Court stands out for its modern facilities, competitive prices, and great Bund views from across the Wai-baidu Bridge. The 32-story Accor-owned hotel attracts European tourists familiar with the brand as well as business travelers. One- to three-bedroom suites all include living rooms and tiny kitchens, but you'll have to request utensils. Standard rooms have thoughtfully designed bathrooms with handy shelves for toiletries. If you want to take full advantage of the view, ■TIP→ **ask for a room above the 18th floor—otherwise your river view will be blocked by a billboard.** Pros: price. Cons: erratic service ⊠*53 Huangpu Lu, Hongkou* ☎*021/5393–0008* 🖷*021/5393–0009* 🛏*62 rooms, 92 suites* ⚤*In-room: safe, kitchen (some), refrigerator, Internet. In-hotel: restaurant, room service, bar, gym, concierge, laundry facilities, laundry service, parking (no fee)* ▤*AE, DC, MC, V.*

HONGQIAO & GUBEI

$$–$$$ 🛏 **Cypress Hotel.** Once part of tycoon Victor Sassoon's estate, the Cypress Hotel's shaded, stream-laced grounds remain a tranquil retreat in noisy Shanghai. From all of the hotel's rooms, you can look out over the garden and actually hear birdsong rather than car horns. The extensive health club boasts a swimming pool and outdoor tennis courts, which help to compensate for the hotel's limited English-speaking staff and location far from downtown Puxi. **Pros:** luxuriously quiet; beautiful environment **Cons:** very, very far from downtown. ⊠*2419 Hongqiao Lu, Hongqiao* ☎*021/6268–8868* 🖷*021/6268–1878* 🛏*141 rooms, 8 suites* ⚤*In-room: safe, refrigerator, Wi-Fi. In-hotel: 2 restaurants, room service, bar, tennis courts, pool, gym, laundry service, airport shuttle, parking (fee), no-smoking rooms* ▤*AE, DC, MC, V.*

$$$$ 🛏 **The Longemont.** Formerly the Regent, the Longemont maintains the original standards of its former brand. All rooms come with 42-inch flat-screen TVs, luxurious rain showers, and dazzling city views. The Longemont is outside the city center on the edge of the Former French Concession. Its quality restaurants, L'Institute de Guerlain Spa, and stunning infinity-edge lap pool, more than compensate for its location. Guests also rave about the studio and corner suite's exceptional showers, which look out through a wall of glass to sweeping views of downtown Shanghai. **Pros:** nice facilities. **Cons:** awkward location. ⊠*1116 Yan'an Xi Lu, Hongqiao* ☎*021/6115–9988* 🖷*021/6115–9977* ⊕*www.regenthotels.com* 🛏*511 rooms, 83 suites* ⚤*In-room: safe, DVD, refrigerator, Internet. In-hotel: 6 restaurants, bars, tennis courts, pool, gym, spa, concierge, laundry service, executive floor, parking (no fee), no-smoking rooms* ▤*AE, DC, MC, V.*

$$$$ 🛏 **Millennium Hongqiao.** Located in the borders of Hongqiao and Gubei, the Millennium offers well-appointed rooms in a pleasant garden environment, which is unfortunately engulfed by larger construction sites. Still, the hotel is quiet and the rooms are good value, with ample working space and flat-screen TVs. **Pros:** good value with lots of amenities; well-situated for those doing business in Hongqiao. **Cons:** awkward location; erratic service quality. ⊠ *2588 Yan An Xi Lu, near Shuicheng Lu, Changning* ☎*021/6208–5888* 🖷*021/6295–1390* ⊕*www.millennium hongqiao.com* 🛏*340 rooms, 19 suites* ⚤*In-room: safe, refrigerator,*

CLOSE UP

Up and Coming Hotels in Shanghai

Shanghai's rapidly growing and changing landscape is marked by an ever-expanding number of luxury hotels. The following hotels, at the time of publication set to open in late 2008, are generating buzz in the hospitality world and promise to redefine service in China.

The Conrad Shanghai ($$$$). Rounding out Xintiandi's luxury-hotel contingent is the Conrad Shanghai, which will be opening in December 2008. With an eye-catching façade and a full slate of luxury amenities, the Conrad promises to be a premium experience. ⊠ *99 Madang Rd., Xintiandi* ☎ *021-6386-9888* ⌂ *337 rooms, 25 suites* ♿ *In-room: safe, Wi-Fi, refrigerator. In-hotel: 4 restaurants, room service, bars, pool, gym, spa, concierge, laundry service, executive floor, parking, no-smoking rooms* ▤ *AE, DC, MC, V.*

Jumeirah HangTang Xintiandi Shanghai ($$$$). The first entry into the far Eastern market for Dubai-based ultraluxury brand Jumeirah, the Jumeirah HangTang Xintiandi Shanghai promises superb facilities and deca-

dent service behind its jaw-breaking name. Located in the center of Xintiandi, the Jumeirah is scheduled to open in December 2008. ⊠ *88 Shongshan Rd., Xintiandi* ☎ *021/6387-7888* ⌂ *309 rooms, 46 suites* ♿ *In-room: safe, refrigerator, Wi-Fi. In-hotel: 2 restaurants, room service, bar, pool, gym, spa, concierge, laundry service, executive floor, no-smoking rooms* ▤ *AE, DC, MC, V.*

Park Hyatt Shanghai ($$$$). Towering over the city from its perch atop the Shanghai World Financial Center, the Park Hyatt will succeed its sister Grand Hyatt next door as the highest hotel in the world. Amenities promise to be spectacular, with prices to match. Scheduled to open fall 2008. ⊠ *Shanghai World Financial Center, 100 Century Ave., Lujiazui* ☎ *021/6888-1234* ⊕ *shanghai.park. hyatt.com* ⌂ *142 rooms, 32 suites* ♿ *In-room: safe, refrigerator, Wi-Fi. In-hotel: 3 restaurants, room service, bars, pool, gym, spa, concierge, laundry service, executive floor, parking (fee), no-smoking rooms* ▤ *AE, DC, MC, V.*

6

Internet. In-hotel: 3 restaurants, room service, bar, pool, gym, concierge, laundry service, executive floor, no-smoking rooms ▤*AE, DC, MC, V.*

$$$$ **Renaissance Yangtze.** Next door to the Sheraton Grand Tai Ping Yang, the Renaissance does not quite match its neighbor's detailed elegance and service—or lower prices, for that matter. It is nonetheless a great option in the Hongqiao area, with eight executive floors catering to conventioneers and corporate types with business at INTEX and Shanghai Mart. There's a good-size gym and pool and an often-overlooked cigar bar. The hotel's long-standing reputation for top-quality catering at its five restaurants is well deserved, particularly at its Chinese restaurant, Dynasty. Rooms are warm, with sunrise-golden comforters and drapes, vermilion club chairs, and auburn-tiled bathrooms. The general manager is often to be found chatting with guests in the lobby or greeting staff by their first name, a surprisingly personal touch among Shanghai's five-star hotels. **Pros:** quality hotel at a good price. **Cons:**

awkward location for on-foot exploration. ✉*2099 Yanan Xi Lu, Hongqiao* ☎*021/6275–0000 or 888/236–2427* 🖷*021/6275–0750* ⊕*www.renaissancehotels.com* ➷*521 rooms, 23 suites* ⚒*In-room: safe, refrigerator, Internet. In-hotel: 5 restaurants, room service, bars, pool, gym, concierge, laundry service, executive floor, parking (no fee), no-smoking rooms* ▭*AE, DC, MC, V.*

$$$$ 🖵**Shanghai Marriott Hongqiao.** With eight stories, the unpretentious Marriott Hongqiao feels like a boutique hotel compared to its soaring competitors in Hongqiao. The hotel is quiet; inside Premier rooms have balconies overlooking the third-floor poolside courtyard. Porcelain vases and Ming-influenced furniture add some Chinese flair to the generously sized rooms. The Manhattan Steakhouse serves tender, juicy steaks; the Marriott Café has an excellent Sunday brunch; and the Champions Bar offers many after-work promotions. When making reservations, be sure to ask about special rates and packages, especially on weekends. **Pros:** attractive surroundings; quiet atmosphere. **Cons:** accessible only by taxi. ✉*2270 Hongqiao Lu, Gubei* ☎*021/6237–6000 or 800/228–9290* 🖷*021/6237–6222* ⊕*www. marriott.com* ➷*312 rooms, 13 suites* ⚒*In-room: safe, DVD (some), refrigerator, Internet. In-hotel: 4 restaurants, room service, bars, tennis court, pool, gym, concierge, laundry service, executive floor, airport shuttle, parking (no fee), no-smoking rooms* ▭*AE, DC, MC, V.*

$$$$ 🖵**Sheraton Grand Tai Ping Yang.** Even after 16 years, the Sheraton Grand
Fodor'sChoice is still the go-to hotel for savvy business travelers staying in Hongq-
★ iao. Formerly the Westin, this Japanese-managed property has four club floors, one-touch service by phone, and golf privileges at Shanghai International Golf Club. Oriental rugs, antique pottery, folding Chinese screens, and wooden masks and statues, all chosen by the hotel's general manager on his travels, add personal touches that cannot be found at any other hotel in town. Spacious standard rooms include large desks and ergonomic chairs, and the plush grand rooms have Oriental carpets and overstuffed chairs in the separate bed and sitting rooms. A grand staircase sweeps you from the formal lobby up to the second floor and the exceptional Bauernstube deli. Giovanni's serves Italian food as impressive as its views from atop the 27th floor. **Pros:** beautifully decorated. **Cons:** far from downtown. ✉*5 Zunyi Nan Lu, Hongqiao* ☎*021/6275–8888 or 888/625–5144* 🖷*021/6275–5420* ⊕*www. sheratongrand-shanghai.com* ➷*474 rooms, 22 suites* ⚒*In-room: safe, DVD, refrigerator, Internet. In-hotel: 5 restaurants, room service, bars, tennis court, pool, gym, concierge, laundry service, executive floor, parking (fee), no-smoking rooms, Wi-Fi* ▭*AE, DC, MC, V.*

PLACES TO STAY	PINYIN	CHINESE
88 Xintiandi	88 xīntiāndì jiǔdiàn	88 新天地酒店
Anting Villa Hotel	Antíng biéshù huāyuán jiǔdiàn	安亭别墅花园酒店
Astor House Hotel	Pǔjiāng fàndiàn	浦江饭店
Broadway Mansions	Shànghǎi dàshà	上海大厦
Captain Hostel	Chuánzhǎng qīngnián jiǔdiàn	船长青年酒店
Changhang Merrylin Hotel	Chánghàng Meǐlín'gé fàjiǔdiàn	长航美林阁大酒店
City Hotel	Chéngshì jiǔdiàn	城市酒店
Conrad Shanghai	Shànghǎi Kāngláidé jiǔdiàn	上海康莱德酒店
Crowne Plaza	Yínxīng Huángguān Jiàrì Jiǔdiàn	银星皇冠假日酒店
Cypress Hotel	Longbài fàndiàn	龙柏饭店
Four Seasons Hotel	Sìjì jiǔdiàn	四季酒店
Grand Hyatt	Shànghǎi jīnmào jūnyuè dàjiǔdiàn	上海金茂君悦大酒店
Heng Shan Moller Villa	Héngshānmàle biěshuˇ fàndiàn	衡山马勒别墅饭店
Hilton Hotel	Shànghǎi Jìng'ānxīěrdùn jiǔdiàn	上海静安希尔顿酒店
Holiday Inn Pudong Shanghai	Shànghǎi Pǔdōng Jiàrì jiǔdiàn	上海浦东假日酒店
Hotel InterContinental	Jǐnjiāngtāngchén zhōujì dàjiǔdiàn	锦江汤臣洲际大酒店
Hyatt on the Bund	Shànghǎi Wàitānmàoyuè dàjiǔdiàn	上海外滩茂悦大酒店
JC Mandarin	Jǐncāng wénhuà dàjiǔdiàn	锦沧文化大酒店
JIA	Shànghǎijiā jiǔdiàn	上海家酒店
Jinjiang Hotel	Jǐnjiāng fàndiàn	锦江饭店
Jing An	Jìng'ān bīnguǎn	静安宾馆
Jumeirah Shanghai	Shànghǎi Zhūměilā jiǔdiàn	上海朱美拉酒店
JW Marriott	J.W.wànháo jiǔdiàn	JW 万豪酒店
Le Royal Meridien	Shànghǎi Shìmàohuángjiāàiměi jiǔdiàn	上海世茂皇家艾美酒店
The Longemont	Shànghǎi Lóngzhīmèng Lìjīng dàjiǔdiàn	上海龙之梦丽晶 大酒店*
Mason Hotel	Měichén dàjiǔdiàn	美臣大酒店
Millennium Hongqiao	Shànghǎi Qiānxīhǎiōu dàjiǔdiàn	上海千禧海鸥大酒店
Nanjing Hotel	Nánjīng fàndiàn	南京饭店
Okura Garden Hotel	Huāyuán fàndiàn	花园饭店
Old House Inn	Lǎoshíguāng jiǔdiàn	老时光酒店
Pacific Hotel	Jīnmén dàjiǔdiàn	金门大酒店
Panorama Century Court	Hǎiwān dàshà	海湾大厦

6

PLACES TO STAY	PINYIN	CHINESE
Park Hotel	Guójì fàndiàn	国际饭店
Park Hyatt	Shànghǎi Bǎiyuè jiǔdiàn	上海柏悦酒店
The Portman Ritz-Carlton	Bōtèmàn Lìjiā jiǔdiàn	波特曼丽嘉酒店
Pudong Shangri-La	Pǔdōng Xiānggélǐlā jiǔdiàn	浦东香格里拉酒店
Radisson Hotel Shanghai New World	Xīnshìjiè Lìshēng dàjiǔdiàn	新世界丽笙大酒店
Radisson Plaza Xing Guo Hotel Shanghai	Shànghǎi Xīngguó bīnguǎn	上海兴国宾馆
Ramada Plaza	Nánxīn Yǎhuáměidá dàjiǔdiàn	南新雅华美达大酒店
Regal International East Asia	Fùháo Huánqiúdōngyà jiǔdiàn	富豪环球东亚酒店
Renaissance Yangtze Shanghai Hotel	Shànghǎi Yangzǐjiāngwànlì dàjiǔdiàn	上海扬子江万丽大酒店
Ruijin Hotel	Ruìjīn bīnguǎn	瑞金宾馆
Shanghai Hotel	Shànghǎi bīnguǎn	上海宾馆
Shanghai Marriott Hongqiao	Shànghǎi wànhào hongqiào dàjiǔdiàn	上海万豪虹桥大酒店
Sheraton Grand Tai Ping Yang	Shànghǎi tàipìngyang Dàfàndiàn	上海太平洋大饭店
Sofitel Hyland Hotel	Suǒfēitè hǎilún bīnguǎn	索菲特海仑宾馆
Somerset Grand	Shèngjiè gāojí fúwù gōngyù	盛捷高级服务公寓
Somerset Xuhui	Xúhuì Shèngjié fúwù gōngyù	徐汇盛捷服务公寓
The St. Regis	Shànghǎi Ruìjí Hóngtà dàjiǔdiàn	上海瑞吉红塔大酒店
URBN	Yàyuè jiǔdiàn	雅悦酒店
Westin	Wēisītīng dàfàndiàn	威斯汀大饭店
YMCA	Qīngniánhuì jiǔdiàn	青年会酒店

Side Trips

ZHEJIANG & FUJIAN

Hangzhou's Buddhist Lingyin Temple Hall of the 500 Arhats

WORD OF MOUTH

"Xiamen deserves its title of 'Garden on the Sea.' The perpetual spring with its luxuriant flowers and trees gives it another name, 'Green Island.' The legend that it was once a habitat of egrets brings about another beautiful name 'Egret Island.'"

—chinajack

SIDE TRIPS PLANNER

Follow the Coast

Few tour routes these days have exclusive planners just for China's central coast, which is a pity. After all, the provinces of Zhejiang and Fujian have much to offer for bicyclists, hikers, ocean swimmers, and wind-surfers. And as one of China's first Special Economic Zones, Xiamen is currently awash with cash but still hasn't lost its old-world charm. Fall and spring are the ideal times to visit the region. Spring, especially April and May, has very comfortable temperatures and the trees and flowers are in full bloom. Hot and muggy summer is not the best time to visit—many of the cities are uncomfortable from mid-June though August. The region has a long and very pleasant fall season—moderate weather and clear skies last into early December. Chinese tourists flood in during the two "Golden Week" holidays at the start of May and October, so try to avoid those two weeks. Most of the region's sights are open daily.

With the Kids

China loves children, and the Chinese family revolves around its youngest members. If you follow basic safety guidelines, you can have a great family vacation in China.

Travel by the most comfortable option possible. If there is a tourist train or bus available, take it. Traveling on local transport is hot, crowded, and often unpleasant, especially for kids.

China maintains very lax standards about personal safety, so always keep an eye on your children. Things to look out for are missing railings on stairs, pools, towers, and cliffs, poor footing, unprotected cooking implements, and hazard-ous traffic.

When in doubt, you can always find a fast-food outlet. Fa-miliar food can go a long way toward keeping kids happy in an unfamiliar place.

The Chinese, especially the older generation, love chil-dren. Don't lose your cool if older people approach your children and want to touch their hair, faces, and hands. They are just curious, and can be gently redirected away from your children.

When to Go

Eastern China has mildly cool winters (the temperature rarely dips below zero) and long, hot summers. The mon-soon period extends from April through June, and typhoons can strike at any time through the late summer and autumn. If at all possible avoid traveling around the big Chinese national festivals (National Day, Oct.1; May Day, May 1; and the Lunar New Year, late January or early February).

Getting Here & Around

Shanghai is generally the best place to begin exploring Eastern China. It has good amenities, and with two airports and train stations, it offers myriad connectors across the country. Do not travel by bus unless it's absolutely necessary: even the smaller cities can be reached by rail, and buses should be reserved as a final recourse. Most major travel agents in Shanghai speak English, and they can be very useful in helping you plan out your trip. If you want to make Hangzhou your base, many cheap flights are available, although choice of destinations is more limited. Talk to your travel agent for the best deals.

Money Matters

Prices are negotiable everywhere except supermarkets. Be sure to ask for a discount, do not accept prices quoted in foreign currency, and never pay more than you think the article is really worth. Tourist markups can hit 1,000% in major attractions. Don't be afraid to shout Tai gui le! ("too expensive"), laugh at the seller, and walk away. He or she will probably call you back with a better price.

China is not a tipping country; however, if you are happy with your tour guide, do tip. Tips constitute the majority of a tour guide's income.

What It Costs in Yuan

¢	$	$$	$$$	$$$$
Restaurants				
under Y25	Y25–Y49	Y50–Y99	Y100–Y165	over Y165
Hotels				
under Y700	Y700–Y1,099	Y1,100–Y1,399	Y1,400–Y1,800	over Y1,800

Restaurant prices are for a main course, excluding tax and tips. Hotel prices are for a standard double room, including taxes.

On the Menu

Zhejiang cuisine is often steamed or roasted and has a more subtle, salty flavor; specialties include yellow croaker with Chinese cabbage, sea eel, drunken chicken, and stewed chicken. In Shaoxing locals traditionally start the day by downing a bowl or two of huang jiu (rice wine), the true breakfast of champions. Shaoxing's most famous dish is its deep-fried chou dofu, or stinky tofu. Try it with a touch of the local chili sauce.

The cuisine of Fujian is considered by some to have its own characteristics. Spareribs are a specialty, as are soups and stews using a soy-and-rice-wine stock. The coastal cities of Fujian offer a wonderful range of seafood, including river eel with leeks, fried jumbo prawns, and steamed crab.

BE SURE TO AVOID

Shark's fin soup is a delicacy that we do not recommend ordering. The harvesting of shark fins is exceptionally cruel (cutting off the fin and discarding the rest) and the zeal with which the animals are being hunted has lead to a shocking decline in global shark populations. If this information isn't enough to turn you off the dish, shark fins are known to contain high levels of mercury.

7

Updated by
David Taylor

A microcosm of the forces at play in contemporary China is presented in the provinces on the eastern coast of the country. The past's rich legacy and the challenges and aspirations for China's future combine in a present that is dizzying in its variety and speed of transformation. Zhejiang and Fujian have historically been some of the most affluent provinces in China and today they're once again enjoying prosperity.

Zhejiang has always been a hub of culture, learning, and commerce. The cities, with their elegant gardens, elaborate temples, and fine crafts, evoke the sophisticated and refined world of classical China's literati. Since the Southern Song Dynasty (1127–79), large numbers of Fujianese have emigrated around Southeast Asia. As a result, Fujian province has strong ties with overseas Chinese. In 1979 Fujian was allowed to form the first Special Economic Zone (SEZ)—a testing ground for capitalist market economy—at Xiamen. Today Xiamen is a pleasant city with a vibrant economy.

ZHEJIANG

The province of Zhejiang showcases the region's agricultural prowess and dedication to nature, even as it is one of the most populous urban regions of China. The capital city of Hangzhou is famous for its West Lake, which is visited by millions of tourists annually. A center of culture and trade, Zhejiang is also one of China's wealthiest provinces. Hangzhou served as one of the eight ancient capital cities of the country, after the Song Dynasty rulers fled Jurchen invaders. Throughout history, the city also benefited from its position as the last stop on the Grand Canal, the conduit for supplying grains and goods to the imperial north.

Shaoxing showcases another aspect of Zhejiang life. The small-town flavor of this city-on-canals remains, despite a growing population and overall economic boom in the province. Several high-profile figures helped put Shaoxing on the map, including former Premier Zhou Enlai, and novelist Lu Xun.

Geographically, the river basin's plains in the north near Shanghai give way to mountains in the south of the province. Besides grain, the province also is recognized in China for its tea, crafts, silk production, and long tradition of sculpture and carving.

HANGZHOU

180 km (112 mi) southwest of Shanghai.

Residents of Hangzhou are immensely proud of their city, and will often point to a classical saying that identifies it as an "earthly paradise." Indeed, Hangzhou is one of the country's most enjoyable cities. The green spaces and hilly landscape that surround the city make Hangzhou unique in Eastern China. Add to the experience a thriving arts scene, sophisticated restaurants, and vibrant nightlife, and Hangzhou vies with nearby Shanghai as the hippest city in the East.

GETTING HERE & AROUND

Hangzhou is best accessed by train, with the tourist express taking around an hour from Shanghai. There are buses that will get you to Shanghai in two hours or to Suzhou in 2½ hours. Hangzhou has several bus stations spread around the city serving different destinations—

buses to Shanghai use the East Bus Station, whereas those to Suzhou use the North Bus Station. Be careful to check that you are headed to the correct terminal.

BY AIR

Hangzhou Xiaoshan International Airport, about 27 km (17 mi) southeast of the city, has frequent flights to Hong Kong, Guangzhou, and Beijing, which are all about two hours away. There are also flights to other major cities around the region.

Major hotels offer limousine service to the airport. Taxis to the airport cost around Y120. A bus leaves from the CAAC office on Tiyuchang Lu every 30 minutes between 5:30 AM and 8:30 PM. It costs Y15 per person.

BY BOAT & FERRY

You can travel overnight by ferry between Hangzhou and Suzhou on the Grand Canal. Tickets are available through CITS or at the dock. It's a slow trip compared to buses and trains, and it's at night, so there's little to see.

One of the best ways to experience the charm of West Lake is on one of the many boats that ply the waters. Ferries charge Y35 for trips to the main islands. They depart when there are enough passengers, usually about every 20 minutes. Small private boats charge Y80 for up to four people, but you can choose your own route. You can head out on your own boat for Y20, but you can't dock at the islands. Prices are fixed but boat operators often try to overcharge you.

BY BUS

Hangzhou is the bus hub for the province and has four stations. The West Bus Station (Xi Zhan) has several buses daily to the Yellow Mountain, as well as to Nanjing. The East Bus Station (Dong Zhan) is the town's biggest, with several hundred departures per day to destinations like Shaoxing (1 hour), Suzhou (2½ hours), and Shanghai (2 hours). About 9 km (5 mi) north of the city is the North Bus Station (Bei Zhan), where there are buses to Nanjing (4 to 4½ hours).

Make sure you check with your hotel or travel agent which bus station you need to use.

Within Hangzhou, in addition to regular city buses, a series of modern, air-conditioned buses connects most major tourist sights. They are an easy way to get to more isolated sights. Bus Y1 connects Baidi

Causeway, Solitary Hill Island, Yue Fei Mausoleum, the Temple of the Soul's Retreat, and Orioles Singing in the Willow Waves. Bus Y3 runs to Precious Stone Hill, the China National Silk Museum, and the China Tea Museum.

BY TAXI

Hangzhou's clean, reliable taxi fleet makes it easy to get from West Lake to far-flung sights like the Temple of the Soul's Retreat and the China Tea Museum (Y30–Y45).

BY TRAIN

Travel between Shanghai and Hangzhou is very efficient. Fast trains take about an hour, while local trains take two or more. The train station can be chaotic, but hotel travel desks can often book advance tickets for a small fee. Trains also run to Suzhou (3 hours), Nanjing (5½ hours), and most cities in Fujian.

> **RENT A BIKE**
>
> Shaded by willow trees, West Lake is one of the country's most pleasant places for bicycling. This path, away from car traffic, is also a quick way to move between the area's major sights. There are numerous bike-rental shops around Orioles Singing in the Willow Waves Park. The rental rate is about Y10 per hour. A deposit and some form of identification are usually required.

ESSENTIALS

Air Contacts CAAC (⊠ *390 Tiyuchang Lu* ☎ *0571/8515-4259*). **Dragonair** (⊠ *Radisson Plaza Hotel Hangzhou, 5th fl., 333 Ti Yu Chang Lu* ☎ *0571/8506-8388*). **Hangzhou Xiaoshan International Airport** (⊠ *Hangzhou Xiaoshan District* ☎ *0571/8666-1234*).

Bank Bank of China (⊠ *140 Yan An Lu* ☎ *0571/8501-8888*).

Boat & Ferry Contacts CITS (⊠ *Huancheng Bei Lu* ☎ *0571/8515-3360*).

Bus Contacts East Bus Station (⊠ *71 Genshan Xi Lu* ☎ *0571/8694-8252, 0571/8696-4011 for tickets*). **North Bus Station** (⊠ *766 Moganshan Lu* ☎ *0571/8604-6666, 0751/8809-7761 for tickets*). **West Bus Station** (⊠ *357 Tianmushan Lu, Hangzhou* ☎ *0571/8522-2237*).

Medical Assistance Hangzhou Red Cross Hospital (⊠ *208 Huancheng Dong Lu* ☎ *0571/5610-9588*). **Zhejiang Medical University Affiliated Hospital No. 1** (⊠ *261 Qingchun Lu, Hangzhou* ☎ *0571/8707-2524*).

Train Information Hangzhou Train Station (⊠ *1 Huan Cheng Dong Lu, near intersection of Jiang Cheng Lu and Xihu Da Dao* ☎ *0571/8782-9418*).

Visitor & Tour Info Hangzhou Travel and Tourism Bureau (⊠ *484 Yanan Lu* ☎ *0571/8515-2645*). **Zhejiang CITS** (⊠ *1 Shihan Lu ✛ next to the Hangzhou Tourism Bureau* ☎ *0571/8516-0877*). **Zhejiang Comfort Travel** (⊠ *Shangri-La Hotel Hangzhou, 78 Beishan Lu* ☎ *0571/8796-5005*). **Zhejiang Women's International Travel Service** (⊠ *1 508 Wensan Lu* ☎ *0571/8822-5166*).

EXPLORING HANGZHOU

WEST LAKE ATTRACTIONS

West Lake (*Xihu*). With arched bridges stretching over the water, West Lake is the heart of leisure in Hangzhou. Originally a bay, the whole area was built up gradually throughout the years, a combination of natural changes and human shaping of the land. The shores are idyllic and immensely photogenic, enhanced by meandering paths, artificial islands, and countless pavilions with upturned roofs.

Two pedestrian causeways cross the lake: **Baidi** in the north and **Sudi** in the west. They are named for two poet–governors from different eras who invested in landscaping and developing the lake. Ideal for strolling or biking, both walkways are lined with willow and peach trees, crossed by bridges, and dotted with benches where you can pause to admire the views. ⊠ *East of the city, along Nanshan Lu.*

The Bai Causeway ends at the largest island on West Lake, **Solitary Hill Island** *(Gushan)*. A palace for the exclusive use of the emperor during his visits to Hangzhou once stood here. On its southern side is a small, carefully composed park around several pavilions and a pond. A path leads up the hill to the **Seal Engraver's Society** (*Xiling Yinshe* ☎ *0571/8781–5910* 💴 *Y5* 🕙 *Daily 9–5*). Professional carvers here will design and execute seals. The trip up the hill to the society is worth it, even for those who aren't particularly interested in this unusual art form. The society's garden has one of the best views of the lake. Solitary Hill Island is home to the **Zhejiang Provincial Museum** (*Zhejiang Bowuguan* ☎ *0571/8797–1177* ⊕ *www.zhejiangmuseum.com* 💴 *Free* 🕙 *Weekdays 8:30–4:30*). The museum has a good collection of archaeological finds, as well as bronzes and paintings. ⊠ *West Lake* 💴 *Free* 🕙 *Daily 8–dusk.*

NEED A BREAK?

On the crest of the hill inside the Seal Engraver's Society is a small teahouse where you can drink local teas. Order a cup and have a seat on the hilltop veranda. The view will make clear why locals have loved this place for centuries.

FodorsChoice ★

On the southeastern shore of West Lake is the **Evening Sunlight at Thunder Peak Pagoda** *(Leifeng Xizhao)*. Local legend says that the original Thunder Peak Pagoda was constructed to imprison a snake-turned-human who lost her mortal love on West Lake. The pagoda collapsed in 1924, perhaps finally freeing the White Snake. A new tower, completed in 2002, sits beside the remains of its predecessor. There's a sculpture on each level, including a carving that depicts the tragic story of the White Snake. The foundation dates to AD 976 and is an active archaeological site, where scientists uncovered a miniature silver pagoda containing what is said to be a lock of the Buddha's hair, on display in a separate hall. The view of the lake is breathtaking, particularly at sunset. ⊠ *15 Nanshan Lu* ☎ *0571/8796–4515* ⊕ *www.leifengta.com.cn* 💴 *Y40* 🕙 *Mar. 16–Nov. 15, daily 8 AM–9 PM; Nov. 16–Mar. 15, daily 7:30 AM–5:30 PM; last admission 30 mins before closing.*

On the southern side of the lake is the man-made island of **Three Pools Reflecting the Moon** *(Santan Yin Gyue)*. Here you'll find walkways surrounding several large ponds, all connected by zigzagging bridges. Off the island's southern shore are three stone Ming Dynasty pagodas. During the Mid-Autumn Moon Festival, held in the middle of

September, lanterns are lit in the pagodas, creating the three golden disks that give the island its name. Boats charging between Y35 and Y45 run between here and Solitary Hill Island. ⊠ *West Lake* 🖃*Y20* ⏰*Daily 7–5:30.*

The slender spire of Protecting Chu Pagoda rises atop **Precious Stone Hill** *(Baoshi Shan)*. The brick and stone pagoda is visible from just about anywhere on the lake. From the hilltop, you can see around West Lake and across to Hangzhou City. Numerous paths from the lakeside lead up the hill, which is dotted with Buddhist and Taoist shrines. Several caves provide shade and relief from the hot summer sun. ⊠*North of West Lake.*

Along the eastern bank of the lake is **Orioles Singing in the Willow Waves** *(Liulang Wenying)*, a nice place to watch boats on the lake. This park comes alive during the Lantern Festival, held in the winter. Paper lanterns are set afloat on the river, under the willow bows. ⊠*Near the intersection of Hefang Jie and Nanshan Lu.*

OTHER MAIN ATTRACTIONS

From worm to weave, the **China National Silk Museum** *(Zhongguo Sichou Bowuguan)* explores traditional silk production, illustrating every step of the way. By the end, you'll comprehend the cost of this fine fiber made from cocoons of mulberry-munching larvae. On display are looms, brocades, and a rotating exhibit of historical robes from different Chinese dynasties. The first-floor shop has the city's largest selection of silk, and sells it by the meter. The museum is south of West Lake, on the road to Jade Emperor Hill. ⊠*73-1 Yuhuangshan Lu* ☎*0571/8706–2129* ⊕*www.chinasilkmuseum.com* 🖃*Free* ⏰*Daily 8:30–4:30.*

★ The fascinating **China Tea Museum** *(Zhongguo Chaye Bowuguan)* explores all the facets of China's tea culture, such as the utensils used in the traditional ceremony. Galleries contain fascinating information about the varieties and quality of leaves, brewing techniques, and gathering methods, all with good English explanations. A shop also offers a range of tea for sale, without the bargaining you'll encounter at Dragon Well Tea Park. ⊠*Off Longjing Lu, north of Dragon Well Tea Park* ⊕*www.teamuseum.cn* 🖃*Free* ⏰*Daily 8:30–4:30.*

Equally celebrated as West Lake, and a short ride southwest of the lake is **Dragon Well Tea Park** *(Longjing Wencha)*, set amid rolling tea plantations. This park is named for an ancient well whose water is considered ideal for brewing the famous local Longjing tea. Distinguishing between varieties and grades of tea can be confusing for novices, especially under the high pressure of the eager hawkers. It is worth a preliminary trip to the nearby tea museum to bone up first. The highest quality varieties are very expensive, but once you take a sip you will taste the difference. Opening prices are intentionally high, so be sure to bargain. ⊠*Longjing Lu, next to Dragon Well Temple.*

One of the major Zen Buddhist shrines in China, the **Temple of the Soul's Retreat** *(Lingyin Si)* was founded in AD 326 by Hui Li, a Buddhist monk from India. He looked at the surrounding mountains and exclaimed, "This is the place where the souls of immortals retreat," hence the name. This site is especially notable for religious carvings on the nearby **Peak That Flew from Afar** (Feilai Feng). From the 10th to the 14th century, monks and artists sculpted more than 300 iconographical images on the mountain's face and inside caves. Unfortunately, the destruction wrought by the Red Guards during the Cultural Revolution is nowhere more evident than here. The temple and carvings are among the most popular spots in Hangzhou. To avoid the crowds, try to visit during the week. The temple is about 3 km (2 mi) southwest of West Lake. ⊠*End of Lingyin Lu* ☎*0571/8796–9691* ⊠*Park Y35, temple Y30* ⊙*Park daily 5:30 AM–6 PM, temple daily 7–5.*

IF YOU HAVE TIME

Atop **Moon Mountain** (Yuelin Shan) stands the impressive **Pagoda of Six Harmonies** *(Liuhe Ta)*. Those who climb to the top of the seven-story pagoda are rewarded with great views across the Qiantang River. Originally lanterns were lighted in its windows, and the pagoda served as a lighthouse for ships navigating the river. On the 18th day of the 8th lunar month, the pagoda is packed with people wanting the best seat for Qiantang Reversal. On this day the flow of the river reverses itself, creating large waves that for centuries have delighted observers. Behind the pagoda in an extensive park is an exhibit of 100 or so miniature pagodas, representing every Chinese style. The pagoda is 2½ km (1½ mi) south of West Lake. ⊠*Fuxing Jie, on the Qiantang River* ⊠*Y15* ⊙*Daily 6 AM–6:30 PM.*

In the hills southwest of the lake is **Running Tiger Spring** *(Hupao Quan)*. According to legend, a traveling monk decided this setting would be a perfect location for a temple, but was disappointed to discover that there was no source of water. That night he dreamed of two tigers that ripped up the earth around him. When he awoke he was lying next to a spring. On the grounds is an intriguing "dripping wall," cut out of the mountain. Locals line up with jugs to collect the water that pours from its surface, believing the water has special qualities—and it does. Ask someone in the temple's souvenir shop to float a coin on the surface of the water to prove it. ⊠*Hupao Lu, near the Pagoda of Six Harmonies* ⊠*Y15* ⊙*Daily 6 AM–6 PM.*

At the foot of Qixia Hill is **Yellow Dragon Cave** *(Huanglong Dong)*, famous for a never-ending stream of water spurting from the head of a yellow dragon. Nearby is a garden and a stage for traditional Yue opera performances that are given daily. In a nearby grove you'll see examples of rare "square bamboo." ⊠*Shuguang Lu* ☎*0571/8798–5860* ⊠*Y15* ⊙*Daily 7:30–6.*

The Qiantang Tidal Bore

During the autumnal equinox, when the moon's gravitational pull is at its peak, huge waves crash up the Qiantang River. Every year at this time, crowds gather at a safe distance to watch what begins as a distant line of white waves approaching. As it nears, it becomes a towering, thundering wall of water.

The phenomenon, known as a tidal bore, occurs when strong tides surge against the current of the river. The Qiantang Tidal Bore is the largest in the world, with speeds recorded up to 25 mph, and heights of 30 feet. The Qiantang has the best conditions in the world to produce these tidal waves. Incoming tides are funneled into the shallow riverbed from the Gulf of Hangzhou. The bell shape narrows and concentrates the wave. People have been swept away in the past, so police now enforce a strict viewing distance.

Near Solitary Hill Island stands the **Yue Fei Mausoleum** *(Yue Fei Mu)*, a shrine to honor General Yue Fei (1103–42), who led Song armies against foreign invaders. As a young man, his mother tattooed his back with the commandment to "Repay the nation with loyalty." This made Yue Fei a hero of both patriotic loyalty and filial piety. At the height of his success, a jealous rival convinced the emperor to have Yue Fei executed. A subsequent leader pardoned the warrior and enshrined him as a national hero. Statues of Yue Fei's accusers kneel in shame nearby. Traditionally, visitors would spit on statues of the traitors, but a recent sign near the statue asks them to glare instead. ⊠*Beishan Lu, west of Solitary Hill Island* ☜*Y25* ⊘*Daily 7:30–6.*

7

TOURS

Hotels can set up tours of the city's sights. You can also hire a car, driver, and translator through CITS, which has an office east of West Lake in the building of the Zhejiang Tourism Board. It's relatively inexpensive, and you'll be privy to discounts you wouldn't be able to negotiate for yourself. Smaller travel services tend to be less reliable and less experienced with the needs of foreign travelers.

Taxi drivers at the train station or in front of hotels will often offer tours. Although these can be as good as official ones, your driver's knowledge of English is often minimal.

Contact **CITS** (⊠*1 Shihan Lu, Hangzhou* ☎*0571/8515–2888*).

WHERE TO EAT

$$ ╳**Haveli.** A sign of the city's cosmopolitan atmosphere, Nanshan Lu
INDIAN is home to several good international restaurants. The best of these is this authentic Indian restaurant, with a solid menu of dishes ranging from lamb vindaloo to chicken tandoor cooked in a traditional oven. End your meal with a fantastic mango-flavored yogurt drink. Choose between the dining room with a high peaked ceiling and exposed wood beams or the large patio. A belly dancer performs nightly. ⊠*77 Nanshan Lu, south of Orioles Singing in the Willow Waves* ☎*0571/8702–9177* ⌲*Reservations essential* ▤*AE, DC, MC, V.*

$-$$ ✕ **Lingyin Si Vegetarian Restaurant.** Inside the Temple of the Soul's Retreat,
VEGETARIAN   this restaurant has turned the Buddhist restriction against eating meat
into an opportunity to invent a range of delicious vegetarian dishes. Soy
replaces chicken and beef, meaning your meal is as benevolent to your
health as to the animal world. ⊠*End of Lingyin Si Lu, western shore
of West Lake* ☎*0571/8796–9691* ⊟*No credit cards* ⊘*No dinner.*

$$-$$$ ✕ **Louwailou Restaurant.** Back in 1848, this place opened as a fish shack
CHINESE   on West Lake. Business boomed and it became the most famous restau-
FUSION   rant in the province. Specializing in Zhejiang cuisine, Louwailou makes
Fodor'sChoice   special use of lake perch, which is steamed and served with vinegar
★   sauce. Another highlight is the classic *su dongpo* pork, slow cooked in
yellow-rice wine and tender enough to cut with chopsticks. Hangzhou's
most famous dish, Beggar's Chicken, is wrapped in lotus leaves and
baked in a clay shell. It's as good as it sounds. ⊠*30 Gushan Lu, southern tip of Solitary Hill Island* ☎*0571/8796–9682* ⊟*AE, MC, V.*

¢-$$$ ✕ **Zhiweiguan Restaurant.** In business for nearly a century, this restau-
CHINESE   rant's bustling first floor is a pay-as-you-go dim-sum counter. No menu
FUSION   is necessary: you point to order a bamboo steamer filled with its famous
dumplings or a bowl of wonton soup. The second floor is for proper
dinner, where the menu is full of well-prepared fish dishes. ⊠*83 Renhe
Lu, east side of West Lake* ☎*0571/8701–8638* ⊟*No credit cards.*

WHERE TO STAY

¢   🏨 **Dong Po Hotel.** This budget business hotel is clean and comfortable.
The smaller rooms are rather utilitarian, but the location in the center
of town—two blocks from the lake and two blocks from the night mar-
ket—makes this a good choice. **Pros:** convenient location, low price.
Cons: small and boring rooms, poor service, little English is spoken.
⊠*52 Renhe Lu* ☎*0571/8706–9769* ➪*99 rooms, 3 suites* ⚖*In-hotel:
restaurant* ⊟*MC, V.*

$$ 🏨 **Dragon Hotel.** Within walking distance of Precious Stone Hill and the
Yellow Dragon Cave, this hotel stands in relatively peaceful and attrac-
tive surroundings. It's a massive place, but feels much smaller because its
buildings are spread around peaceful courtyards with ponds, a waterfall, and a gazebo. Two towers house the medium-size guest rooms,
which are decorated in pale greens and blues. Although it has plenty
of facilities, the hotel lacks the polish of its Western competitors. **Pros:**
good location, newly renovated. **Cons:** indifferent service, little English
is spoken. ⊠*120 Shuguang Lu, at Hangda Lu* ☎*0571/8799–8833*
⊕*www.dragon-hotel.com* ➪*499 rooms, 29 suites* ⚖*In-room: safe,
dial-up. In-hotel: 4 restaurants, room service, bar, tennis court, pool,
gym, bicycles, concierge, laundry service, no-smoking rooms, Ethernet*
⊟*AE, DC, MC, V.*

¢   🏨 **Hangzhou Overseas Chinese Hotel.** A budget hotel with a five-star location, the Overseas Chinese Hotel is steps from West Lake. The chipped
woodwork and beige color scheme makes it less flashy than its competitors, but the low price makes this hotel a good pick. Rooms on the fifth
floor have the best views over the water. You can hire a car and driver
through the hotel to tour the outlying area. **Pros:** phenomenal location,
good price. **Cons:** worn, dingy decor, inadequate dining. ⊠*39 Hubin
Lu* ☎*0571/8768–5555* ➪*218 rooms, 4 suites* ⚖*In-room: safe. In-*

hotel: 5 restaurants, bars, laundry service ⊟AE, DC, MC, V.

$$$–$$$$
Fodor's Choice
★
Hyatt Regency Hangzhou. Hangzhou's newest luxury hotel, the Hyatt Regency combines careful service, comfortable rooms, and a great location. A large pool overlooks West Lake. Inside there's a day spa, as well as excellent Chinese

and Western restaurants. About two blocks north is Hubing Yi Park Boat Dock, where you can catch boats that ply the lake. The rooms are sleekly furnished, and unlike many hotels in China, the beds are truly soft. Ask for a room on an upper floor for an unobstructed view. **Pros:** gorgeous view, good service, excellent pool. **Cons:** location could be quieter, long check-in time. ⊠28 Hu Bin Lu ☎0571/8779–1234 ⊕www.hyatt.com ➵390 rooms, 23 suites ⌂In-room: safe, Ethernet. In-hotel: 3 restaurants, room service, bars, tennis court, pool, gym, spa, concierge, children's programs (ages 1–12), laundry service, no-smoking rooms ⊟AE, DC, MC, V.

$$$–$$$$
Lakeview Wanghu Hotel. True to its name, this hotel has good views of the water from its position near the northeastern shore of West Lake. It's oriented toward business travelers, which is why it emphasizes its meeting facilities and 24-hour business center. An on-site travel agency employs several guides who specialize in working with English-speaking travelers. **Pros:** good location, convenient travel services. **Cons:** poor customer service, small rooms. ⊠2 Huancheng Xi Lu ☎0571/8707–8888 ⊕www.wanghuhotel.com ➵348 rooms, 9 suites ⌂In-hotel: 2 restaurants, bar, pool, gym ⊟AE, MC, V.

$$$–$$$$
Fodor's Choice
★
Shangri-La Hotel Hangzhou. Set on the site of an ancient temple, the Shangri-La is a scenic and historic landmark. The hotel's 40 hillside acres of camphor and bamboo trees merge seamlessly into the nearby gardens and walkways surrounding West Lake. Spread through two wings, the large rooms have a formal feel, with high ceilings and heavy damask fabrics. Request a room overlooking the lake. The gym and restaurants are all top caliber. A first-floor garden bar is an elegant spot to relax with a drink. Staff speaks fluent English. **Cons:** poor customer service, long check-in times. ⊠78 Beishan Lu ☎0571/8797–7951 ⊕www.shangri-la.com ➵355 rooms, 37 suites ⌂In-room: safe, dial-up. In-hotel: 3 restaurants, room service, bar, tennis court, pool, gym, bicycles, concierge, laundry service, executive floor, airport shuttle, no-smoking rooms, Ethernet ⊟AE, DC, MC, V.

$$$$
★
Sofitel Westlake Hangzhou. A stone's throw from West Lake, this high-end hotel is in a lively neighborhood of restaurants, bars, and shops. Gauzy curtains and etched-glass-and-wood columns divide the distinctive lobby, distinguished by a gold-and-black mural of the city's landmarks. The rooms—most of which have lake views—are thoughtfully designed, with sleek oval desks, fabric-covered headboards, and a glass privacy screen in the bathroom. A Roman-style pool overcomes its drab basement location. The hotel is a block north of Orioles Singing in the

7

Willow Waves. Pros: good location, helpful staff. Cons: small rooms, many rooms with poor views. ✉*333 Xihu Dadao* ☎*0571/8707–5858* ⊕*www.accor.com* ⇝*186 rooms, 15 suites* ⅊*In-room: safe, dial-up, Wi-Fi. In-hotel: 4 restaurants, room service, bar, pool, gym, spa, concierge, laundry service, executive floor, airport shuttle, no-smoking rooms* ⊟*AE, DC, MC, V.*

NIGHTLIFE & THE ARTS

The city's most exciting bar is the **Travelers Pub** (✉*176 Shuguang Lu* ☎*0571/8796–8846*), the only venue for live jazz and folk music. A bohemian crowd gathers here during the week, and on weekends hipsters fill the place to capacity. Subtle political murals decorate the wall, and there's even a bulletin board for those looking to meet fellow travelers and artists looking for collaborators.

The laid-back **Kana Pub** (✉*152 Nanshan Lu* ☎*0571/8706–3228*) is an expat favorite for its well-mixed cocktails, live music, and friendly proprietor. The personable staff at the **Shamrock** (✉*70 Zhongshan Zhong Lu* ☎*0571/8702–8760*), the city's first Irish pub, serves Guinness and Kilkenny pints, bottled-beer specials, along with great food.

Yue opera performances take place daily from 8:45 AM to 11:30 AM and 1:45 PM to 4:30 PM at the **Yuanyuan Minsu Theater** (✉*69 Shuguang Lu* ☎*0571/8797–2468*), at the Yellow Dragon Cave. The performances are free with the Y15 park admission.

SHOPPING

The best souvenirs to buy in Hangzhou are green tea and silk, but all sorts of wooden crafts, silk fans and umbrellas, and antiques are available in small shops sprinkled around town. For the best Longjing tea, head to Dragon Well Tea Park or the China Tea Museum. Around town, especially along Yan'an Lu, you can spot the small tea shops by the wok-like tea roasters at the entrances.

China Silk City (*Zhongguo Sichou Cheng* ✉*217 Xinhua Lu, between Fengqi Lu and Tiyuchang Lu* ☎*0571/8510–0192*) sells silk ties, pajamas, and shirts, plus silk straight off the bolt. A combination health-food store and apothecary, **Fulintang** (✉*147 Nanshan Lu* ☎*0571/8702–6639*) sells herbs and other health-enhancing products. About three blocks north of the China Tea Museum, the **Xihu Longjing Tea Company** (✉*108 Longjing Lu* ☎*0571/8796–2219*) has a nice selection of Longjing tea.

Hangzhou's **Night Market** (✉*Renhe Lu, east of Huansha Lu*) is thriving. In addition to Hangzhou's best selection of late-night snacks, you'll find accessories of every kind—ties, scarves, pillow covers—as well as knockoff designer goods and fake antiques. You'll find the same merchandise at many stalls, so don't hesitate to walk away if the price isn't right. It's open nightly 6 PM–10:30 PM.

SHAOXING

68 km (42 mi) east of Hangzhou.

★ Shaoxing is alive in the Chinese imagination thanks to the famous writer Lu Xun, who set many of his classic works in this sleepy southern town. A literary revolutionary, Lu Xun broke tradition by writing in the vernacular of everyday Chinese, instead of the stiff, scholarly prose previously held as the only appropriate language for literature.

Today, much of the city's charm is in exploring its narrow cobbled streets. The older sections of the city are made of low stone houses, connected by canals and crisscrossed by arched bridges. East Lake is no match for the grandeur of Hangzhou's West Lake, but its bizarre rock formations and caves make for interesting tours. Shaoxing is also famous for its celebrated yellow-rice wine, used by cooks everywhere.

GETTING HERE & AROUND

The most reliable and comfortable way to travel to Shaoxing is by train. Regular train and luxury bus services run to Shaoxing from Hangzhou and Shanghai a few times a day. Check with your hotel concierge for details

BY BUS

Hangzhou's East Bus Station has dozens of buses each day to Shaoxing. In Shaoxing, buses to Hangzhou leave from the main bus station in the north of town, at the intersection of Jiefang Bei Lu and Huan Cheng Bei Lu. Luxury buses take about an hour.

BY TAXI

Although Shaoxing is small enough that walking is the best way to get between many sights, the city's small red taxis are relatively inexpensive. Most trips are Y15.

BY TRAIN

Trains between Hangzhou and Shaoxing take about an hour, but do not leave as frequently as buses. The Shaoxing Train Station is 2½ km (1½ mi) north of the city, near the main bus station.

ESSENTIALS

Bank **Bank of China** (⊠ *568 Zhongxing Bei Lu, Shaoxing* ☎ *0575/8514-3571*).

Bus Contacts **Shaoxing North Bus Station** (⊠ *2 Jiefang Bei Lu* ☎ *0575/8513-0794*).

Medical Assistance **Shaoxing People's Hospital** (⊠ *61 Shaoxing Dongjie* ☎ *0575/8822-8888*).

Train Contacts **Shaoxing Train Station** (⊠ *Shaoxing Chezhan Lu* ☎ *0575/8802-2584*).

Visitor & Tour Info **Welcome to Shaoxing** (⊕ *www.shaoxing.gov.cn/en/index.htm*).

EXPLORING SHAOXING

MAIN ATTRACTIONS

The city's quiet northern neighborhoods are especially amenable to wandering, with several historic homes and temples that are now preserved as museums. The largest is the **Cai Yuanpei's House** (✉*13 Bifei alley, Xiaoshan Lu* ☎*0575/8511–0652* 🎫*Y5* ⏱*Daily 8–5*). The owner was a famous educator during the republic, and his family's large compound is decorated with period furniture.

In a city of bridges, **Figure 8 Bridge** *(Bazi Qiao Bridge)* is the city's finest and best known. Its long, sloping sides rise to a flat crest that looks like the character for eight, an auspicious number. The current bridge is over 800 years old, and is draped with a thick beard of ivy and vines. It sits in a quiet area of old stone houses with canal-side terraces where people wash clothes and chat with neighbors. ✉*Bazi Qiao Zhi Jie, off Renmin Zhong Lu.*

The **Lu Xun Family Home** *(Lu Xun Gu Ju)* was once the stomping grounds of literary giant and social critic Lu Xun. The extended Lu family lived around a series of courtyards. Nearby is the local school where Lu honed his writing skills. This is a great place to explore a traditional Shaoxing home and see some beautiful antique furniture. This is a popular destination, so it's wise to book a tour in high season. Consult your concierge for details. ✉*398 Lu Xun Zhong Lu, 1 block east of Xianhen Hotel* ☎*0575/8513–2080* 🎫*Free with ID or passport* ⏱*Daily 8:30–5.*

IF YOU HAVE TIME

Near the Figure 8 Bridge is the bright pink **Catholic Church of St. Joseph,** dating from the turn of the 20th century. A hybrid of styles, the Italian-inspired interior is decorated with passages from the Bible in Chinese calligraphy. ✉*Bazi Qiao Zhi Jie, off Renmin Zhong Lu.*

The narrow **East Lake** *(Dong Hu)* runs along the base of a rocky bluff rising up from the rice paddies of Zhejiang. The crazily shaped cliffs were used as a rock quarry over the centuries, and today their sheer gray faces jut out in sheets of rock. You can hire a local boatman to take you along the base of the cliffs in a traditional black awning boat for Y40. ✉*Yundong Lu, 3 km (2 mi) east of the city center* 🎫*Y25* ⏱*Daily 7:30–5:30.*

The **Zhou Enlai Family Home** (✉*369 Laodong Lu* ☎*0575/8513–3368* 🎫*Y18* ⏱*Daily 8–5*) belonged to the first premier of Communist China, who came from a family of prosperous Shaoxing merchants.

Zhou is credited with saving some of China's most important historical monuments from destruction at the hands of the Red Guards during the Cultural Revolution. The compound, a showcase of traditional architecture, has been preserved and houses exhibits on Zhou's life, ranging from his high-school essays to vacation snapshots with his wife.

> **WORD OF MOUTH**
>
> "Local dishes made with the famous Shaoxing 'yellow wine' are worth trying, and you can get all the same Huaiyang dishes you can get in Hangzhou, too." –PeterN_H

WHERE TO EAT

¢–$ ╳**Sanwei Jiulou.** This restaurant serves up local specialties, including
CHINESE warm rice wine served in Shaoxing's distinctive tin kettles. Relaxed and
FUSION distinctive, it's in a restored old building and appointed with traditional wood furniture. The second story looks out over the street below. ✉*2 Lu Xun Lu* ☎*0575/8893–5578* 🚫*No credit cards.*

¢ ╳**Xianheng Winehouse** *(Xianheng Jiudian).* Shaoxing's most famous
CHINESE fictional character, the small-town scholar Kong Yiji, would sit on a bench here, dining on wine and boiled beans. Forgo the beans, but the fermented bean curd is good, especially with a bowl of local wine. ✉*179 Lu Xun Zhong Lu, 1 block east of the Sanwei Jiulou* ☎*0575/8511–6666* 🚫*No credit cards.*

WHERE TO STAY

$–$$ ▦**Shaoxing International Hotel** *(Shaoxing Guoji Dajiudian).* Surrounded by pleasant gardens, this hotel offers bright, well-appointed rooms and a range of facilities. It's near the West Bus Station. **Pros:** reasonable price. **Cons:** no Internet, dated decor. ✉*100 Fushan Xi Lu* ☎*0575/516–6788* 🛏*302 rooms* 🛎*In-hotel: 2 restaurants, tennis court, pool, gym* 🚫*AE, DC, MC, V.*

$–$$ ▦**Shaoxing Xianheng Hotel.** Conveniently located near many of the city's restaurants, the Shaoxing Xianheng offers modern, comfortable rooms and good service. **Pros:** centrally located, good value. **Cons:** inconsistent English, some rooms need updating. ✉*680 Jiefang Nan Lu* ☎*0575/8806–8688* 🛏*221 rooms, 8 suites* 🛎*In-hotel: 2 restaurants, bar, tennis court, pool, gym* 🚫*AE, MC, V.*

SHOPPING

Shaoxing has some interesting local crafts, mainly related to calligraphy and rice wine. The most convenient place to buy souvenirs is the shopping street called **Lu Xun Zhong Lu.** In addition to calligraphy brushes, and fans, scrolls, and other items decorated with calligraphy, look for shops selling the local tin wine pots. The traditional way of serving yellow-rice wine, the pots are placed on the stove to heat up wine for a cold winter night. Also popular are traditional boatmen's hats, made of thick, waterproof, black felt.

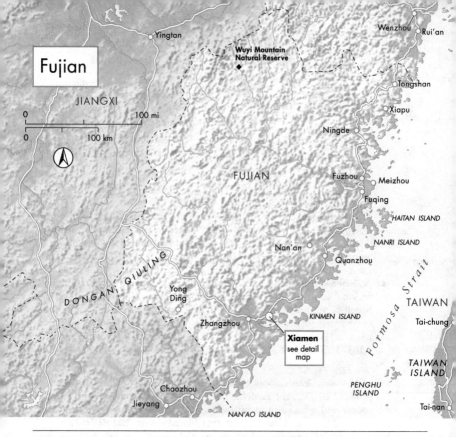

FUJIAN

One of China's most beautiful provinces, Fujian has escaped the notice of most visitors. This is because the region, though not too far off the beaten path, is usually passed over in favor of more glamorous destinations like Hong Kong or Shanghai. The city of Xiamen is clean and beautiful, and the surrounding area has some of the best beaches north of Hainan. And Gulangyu is a rarity in modern China: a tree-filled island with undisturbed colonial architecture and absolutely no cars.

XIAMEN

200 km (124 mi) southwest of Fuzhou; 500 km (310 mi) northeast of Hong Kong.

By Chinese standards, Xiamen is a new city: its history only dates to the late 12th century. Xiamen was a stronghold for Ming loyalist Zheng Chenggong (better known as Koxinga), who later fled to Taiwan after China was overrun by the Qing. Xiamen's place as a dynasty-straddling city continues to this day due to its proximity to Taiwan. Some see Xiamen as a natural meeting point between the two sides in the decades-long separation. Only a few miles out to sea are islands that still technically belong to "The Republic of China," as Taiwan is still officially known.

A prosperous city due to its importance as a trading port, Xiamen suffered because of China's anxieties over Taiwan. But as one of the first cities opened to foreign trade, Xiamen saw the money come rolling in again. It is today one of the most prosperous cities in China, with beautiful parks, amazing temples, and waterfront promenades that neatly complement the port city's historic architecture. Xiamen has a number of wonderful parks and temples well worth visiting.

GETTING HERE & AROUND

The best way to reach Xiamen is by plane. The city is also accessible by long-distance train or sleeper bus, but these types of transportation entail much longer travel times.

BY AIR

Xiamen Airport, one of the largest and busiest in China, lies about 12 km (7 mi) northeast of the city. A taxi from downtown should cost no more than Y60. Most carriers service Xiamen, which has connections to many cities in China, as well as international destinations like Jakarta, Manila, Penang, and Singapore.

BY BUS

Xiamen has luxury bus service to all the main cities along the coast as far as Guangzhou and Shanghai. The long-distance bus station is on Hubin Nan Lu, just south of Yuandang Lake.

BY TAXI

In Xiamen, taxis can be found around hotels or on the streets; they're a convenient way to visit the sights on the edge of town. Most taxi drivers do not speak English, so make sure that all your addresses are written in Chinese. Any hotel representative will be happy to do this for you.

BY TRAIN

Rail travel to and from Xiamen isn't as convenient as in many other cities. Many journeys involve changing trains at least once. There is, however, direct service to Shanghai, which takes 27 hours. Service between Xiamen and Beijing takes 34 hours, and service between Xiamen and Kunming takes a whopping 41 hours. For this reason, most visitors to Xiamen prefer to fly.

The railway station is about 3 km (2 mi) northeast of the port; bus service between the station and port is frequent.

ESSENTIALS

Air Contacts **Dragonair** (⊠ Seaside Bldg., Jiang Dao Lu, Xiamen ☎ 0592/202–5433). **Philippine Airlines** (⊠ Xiamen Airport ☎ 0592/239–4729 ⊕ www.philippineair lines.com). **Xiamen Airlines** (⊠ 22 Dailiao Lu, Xiamen ☎ 0592/602–2961 ⊕ www. xiamenair.com.cn). **Xiamen Airport** (☎ 0592/602–0017).

Banks **Bank of China** (⊠ 10 Zhongshan Lu, Xiamen ☎ 0592/506–6466). **HSBC** (⊠ 189 Xiahe Lu, Xiamen ☎ 0592/239–7799).

Continued on page 215

SPIRITUALITY IN CHINA

Even though it's officially an atheist nation, China has a vibrant religious life. But what are the differences between China's big three faiths of Buddhism, Taoism, and Confucianism? Like much else in the Middle Kingdom, the lines are often blurred.

Walking around the streets of any city in China in the early 21st century, it's hard to believe that only three decades ago the bulk of the Middle Kingdom's centuries-old religious culture was destroyed by revolutionary zealots, and that the few temples, mosques, monasteries, and churches that escaped outright destruction were desecrated and turned into warehouses and factories, or put to other ignoble uses. Those days are long over, and religion in China has sprung back to life. Even though the official line of the Chinese Communist Party is that the nation is atheist, China is rife with religious diversity.

Perhaps the faith most commonly associated with China is Confucianism, an ethical and philosophical system developed from the teachings of the sage Confucius. Confucianism stresses the importance of relationships in society and of maintaining proper etiquette. These aspects of Confucian thought are associated not merely with China (where its modern-day influence is dubious at best, especially in a crowded subway car), but also with East Asian culture as a whole. Confucianism also places great emphasis on filial piety, the respect that a child should show an elder (or subjects to their ruler). This may account for

(left) Offering up joss sticks.
(below) The Yong he Gong Lama temple in Beijing.

Confucianism's status as the most officially tolerated of modern China's faiths.

Taoism is based on the teachings of the *Tao Te Ching*, a treatise written in the 6th century BC, and blends an emphasis on spiritual harmony with that of the individual's duty to society. Taoism and Confucianism are complementary, though to the outsider, the former might seem more steeped in ritual and mysticism. Think of it this way: Taoism is to Confucianism as Catholicism is to Protestantism. Taoism's mystic quality may be why so many westerners come to China to study "the way," as Taoism is sometimes called.

Tian Tan, The Temple of Heaven in Beijing.

Buddhism came to China from India in the first century AD and quickly became a major force in the Middle Kingdom. The faith is so ingrained here that many Chinese openly scoff at the idea that the Buddha wasn't Chinese. In a nutshell, Buddhism teaches that attachment leads to suffering, and that the best way to alleviate the world's suffering is to purify one's mind, to abstain from evil, and to cultivate good. In China, there are three major schools: the Chinese school, embraced mainly by Han Chinese; the Tibetan school (or Lamaism) as practiced by Tibetans and Mongolians; and Theravada, practiced by the Dai and other ethnic minority groups in the southwest of the country.

TEMPLE FAUX PAS

Chinese worshippers are easygoing. Even at the smallest temple or shrine, they understand that some people will be visitors and not devotees. Temples in China have relaxed dress codes, but you should follow certain rules of decorum.

■ You're welcome to burn incense, but it's not required. If you do decide to burn a few joss sticks, take them from the communal pile and be sure to make a small donation. This usually goes to temple upkeep or local charities.

The Buddha

■ When burning incense, two sticks signify marriage, and four signify death.

■ Respect signs reading NO PHOTO in front of altars and statues. Taoist temples seem particularly sensitive about photo taking. When in doubt, ask.

■ Avoid stepping in front of a worshipper at an altar or censer (where incense is burned).

■ Speak quietly and silence mobile phones inside of temple grounds.

■ Don't touch Buddhist monks of the opposite sex.

■ Avoid entering a temple during a ceremony.

TEMPLE OBJECTS

For many, temple visits are among the most culturally edifying parts of a China trip. Large or small, Chinese temples incorporate a variety of objects significant to religious practice.

INCENSE

Incense is the most common item in any Chinese temple. In antiquity, Chinese people burned sacrifices both as an offering and as a way of communicating with spirits through the smoke. This later evolved into a way of showing respect for one's ancestors by burning fragrances that the dearly departed might find particularly pleasing.

BAGUA

Taoist temples will have a bagua: an octagonal diagram pointing toward the eight cardinal directions, each representing different points on the compass, elements in nature, family members, and more esoteric meanings. The bagua is often used in conjunction with a compass to make placement decisions in architectural design and in fortune-telling.

"GHOST MONEY"

Sometimes the spirits need more than sweet-smelling smoke, and this is why many Taoists burn "ghost money" (also known as "hell money"), a scented paper resembling cash. Though once more popular in Taiwan and Hong Kong (and looked upon as a particularly capitalist superstition on the mainland), the burning of ghost money is now gaining ground throughout the country.

CENSER

Every Chinese temple will have a censer in which to place joss sticks, either inside the hall or out front. Larger temples often have a number of them. These large stone or bronze bowls are filled with incense ash from hundreds of joss sticks placed by worshippers. Some incense censers are ornate, with sculpted bronze rising above the bowls.

STATUES

Chinese temples are known for being flexible, and statues of various deities and mythical figures abound. Confucius is usually rendered as a wizened man with a long beard, and Taoist temples have an array of demons deities.

PRAYER WHEEL

Used primarily by Tibetan Buddhists, the prayer wheel is a beautifully embossed hollow metal cylinder mounted on a wooden handle. Inside the cylinder is a tightly wound scroll printed with a mantra. Devotees believe that the spinning of a prayer wheel is a form of prayer that's just as effective as reciting the sacred texts aloud.

CHINESE ASTROLOGY

According to legend, the King of Jade invited 12 animals to visit him in heaven. As the animals rushed to be the first to arrive, the rat snuck a ride on the ox's back. Just as the ox was about to cross the threshold, the rat jumped past him and arrived first. This is why the rat was given first place in the astrological chart. Find the year you were born to determine what your astrological animal is.

RAT

1924 · 1936 · 1948 · 1960 · 1972 · 1984 · 1996 · 2008

Charming and hardworking, Rats are goal setters and perfectionists. Rats are quick to anger, ambitious, and lovers of gossip.

OX

1925 · 1937 · 1949 · 1961 · 1973 · 1985 · 1997 · 2009

Patient and soft-spoken, Oxen inspire confidence in others. Generally easygoing, they can be remarkably stubborn, and they hate to fail or be opposed.

TIGER

1926 · 1938 · 1950 · 1962 · 1974 · 1986 · 1998 · 2010

Sensitive, and thoughtful, Tigers are capable of great sympathy. Tigers can be short-tempered, and are prone to conflict and indecisiveness.

RABBIT

1927 · 1939 · 1951 · 1963 · 1975 · 1987 · 1999 · 2011

Talented and articulate, Rabbits are virtuous, reserved, and have excellent taste. Though fond of gossip, Rabbits tend to be generally kind and even-tempered.

DRAGON

1928 · 1940 · 1952 · 1964 · 1976 · 1988 · 2000 · 2012

Energetic and excitable, short-tempered and stubborn, Dragons are known for their honesty, bravery, and ability to inspire confidence and trust.

SNAKE

1929 · 1941 · 1953 · 1965 · 1977 · 1989 · 2001 · 2013

Snakes are deep, possessing great wisdom and saying little. Snakes can often be vain and selfish while retaining sympathy for those less fortunate.

HORSE

1930 · 1942 · 1954 · 1966 · 1978 · 1990 · 2002 · 2014

Horses are thought to be cheerful and perceptive, impatient and hot-blooded. Horses are independent and rarely listen to advice.

GOAT

1931 · 1943 · 1955 · 1967 · 1979 · 1991 · 2003 · 2015

Wise, gentle, and compassionate, Goats are elegant and highly accomplished in the arts. Goats can also be shy and pessimistic, and often tend toward timidity.

MONKEY

1932 · 1944 · 1956 · 1968 · 1980 · 1992 · 2004 · 2016

Clever, skillful, and flexible, Monkeys are thought to be erratic geniuses, able to solve problems with ease. Monkeys are also thought of as impatient and easily discouraged.

ROOSTER

1933 · 1945 · 1957 · 1969 · 1981 · 1993 · 2005 · 2017

Roosters are capable and talented, and tend to like to keep busy. Roosters are known as overachievers, and are frequently loners.

DOG

1934 · 1946 · 1958 · 1970 · 1982 · 1994 · 2006 · 2018

Dogs are loyal and honest and know how to keep secrets. They can also be selfish and stubborn.

PIG

1935 · 1947 · 1959 · 1971 · 1983 · 1995 · 2007 · 2019

Gallant and energetic, Pigs have a tendency to be single-minded and determined. Pigs have great fortitude and honesty, and tend to make friends for life.

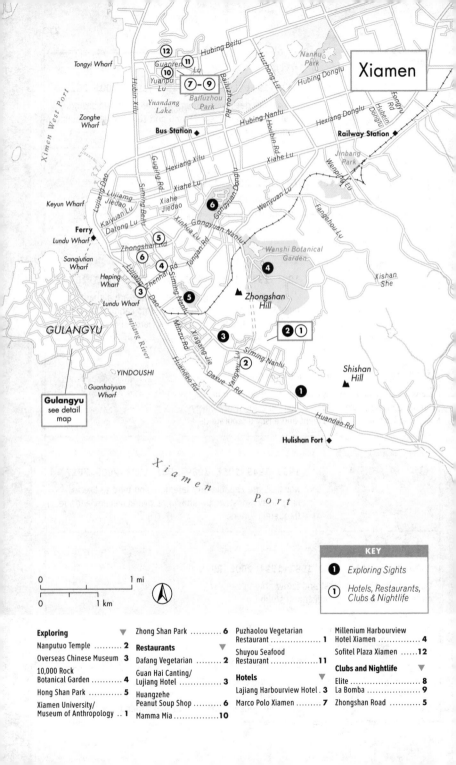

Bus Contacts **Long-Distance Bus Station** (✉ *56 Hubin Nan Lu, Xiamen* ☎ *0592/203–1246*).

Internet **Javaromas** (✉ *31-13 Jianye Lu, Xiamen* ☎ *0592/514–5677*).

Medical Assistance **Lifeline Medical System** (✉ *Hubin Bei Lu, Xiamen* ☎ *0592/203–2834*).

Train Contacts **Xiamen Train Station** (✉ *Xiahe Lu* ☎ *0592/203–8888*).

Visitor & Tour Info **CTS** (✉ *2 Zhongshan Lu, Xiamen* ☎ *0592/212–6917* ✉ *Hubin Bei Lu, Xiamen* ☎ *0592/505–1822*).

EXPLORING XIAMEN

MAIN ATTRACTIONS

⑤ The rather hilly **Hong Shan Park** *(Hong Shan Gong Yuan)* has a small Buddhist temple, a lovely waterfall, and beautiful views of the city and the harbor. There's also a lovely tea shop serving Iron Buddha tea, a Fujian specialty. ✉ *Siming Nan Lu, near Nanputuo Temple* ☑ *Free.*

② **Nanputuo Temple** *(Nanputuo Si)* dates from the Tang Dynasty. It has been restored many times, most recently in the 1980s, following the Cultural Revolution. Built in the exuberant style that visitors to Taiwan will find familiar, it has roofs that are decorated with brightly painted flourishes of clustered flowers, sinewy serpents, and mythical beasts. Pavilions on either side of the main hall contain tablets commemorating the suppression of secret societies by the Qing emperors. As the most important of Xiamen's temples, it is nearly always the center of a great deal of activity as monks and worshippers mix with tour groups. Attached to the temple complex is an excellent vegetarian restaurant. To get here, take Bus 1 or 2 from the port. ✉ *Siming Nan Lu, next to Xiamen University* ☑ *Y3* ☉ *Daily 7:30 AM–6:30 PM.*

① Housed in a fascinating mix of traditional and colonial buildings close to Nanputuo Temple is **Xiamen University** *(Xiamen Daxue)*. It was founded in the 1920s with the help of Chinese people living abroad. The **Museum of Anthropology** *(Renlei Bowuguan)*, dedicated to the study of the Neolithic era, is one of the most popular destinations. It has a very good collection of fossils, ceramics, paintings, and ornaments. It's open daily 8:30 to 11 and 3 to 5. ✉ *End of Siming Nan Lu.*

④ Surrounding a pretty lake, the **10,000 Rock Botanical Garden** *(Wanshi Zhiwuyuan)* has a fine collection of more than 4,000 species of tropical and subtropical flora, ranging from eucalyptus and bamboo trees to orchids and ferns. There are several pavilions, of which the most interesting are those forming the **Temple of the Kingdom of Heaven** *(Tianjie Si)*. ✉ *Huyuan Lu, off Wenyuan Lu* ☑ *Y10* ☉ *Daily 8–6.*

IF YOU HAVE TIME

③ In the southern part of the city, the **Overseas Chinese Museum** *(Huaqiao Bowuguan)* was founded by the wealthy industrialist Tan Kah-kee. Three halls illustrate, with the help of pictures and documents, personal items, and relics associated with the great waves of emigration from southeastern China during the 19th century. ✉ *493 Siming Nan Lu* ☎ *0592/208–5345* ☑ *Free* ☉ *Tues.–Sun. 9:30–4.*

6   Commemorating Dr. Sun Yat-sen, **Zhong Shan Park** *(Zhong Shan Gong Yuan)* is centered around a statue to the great man. There is a small zoo, lakes, and canals you can explore by paddleboat. The annual Lantern Festival is held here. ⊠ *Zhong Shan Lu and Zhenhai Lu* 🎫 *Free.*

WORD OF MOUTH

"Xiamen's main attractions are the warren of streets of the old port area, in which it is easy (and pleasant) to get lost, and the islet of Gulang (Gulang Yu), which has the best-preserved collection of treaty port-era mansions in China, and which still permits no cars."

–PeterN_H

OFF THE BEATEN PATH

Jinmen. History buffs will be fascinated by a trip around this lingering remnant of China's bitter civil war. Though barely a stone's throw from mainland China, this island is still controlled by Taiwan. As of this writing only Xiamen residents are allowed to visit Jinmen, so tour boats only come close enough to let you see Taiwanese guards patrolling the shores or call out to the Taiwanese fishermen netting the waters. However, talks are continually underway between the two sides, and it's entirely possible that rules might be relaxed, allowing casual tourists to visit this cold-war outpost. Tours cost about Y80 per person.

Hakka Roundhouses *(Yong Ding Tu Lou).* Legend has it that when these four-story-tall structures were first spotted by the American military, fear spread that they were silos for some unknown gigantic missile. They were created centuries before by the Hakka, or "Guest People," an offshoot of the Han Chinese who settled all over southeastern China. These earthen homes are made of raw earth, glutinous rice, and brown sugar, reinforced with bamboo and wood. They are the most beautiful example of Hakka architecture. The roundhouses are in Yong Ding, 210 km (130 mi) northwest of Xiamen. To get here, take a bus from Xiamen to Longyan, then transfer to a minibus headed to Yong Ding. ⊠ *Yong Ding* 🎫 *Y20.*

WHERE TO EAT

Although Xiamen is known for its excellent seafood (this is a port city, after all), the city's Buddhist population means it has excellent vegetarian cuisine. Xiamen is probably the best place outside of Taiwan to experience Taiwanese cuisine, and many restaurants advertise their *Taiwan Wei Kou* and *Taiwan Xiao Chi,* meaning "Taiwanese flavor" and "Taiwanese snacks."

¢–$
VEGETARIAN

✕**Dafang Vegetarian Restaurant.** Across from Nanputuo Temple, this reasonably priced restaurant is popular with students. But don't just come for the low prices—it also has excellent food. Try the sweet-and-sour soup or the mock duck. English menus are available. ⊠ *3 Nanhua Lu* 🕾 *0592/209–3236* 🚫 *No credit cards.*

$–$$
SEAFOOD

✕**Guan Hai Canting.** On the rooftop of the waterfront Lujiang Hotel, this terrace restaurant has beautiful views over the bay. The Cantonese chef prepares delicious seafood dishes and dim-sum specialties like sweet pork buns and shrimp dumplings. ⊠ *54 Lujiang Lu, across from ferry terminal* 🕾 *0592/266–2398* 💳 *AE, MC, V.*

¢   ✕ **Huangzehe Peanut Soup Shop.** Peanuts get the star treatment at this pop-
CHINESE   ular restaurant near the waterfront. Peanut soups, peanut sweets, and
FUSION   even peanut dumplings show off the culinary potential of the humble
   goober. ✉ *24 Zhongshan Lu* ☎ *0592/212–5825* ▤ *No credit cards.*

$–$$ ✕ **Mamma Mia.** Across from the Marco Polo Xiamen hotel, Mamma
ITALIAN   Mia serves authentic Italian specialties like risotto, gnocchi, and several
   different types of pasta. There's also a beautiful bar on the third floor
   where you can sink into plush chairs. ✉ *1 Jianye Lu* ☎ *0592/536–2662*
   ▤ *AE, MC, V.*

$–$$ ✕ **Puzhaolou Vegetarian Restaurant.** The comings and goings of monks
VEGETARIAN   add to the atmosphere at this restaurant next to the Nanputuo Temple. Popular dishes include black-fungus soup with tofu and stewed
   yams with seaweed. You won't find any English menus, so ask for
   one of the picture menus. ✉ *Nanputuo Temple, 515 Siming Nan Lu*
   ☎ *0592/208–5908* ▤ *No credit cards.*

$$–$$$ ✕ **Shuyou Seafood Restaurant.** Shuyou means "close friend," and that's
SEAFOOD   how you're treated at this upscale establishment. Considered one of the
★   best seafood restaurants in China (and certainly in Xiamen), Shuyou
   serves fresh seafood in an opulent setting. Downstairs, the tanks are
   filled with lobster, prawns, and crabs, and upstairs diners feast on seafood dishes cooked in Cantonese and Fujian styles. If you're in the
   mood for other fare, the restaurant is also known for its excellent
   Peking duck and goose liver. ✉ *Hubin Bei Lu, between Marco Polo
   and Sofitel hotels* ☎ *0592/509–8888* ▤ *AE, MC, V.*

WHERE TO STAY

$–$$ 🏨 **Lujiang Harbourview Hotel.** In a refurbished colonial building, this
   hotel has an ideal location opposite the ferry pier and the waterfront
   boulevard. A rooftop-terrace restaurant looks over the straits. Many of
   the rooms have ocean views. **Pros:** phenomenal location, good prices.
   Cons: limited English is spoken, rooms are small. ✉ *54 Lujiang Lu*
   ☎ *0592/202–2922* 🖷 *0592/202–4644* 🛏 *153 rooms, 18 suites* ⚷ *In-
   room: safe, Ethernet. In-hotel: 4 restaurants, bar* ▤ *AE, MC, V.*

$$$ 🏨 **Marco Polo Xiamen.** Standing between the historic sights and the com-
   mercial district, the Marco Polo has an excellent location. The hotel's
   glass-roof atrium makes the lobby bar a particularly nice place to
   relax after a day's sightseeing. Nightly entertainment includes a dance
   band from the Philippines. The guest rooms are comfortable and well
   appointed. **Pros:** good location, helpful staff. **Cons:** noise, poor reserva-
   tion service. ✉ *8 Jianye Lu* ☎ *0592/509–1888* ⊕ *www.marcopolohotels.
   com* 🛏 *246 rooms, 38 suites* ⚷ *In-room: safe, Ethernet. In-hotel: 3
   restaurants, bar, pool, gym, no-smoking rooms* ▤ *AE, MC, V.*

$$–$$$$ 🏨 **Millenium Harbourview Hotel Xiamen.** With an excellent location over-
★   looking the harbor, this hotel is among the best in the city. Rooms are
   spacious and comfortable, and the staff is friendly and attentive. The
   hotel's restaurants are particularly good, and the first-floor coffee shop
   is the only place in Xiamen to get a good New York–style deli sand-
   wich. Golfers will want to have a drink at the first-floor bar, which
   has a small putting green. **Pros:** excellent service, travel agents. **Cons:**
   noise, some rooms very dark. ✉ *12–8 Zhenhai Lu* ☎ *0592/202–3333*
   ⊕ *www.millenniumhotels.com/cn/millenniumxiamen/index.html*

7

CLOSE UP

Art for Art's Sake

The contemporary arts scene in Hangzhou grows by the year, with a mix of national and international artists calling Hangzhou home. For current art exhibits, grab a copy of *In Touch* (☎ 0571/8763–0035 ⊕ *www. intouchzj.com*), an English-language magazine available in many hotels and coffee shops.

Some of the country's hottest artists show their work at **Contrasts** (✉ *No. 20-2b Hubin Lu* ☎ *0571/8717–2519* ⊕ *www.contrastsgallery.com*).

At **Loft 49** (✉ *49 Hangyin Lu* ☎ *0571/8823–8782* ⊕ *www.loft49. cn*), industrial spaces have been transformed into studios for the cutting-edge artists, sculptors, and architects. This former printing factory has free galleries and a café.

Frequent exhibits of painting and sculpture are on display at **Red Star** (✉ *280 Jianguo Nan Lu* ☎ *0571/7770–3888* ⊕ *www.redstar hotel.com*).

🛏 334 *rooms, 7 suites* ☆ *In-room: safe, Ethernet. In-hotel: 4 restaurants, bar, pool, gym, no-smoking rooms* 🖃 *AE, MC, V.*

$$$–$$$$ 🏨 **Sofitel Plaza Xiamen.** The newest (and costliest) luxury hotel in Xiamen, the Sofitel Plaza has a beautiful art-deco lobby. Though not on the beach, many of the hotel's nicely appointed guest rooms have a beautiful view of nearby Lake Yuandang. The location is convenient to the city's financial district. The Oasis Bar is a popular spot with Xiamen's trendy set. The guest rooms, with dark-wood furnishings, are beautiful and modern. **Pros:** convenient location, good service, very clean. **Cons:** far from the beach. ✉ *19 Hubin Bei Lu* ☎ *0592/507–8888* ⊕ *www. sofitel.com* 🛏 *383 rooms, 48 suites* ☆ *In-room: safe, Ethernet. In-hotel: restaurant, bar, pool, gym, airport shuttle, no-smoking rooms* 🖃 *AE, MC, V.*

NIGHTLIFE & THE ARTS

Although it has nothing to rival Beijing or Shanghai, Xiamen has a few options for night owls. The stretch of Zhongshan Lu near the ferry pier is charming in the evening when the colonial-style buildings are lighted with gentle neon. This waterfront promenade is a particularly popular spot for young couples walking arm in arm. There are a few small pubs where people stop for drinks.

The dimly lit **La Bomba** (✉ *Jianye Lu.1 block north of Marco Polo Xiamen hotel* ☎ *0592/531–0707*) is popular with locals and expats alike. It has live rock bands on the weekends.

The upscale **Elite** (✉ *Jianye Lu. 1 block north of Marco Polo Xiamen hotel* ☎ *0592/533–0707*) has a dance floor and a lounge where you can check out the crowd.

SPORTS & THE OUTDOORS

Xiamen offers some excellent hiking opportunities. Most notable of these are the hills behind the Nanputuo Temple, where winding paths and stone steps carved into the sheer rock face make for a fairly strenuous climb. For a real challenge, hike from Nanputuo Temple to 10,000

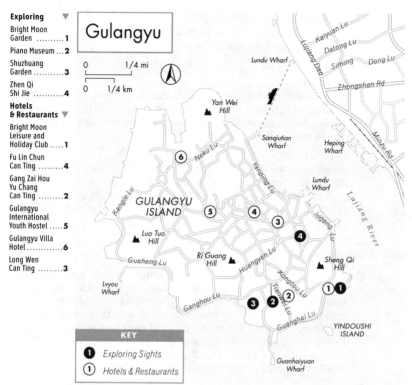

Gulangyu

KEY

❶ *Exploring Sights*

① *Hotels & Restaurants*

Rock Garden. If you're still in the mood for a climb after spending a few hours enjoying the garden's beautiful landscape, another more serpentine trail (a relic of the Japanese occupation) leads to Xiamen University. The hike takes the better part of an afternoon, and is well worth it.

The area around Xiamen is filled with fine public beaches. On nice days, sunbathers abound nearly anywhere along Huandao Lu, the road that circles the island.

GULANGYU

5 minutes by boat from Xiamen.

The best way to experience Gulangyu's charm is to explore its meandering streets, stumbling across a particularly distinctive old mansion or the weathered graves of missionaries and merchants. These quiet back alleys are fascinating to wander, with the atmosphere of a quiet Mediterranean city, punctuated by touches of calligraphy or the click of mah-jongg tiles to remind you where you really are. And unlike most Chinese communities, you won't take your life in your hands when crossing the street because cars are banned on Gulangyu. This island is easy to reach by ferry from Xiamen.

Boats to the island run from early in the morning until midnight and depart from the ferry terminal across from the Lujiang. Electric buses are available on the island.

BY BOAT
Ferry service from the Xiamen Ferry dock starts at 5:45 AM, with departures every 10–15 minutes, and costs Y8. The ferry does not run after midnight, so check the last departure time before you leave Xiamen to avoid getting stranded.

Many sights on Gulangyu charge admission fees, but a tour aboard the island's electric bus includes admission to all sites included on the tour. Island ATMs are available near major tourist sites, but it is best to do your banking before heading out. Ask your hotel concierge for tourist advice.

EXPLORING GULANGYU

❷ Gulangyu holds a special place in the country's musical history, thanks to the large number of Christian missionaries who called the island home in the late-19th and early-20th centuries. Gulangyu has more pianos per capita than any place else in China, with one home in five having one. "Chopsticks" to Chopin—and everything in between—can be heard being played by the next generation's prodigies. The **Piano Museum** *(Island of Drumming Waves)* is a must for any music lover. ✉ *45 Huangyan Lu* ☎ *0592/206–0238* 🎫 *Y30* ⏱ *Daily 8:15–5:15.*

❶ From the ferry terminal, turn left and follow oceanfront Tianwei Lu until you come to **Bright Moon Garden** *(Haoyue Yuan)*. The garden is a fitting seaside memorial to Koxinga, and a massive stone statue of the Ming general stares eastward from a perch hanging over the sea. ✉ *Tianwei Lu* ☎ *No phone* 🎫 *Y15* ⏱ *Daily 8–7.*

❸ Continuing along Tianwei Lu, you'll come to **Shuzhuang Garden** *(Shuzhuang Huayuan)*. The garden is immaculately kept and dotted with pavilions and bridges, some extending out to rocks just offshore. ✉ *Tianwei Lu* ☎ *No phone* 🎫 *Y40* ⏱ *Daily 8–7.*

❹ Skillfully mixing history and oddities, **Zhen Qi Shi Jie** is one of the country's odder museums. Part of the museum displays the usual historical information about Fujian and Taiwan. The other part is a veritable museum of oddities, offering pickled genetic mutations like two-headed snakes, conjoined twin sheep, and a few live exhibits like gigantic tortoises. The room of ancient Chinese sex toys will please some and mystify others. ✉ *38 Huangyan Lu and 4 Donghua Lu* ☎ *0592/206–9933* 🎫 *Y50* ⏱ *Daily 8–6.*

The best—and really, the only—way to see Gulangyu is on foot. Take a morning or afternoon to climb up the narrow, winding streets to see the hundreds of colonial-era mansions (ranging from restored to ram-

What's Cooking

Shaoxing secured its place in the Chinese culinary pantheon with Shaoxing wine, the best yellow-rice wine in the country. Although cooks around the world know the nutty-flavored wine as a marinade and seasoning, in Shaoxing the fermented brew of glutinous rice is put to a variety of uses, from drinking straight up (as early as breakfast) to sipping as a medicine (infused with traditional herbs and remedies). Like grape wines, Shaoxing mellows and improves with age, as its color deepens to a reddish brown. It is local custom to bury a cask when a daughter is born and serve it when she marries.

The wine is excellent accompaniment to Shaoxing snacks such as pickled greens, and the city's most popular street food *chou doufu*, which means "stinking tofu." The golden-fried squares of tender tofu taste great, if you can get past the pungent odor. Also, look for dishes made with another Shaoxing product, fermented bean curd. With a flavor not unlike an aged cheese, it's rarely eaten by itself, but complements fish and sharpens the flavor of meat dishes.

shackle) that are the heart of this fabulous treasure trove of late-19th- and early-20th-century architecture. A good guide is Vivian Wang, a native of the area.

Tour Contact Vivian Wang (☎ *0592/13959–228225*).

WHERE TO EAT

SEAFOOD
✕ **Fu Lin Chun Can Ting.** Serving home-style seafood cooked to order, this closet-size restaurant is almost always packed with locals during peak hours. If it comes from the sea, you'll find it here, with steamed crab, deep-fried shrimp, and whole fish served in a variety of tantalizing styles. ⊠ *109 Long Tou Lu* ☎ *0592/206–2847* ▤ *No credit cards.*

$ ✕ **Gang Zai Hou Yu Chang Can Ting.** The name of this restaurant means
SEAFOOD "Behind Gang Zai Beach," which gives you a clue as to the short distance seafood travels from the ocean to the plate. Gang Zai Hou serves excellent oyster soup, steamed crabs, and just about anything else that swims. ⊠ *14 Gang Hou Lu* ☎ *0592/206–3719* ▤ *No credit cards.*

✕ **Long Wen Can Ting.** Serving fresh seafood dishes, this large restaurant
SEAFOOD near the ferry terminal is popular with tourists from Taiwan. The chef unabashedly admits to being an enthusiastic consumer of his own cuisine—never a bad sign. Specialties include whole steamed fish, oyster soup, and a wide variety of seafood dishes. The decor is traditional Chinese. ⊠ *21 Long Tou Lu* ☎ *0592/206–6369* ▤ *No credit cards.*

WHERE TO STAY

$ 🏨 **Bright Moon Leisure and Holiday Club.** Located in Bright Moon Garden, this lovely little hotel consists of nine wooden houses perched on seaside cliffs. What the place lacks for in amenities it more than makes up with amazing views. **Pros:** quiet, fantastic views. **Cons:** simple amenities, limited English. ⊠ *3 Zhangzhou Lu,* ☎ *0592/206–9730* 🖷 *0592/206–3401* ⬎ *15 rooms* △ *In-hotel: beachfront, laundry service, no elevator* ▤ *AE, MC, V.*

Gulangyu International Youth Hostel. If you're strapped for cash, you'd be hard-pressed to find cheaper accommodations. In the former German Embassy, this place retains a bit of its Bavarian feel. High-ceiling rooms have beds, desks, and antique light fixtures. **Pros:** extremely inexpensive. **Cons:** simple accommodations, no air-conditioning. ✉18 Lu Jiao Lu, ☎0592/206–6066 🖷0592/206–6022 🛏6 rooms ⚉In-room: no a/c (some). In-hotel: laundry facilities, public Internet, no elevator ☰No credit cards.

Gulangyu Villa Hotel. On the west side of the island, this hotel has a peaceful feel. The rooms are clean but simple and the staff is friendly enough. There is a decent Chinese restaurant on the premises. **Pros:** quiet and clean. **Cons:** limited English, no Western food. ✉14 Gusheng Lu, ☎0592/206–0160 or 0592/206–3280 🖷0592/206–0165 🛏75 rooms ⚉In-hotel: restaurant, laundry service ☰No credit cards.

ENGLISH	PINYIN	CHINESE CHARACTERS
10,000 Rock Botanical Garden	Wànshí zhíwùyuán	万石植物园
Air Ticket Office	Mínháng shòupiào chù	民航售票处
American Express	Měiguó yùntōng	美国运通
Baidi	Báidī	白堤
Bank of China	Zhōngguó yínháng	中国银行
Bazi Qiao Bridge	Bāzì qiáo	八字桥
Bright Moon Garden	Hǎoyuè yuán	皓月园
Bright Moon Leisure and Holiday Club***	Hǎoyuè xiūxián dùjià jùlèbù	皓月休闲度假俱乐部
CAAC	Zhōngguó mínháng	中国民航
Cai Yuanpei's House	Cài yuán péi gùjūn	蔡元培故居
Catholic Church of St. Joseph	Tiānzhǔ jiàotáng	天主教堂
China International Travel Service	Zhōngguó guójì lǚxíngshè	中国国际旅行社
China National Silk Museum	Zhōngguó Sīchóu Bówùguǎn	中国丝绸博物馆
China Silk City	Zhōngguó Sīchóuchéng	中国丝绸城
China Tea Museum	Zhōngguó Cháyè Bówùguǎn	中国茶叶博物馆
China Travel Service	Zhōngguó lv3xíngshè	中国旅行社
Dafang Vegetarian	Dàfāng sù shí guǎn	大方素食馆
Dong Po Hotel	Dōngpō bīnguǎn	东坡宾馆
Dragon Hotel	Huánglóng fàndiàn	黄龙饭店
Dragon Well Tea Park	Lóngjǐngwénchá	龙井闻茶

ENGLISH	PINYIN	CHINESE CHARACTERS
Dragonair	Gǎnglóng háng kōng	港龙航空
East Lake	Dōnghú	东湖
Elite**	Míngshì xiànchǎng yīnyuè jiǔbā	名仕现场音乐酒吧
Evening Sunlight at Thunder Peak Pagoda	Léifēngxīzhào	雷锋夕照
Fu Lin Chun Restaurant	Fúlínchūn cāntīng	福林春餐厅
Fujian	Fújiàn	福建
Fulintang	Fúlíntáng	福林堂
Gang Zai Hou Yu Chang Restaurant	Gǎngzáihòu yùchǎng cāntīng	港仔后浴场餐厅
Guan Hai Restaurant	Guānhǎi cāntīng	观海餐厅
Gulangyu	Gǔlàngyǔ	鼓浪屿
Gulangyu International Youth Hostel	Gǔlàngyǔ guójì qīngnián lv3shè	鼓浪屿国际青年旅舍
Gulangyu Villa Hotel	Gǔlàng biéshù fàndiàn	鼓浪别墅饭店
Gushan Island	Gūshān Dǎo	孤山岛
Hakka Roundhouses	kè jiā tǔ lóu	客家土楼
Hangzhou	Hángzhōu	杭州
Hangzhou Aquarium	Hángzhōu Hǎidǐshìjiè	杭州海底世界
Hangzhou East Bus Station	Hángzhōu qìchē dōngzhàn	杭州汽车东站
Hangzhou International Airport	Hángzhōu Xiāoshān guójì jīchǎng	杭州萧山国际机场
Hangzhou North Bus Station	Hángzhōu qìchē běizhàn	杭州汽车北站
Hangzhou Overseas Chinese Hotel	Hángzhōu Huáqiáo fàndiàn	杭州华侨饭店
Hangzhou Red Cross Hospital	Hángzhōu Hóngshízìhuì yīyuàn	杭州红十字会医院
Hangzhou Travel and Tourism Bureau	Hángzhōu shìlǚyóu jún	杭州市旅游局
Hangzhou West Bus Station	Hángzhōu qìchē xīzhàn	杭州汽车西站
Holiday Inn Crowne Plaza Harbourview	Hǎijīnghuángguān jiàrìjiǔdiàn	海景皇冠假日酒店
Huang Shan Park	Huángshān gōngyuán	黄山公园
Huanglong Dong Yuanyuan Mingsu Yuan Theater	Huánglóngdòng Yuányuán mínsú yuán	黄龙洞圆缘民俗园
Huangzehe Peanut Soup Shop	Huángzéhé huāshēng tāngdiàn	黄则和花生汤店
Hyatt Regency Hangzhou	Hángzhōu Kǎiyuè jiǔdiàn	杭州凯悦酒店
Jinmen	Jīnmén	金门

7

ENGLISH	PINYIN	CHINESE CHARACTERS
Kana Pub	Kánà jiǔbā	卡那酒吧
La Bomba	Làbèngbā	辣蹦吧
Lingyin Si Vegetarian Restaurant	Língyǐnsì Sùzhāi	灵隐寺素斋
Liulang Wenying Park	Liǔlàngwényíng Gōngyuán	柳浪闻莺公园
Long Hai White Beach Ancient Crater	Lónghǎi báitán huǒshān kǒu	龙海白滩火山口
Long Wen Restaurant	Lóngwén cāntīng	龙文餐厅
Long-distance bus station	cángtú qìchēzhàn	长途汽车站
Louwailou Restaurant	Lóuwàilóu	楼外楼
Lu Xun Family Home	Lǚxùn gùjū	鲁迅故居
Lujiang Hotel	Lùjiāng bīnguǎn	鹭江宾馆
Marco Polo Xiamen	Mǎkěbōluó dàjiǔdiàn	马可波罗大酒店
Moon Mountain	Yùelúnshān	月轮山
Museum of Anthropology	Rénlèi bówùguǎn	人类博物馆
Nanputuo Temple	Nánpǔtuó sì	南普陀寺
night market	yè shì	夜市
Orioles Singing in the Willow Waves	Liǔlàngwényíng	柳浪闻莺
Overseas Chinese Museum	Huáqiáo bówùguǎn	华侨博物馆
Pagoda of Six Harmonies	Liùhétǎ	六和塔
Peak That Flew from Afar	Fēiláifēng	飞来峰
Piano Museum	gāngqín bówùguǎn	钢琴博物馆
Precious Stone Hill	Bǎoshíshān	宝石山
Protecting Chu Pagoda	Bǎoshūtǎ	宝俶塔
Public Security Bureau	gōng ān jú	公安局
Puzhaolou Vegetarian Restaurant	Pǔzhàolóu sù cài guǎn	普照楼素菜馆
Quanzhou	Quánzhōu	泉州
Redstar Hotel	Hángzhōu Hóngxīng wén-huà dàshà	杭州红星文化大厦
Running Tiger Dream Spring	Hǔpǎomèngquán	虎跑梦泉
Sanwei Jiulou	Sānwèi jiǔlóu	三味酒楼
Seal Engraver's Society	Xīlíngyìnshè	西泠印社
Shamrock	Ai er lan pijiǔbā	爱尔兰啤酒吧
Shangri-La Hotel Hangzhou	Hángzhōu Xiānggélǐlā fàndiàn	杭州香格里拉饭店
Shaoxing	Shāoxìng	绍兴
Shaoxing People's Hospital	Shàoxīng rénmín yīyuàn	绍兴人民医院

ENGLISH	PINYIN	CHINESE CHARACTERS
Shaoxing International Hotel	Shàoxìng guójì dàjiǔdiàn	绍兴国际大酒店
Shaoxing Xianheng Hotel	Shàoxìng Xanhēng dàjiǔdiàn	绍兴咸亨大酒店
Shuyou Seafood Restaurant	Shūyǒu hǎixiān dàjiǔlóu	舒友海鲜大酒楼
Shuzhuang Garden	Shūzhuāng huāyuán	菽庄花园
Sofitel Plaza Xiamen	Suǒfēitè dàjiǔdiàn	索菲特大酒店
Sofitel Westlake Hangzhou	Hángzhōu Suǒfēitè Xīhú Dàjiǔdiàn	杭州索菲特西湖大酒店
Sudi	Sūdī	苏堤
Temple of the Kingdom of Heaven	Tiānjiè sì	天届寺
Temple of the Soul's Retreat	Língyīnsì	灵隐寺
Three Pools Reflecting the Moon	Sāntányìnyuè	三潭印月
Tourist Complaint Hotline	lǚ yóu tóu sù rè xiàn	旅游投诉热线
Wanghu Hotel	Wànghú bīnguǎn	望湖宾馆
Wanshi Botanical Garden	Wànshí zhíwùyuán	万石植物园
West Lake	Xīhú	西湖
Xiamen Airlines	Xiàmén háng kōng	厦门航空
Xiamen Airport	Xiàmén jīchàng	厦门机场
Xiamen City	Xiàmén shì	厦门市
Xiamen Jingdezhen Porcelain****	Jīngdézhèn táocí yìshù zhōngxīn	景德镇陶瓷艺术中心
Xiamen Train Station	Xiàmén huǒchēzhàn	厦门火车站
Xiamen University	Xiàmén dàxué	厦门大学
Xianheng Winehouse	Xánhēng jiǔdiàn	咸亨酒店
Xihu Longjing Tea Company	Xīhú Lóngjǐng cháyè gōngsī	西湖龙井茶叶公司
Yellow Dragon Cave	Huánglóngdòng	黄龙洞
Yue Fei Mausoleum	Yuèfēimù	岳飞墓
Zhejiang	Zhèjiāng	浙江
Zhejiang CITS	Zhèjiāng zhōngguó guójì lǚxíngshè	浙江中国国际旅行社
Zhejiang Medical University Affiliated Hospital No. 1	Zhèjiāng yīkē dàxué dìyī fùshǔ yīyuàn	浙江医科大学第一附属医院
Zhejiang Provincial Museum	Zhéjiāngshěng Bówùguǎn	浙江省博物馆
Zhejiang Women's International Travel Service	Zhèjiāng fùnǚ guójì lǚxíngshè	浙江妇女国际旅行社
Zhen Qi Shi Jie	Zhēnqí shìjiè	珍奇世界
Zhiweiguan Restaurant	Zhīwèiguān	知味观
Zhong Shan Park	Zhōngshān gōngyuán	中山公园

7

ENGLISH	PINYIN	CHINESE CHARACTERS
Zhongshan Park	Zhōngshān Gōngyuán	中山公园
Zhongshan Road	Zhōngshān lù	中山路
Zhou Enlai Family Home	Zhōu ēnlái gùjūn	周恩来故居

UNDERSTANDING SHANGHAI

Vocabulary

CHINESE VOCABULARY

CHINESE	ENGLISH EQUIVALENT	CHINESE	ENGLISH EQUIVALENT
Consonants			
b	**b**oat	p	**p**ass
m	**m**ouse	f	**f**lag
d	**d**ock	t	**t**ongue
n	**n**est	l	**l**ife
g	**g**oat	k	**k**eep
h	**h**ouse	j	and **y**et
q	**ch**icken	x	**sh**ort
zh	ju**dge**	ch	**ch**urch
sh	**sh**eep	r*	**r**ead
z	see**ds**	c	**d**o**ts**
s	**s**eed		
Vowels			
ü	**you**	ia	**ya**rd
üe	**you** + e	ian	**yen**
a	f**a**ther	iang	**young**
ai	k**i**te	ie	**yet**
ao	**now**	o	**a**ll
e	**ea**rn	ou	**go**
ei	**day**	u	w**oo**d
er	c**ur**ve	ua	w**a**ft
i	**yi**eld	uo	w**a**ll
i (after z, c, s, zh, ch, sh)	**th**under		

WORD ORDER

The basic Chinese sentence structure is the same as in English, following the pattern of subject-verb-object:

He took my pen.	Tā ná le wǒ de bě.

s v o   s v o

NOUNS

There are no articles in Chinese, although there are many "counters," which are used when a certain number of a given noun is specified. Various attributes of a noun—such as size, shape, or use—determine which counter is used with that noun. Chinese does not distinguish between singular and plural.

a pen   yìzhī bǐ

a book   yìběn shū

VERBS

Chinese verbs are not conjugated, and they do not have tenses. Instead, a system of word order, word repetition, and the addition of a number of adverbs serves to indicate the tense of a verb, whether the verb is a suggestion or an order, or even whether the verb is part of a question. Tāzaì ná wǒ de bǐ. (He is taking my pen.) Tā ná le wǒ de bǐ. (He took my pen.) Tā you méi you ná wǒ de bǐ? (Did he take my pen?) Tā yào ná wǒ de bǐ. (He will take my pen.)

TONES

In English, intonation patterns can indicate whether a sentence is a statement (He's hungry.), a question (He's hungry?), or an exclamation (He's hungry!). In Chinese, words have a particular tone value, and these tones are important in determining the meaning of a word. Observe the meanings of the following examples, each said with one of the four tones found in standard Chinese: mā (high, steady tone): mother; má (rising tone, like a question): fiber; mǎ (dipping tone): horse; and mà (dropping tone): swear.

PHRASES

You don't need to master the entire Chinese language to spend a week in China, but taking charge of a few key phrases in the language can aid you in just getting by.

COMMON GREETINGS	
Hello/Good morning	Nǐ hǎo/Zǎoshàng hǎo
Good evening	Wǎnshàng hǎo
Good-bye	Zàijiàn
Title for a married woman or an older unmarried woman	Tàitai/Fūrén
Title for a young and unmarried woman	Xiǎojiě
Title for a man	Xiēnshēng
How are you?	Nǐ hǎo ma?
Fine, thanks. And you?	Hěn hǎo. Xièxie. Nǐ ne?
What is your name?	Nǐ jiào shénme míngzi?
My name is . . .	Wǐ jiào . . .

Travel Smart Shanghai

"We took buses and subways whenever possible, they are clean, air conditioned, reasonably priced, fast, and convenient. The stops were announced in both Chinese and accented English. On our arrival we took the Maglev from Pudong Airport into Shanghai. It was worth it for the experience, but not worth it as a means for commuting . . . Taking cash vs. trying to use credit cards seems a good way to go, however, order brand new $100 bills from your bank before you go, since they are very leery of counterfeit currency and will often not accept used bills during the exchange transaction."

—Pat_Rick

GETTING HERE & AROUND

Central Shanghai is cut in two by the Huangpu River. To the east is the city's new financial district, the glittery, modern Pudong, home of the iconic Pearl TV Tower and Jinmao Tower. To the west lies Puxi, the old city, home to most of Shanghai's tourist attractions. Pudong and Puxi are linked by three bridges, three tunnels, three subway crossings, and various ferries.

The focus of Puxi is Huangpu District. It contains the Bund, the linchpin of Shanghai's tourist scene and a good place to start your tour of the city. Nanjing Lu connects the Bund to Renmin (People's) Square; it's Shanghai's answer to 5th Avenue, and you'll find the best shopping on the western stretch in Jing'an District. Also in Puxi are traditional Nanshi, the Former French Concession (sometimes called Old French Concession), which includes once-trendy Xintiandi and is located in the Luwan and Xuhui Districts, and Jing'an, Zhabei, and other areas.

A rough grid system governs the streets of central Shanghai, but deviances abound, as many thoroughfares are paved-over rivers. As in many U.S. cities, some Shanghai's street names change slightly along their length with the addition of a compass point. Thus Beijing Xi Lu and Beijing Dong Lu are Beijing Road East and Beijing Road West, respectively.

Street numbers in Shanghai refer to buildings or to lanes intersecting at major thoroughfares. It's fairly straightforward, but be aware that these numbers tend to reset whenever the street name changes (even when the change is slight). Names do vary in designation between "building" and "lane"—with the latter having their own internal numberings. So, Number 56 and 60 could have between them Lane 58, which could contain as many as dozens of its own numbered entries. Large and mostly newer developments also often have compound building numbers within a single street address. Taxi drivers and pedestrian directions operate by intersection, as Shanghai blocks are manageably short.

Shanghai has a varied array of quality public transit. Look into getting a Shanghai Public Transportation Card, known as the **Jiaotong card.** It's a stored-value card that can be used on most forms of public transport: you just swipe it over the ticket-gate sensor to deduct your fare. You can buy a Jiaotong card in subway stations and in some convenience stores, such as Aldays. You'll pay a refundable deposit of Y30 for the card, then add as much money to it as you think you'll use. It works on the subway and the MagLev (the high-speed train to the airport), as well as in most buses, ferries, and even in taxis.

■TIP→Ask the local tourist board about hotel and local transportation packages that include tickets to major museum exhibits or other special events. But be warned that some of these are much more expensive than normal entry fees.

▌BY AIR

Shanghai is one of China's major international hubs, along with Beijing, Guangzhou, and Hong Kong. You can catch a nonstop flight there from Chicago (14½ hours), San Francisco (17 hours), Los Angeles (16 hours), Sydney (13 hours), and London (12 hours), among others. Flights from the east coast of the United States generally have a stopover in a U.S. city and take between 17 and 25 hours.

Though most airlines say that reconfirming your return flight is unnecessary, some local airlines cancel your seat if you don't reconfirm. Play it safe, and check with your airline.

If you are flying into Asia on a SkyTeam airline (Delta or Continental, for example), you're eligible to purchase its Asia Pass. It includes more than 10 Chinese cities (including Shanghai, Beijing, Xian, and Hong Kong) as well as destinations in 20 other Asian and Australasian countries. The pass works on a coupon basis; the minimum (three coupons) costs $750, whereas six come to $1,410.

China Southern Airlines' China Air Pass is an excellent value if you're planning to fly to several destinations within the country: the minimum three-coupon pass comes to $329, whereas 10 cost $909. The catch? You have to be flying in from abroad on one of its flights. Hong Kong isn't included in the pass, but Shenzhen, just over the border, gets you close enough. Bear in mind that Chinese domestic-flight schedules can be very flexible—flights may be changed or canceled at a moment's notice.

Airlines & Airports **Airline and Airport Links.com** (⊕www.airlineandairportlinks.com) has links to many of the world's airlines and airports.

Airline-Security Issues **Transportation Security Administration** (⊕www.tsa.gov) has answers for almost every question that might come up.

Air-Pass Info **Asia Pass** (SkyTeam ☎800/523–3273 Continental, 800/221–1212 Delta ⊕www.skyteam.com).

China Air Pass (China Southern Airlines ☎888/338–8988 ⊕www.cs-air.com).

AIRPORTS

Shanghai has two major airports: most international flights go through the newer Pudong International Airport (PVG), which is 45 km (30 mi) east of the city, whereas many domestic routes operate out of the older Hongqiao International Airport (SHA), 15 km (9 mi) west of the city center.

Airline security is impressively efficient in Shanghai, even at high-risk times. Carry-on prohibitions vary month-to-month, so check with your airline, hotel, or travel agent in advance. And while customs, immigration, and security are usually quite speedy, they can congest at peak travel times, and then some airlines require particularly early check-ins. Clearing customs and immigration usually only takes a few minutes, but in peak seasons and times there can be a backlog, so be sure to arrive at least two hours before your scheduled flight time. Check in advance with your airline about check-in cut-offs as each company has a different policy. The lettered row of your airline's check-in counter is displayed on screens by each door and around the main hall at the Pudong Airport; look for numbered rows at Hongqiao. Pudong's second terminal has now opened, so check in advance which one your flight leaves from. Hongqiao looks worn and tattered in comparison to Pudong, but fewer passengers and a more practical design make both departure and arrival processes smoother and quicker. Indeed, many business travelers prefer to fly via the quieter, more centrally located Hongqiao.

At both airports, both Chinese and Western-style fast-food outlets abound—Starbucks and KFC are two names you'll recognize—but quality is generally poor. Most are open from around 7 AM to 11 PM. Be warned that prices for even a soft drink vary wildly from place to place. The best options are vending machines in Terminal One and the offerings in gift stores in both terminals; they cost a fraction of the dedicated concessions. Take ample distractions in case of delays: the shopping in both airports is slowly improving, but even airline business-class lounges have limited Internet access and little entertainment.

While wandering either airport, someone may approach you offering to carry your luggage, or even just give you directions. This "helpful" stranger will almost certainly expect payment. Many of the

X-ray machines used for large luggage items aren't film-safe, so keep film in your carry-on luggage.

Airport Information **Hongqiao International Airport** (☎021/6268–8918 ⊕www.shanghaiairport.com). **Pudong International Airport** (☎021/9608–1388 ⊕www.shanghaiairport.com).

GROUND TRANSPORTATION

Taking a taxi is the most comfortable way into town from Pudong International Airport. Expect to pay around Y120 to Y160 for the hour-long or so trip to Puxi; getting to the closer Pudong area takes 40 minutes and should cost no more than Y100. Note that at rush hour, journey times can easily double. There is also a network of comfortable, clean buses servicing all parts of the city from the Pudong Airport, with departures between 7 AM and 11 PM. Attendants do not speak English, but there is an information desk where directions in English are usually provided.

From Hongqiao, a taxi to Puxi starts at Y30 and takes 30 to 40 minutes; expect an hour for the costlier trip to Pudong hotels. A taxi from one airport to the other takes about an hour and costs Y200 to Y240.

When you arrive, head for the clearly labeled taxi stand just outside each terminal. The (usually long) line moves quickly—unless you're at Hongqiao after a holiday, when it will take longer than your flight. Ignore offers from drivers trying to coax you away from the official taxi line; they're privateers looking to rip you off. Insist that drivers use their meters, and do not negotiate a fare. It's illegal for drivers to refuse to use the meter and to refuse a customer for reasons like the distance to the destination (which many do between Pudong and Puxi). If the driver is unwilling to comply, feel free to change taxis. Threatening to report them to the police, taking down their ID number, and/or taking their picture can help sub-

due illegal behavior from taxi drivers, but extreme belligerence can lead to altercations. As long as you're in a public place where other cars are available, it's better to just change to another one.

Many hotels offer free airport transfers to their guests. Ask when you book. Otherwise, shuttle buses link Pudong Airport with a number of hotels (routes starting with a letter) and transport hubs (routes starting with a number) in the city center. Timetables vary, but most services run every 10 to 20 minutes between roughly 7 AM and the last flight arrival (usually around midnight). Trips to Puxi take about 1½ hours and cost between Y19 and Y30. From Hongqiao, Bus 925 runs to People's Square, but there's little room for luggage. It costs Y4.

Contacts **Dazhong Taxi Company** (☎021/96822). **Jinjiang Taxi** (☎021/96961). **Pudong Airport Shuttle Buses** (☎021/6834–6612). **Qiangsheng Taxi** (☎021/6258–0000).

Taxi Complaints (☎021/962000).

TO AND FROM PUDONG AIRPORT		
MODE OF TRANSPORT	DURATION	PRICE TO PUXI/ PUDONG AREAS
Taxi	60 min/ 40 min	Y160/Y120
Bus	90 min/ 60 min	Y8–Y30/ Y6–Y12

FLIGHTS

Air China is China's flagship carrier. It operates nonstop flights from Shanghai to various North American and European cities. Although it once had a slightly sketchy safety record, the situation has improved dramatically, and it is now part of Star Alliance. So is the excellent Shanghai Airlines, which is expanding international offerings. Shanghai Airlines and China Eastern are the major carriers for domestic routes and connect Shanghai to cities all over the country. China

Southern, Hainan, and Xiamen Airlines also ply many domestic routes.

The service on most Chinese airlines is on par with, if not better than, most American carriers: be prepared for limited legroom, iffy food, and possibly no personal TV. More importantly, always arrive at least two hours before departure, as chronic overbooking means latecomers sometimes don't get on. Technically travelers in economy class are only allowed one carry-on, but this rule is almost never enforced.

You can make reservations and buy tickets in the United States directly through airline Web sites or with travel agencies. It's worth contacting a Chinese travel agency like China International Travel Service (CITS) *(⇨ Visitor Information, below)* to compare prices, as these can vary substantially. The best option, though, is to visit the English sites of C-trip and eLong, which have searchable flight schedules and rates and convenient bookings using cash or credit card.

Airline Contacts Air Canada (☎021/6279–2999 ⊕www.aircanada. com). **Air China** (☎021/5239–7227, 021/6269–2999, or 800/820–1999 ⊕www. fly-airchina.com). **Asiana** (☎021/6219–4000 ⊕www.us.flyasiana.com). **British Airways** (☎800/810–8012 ⊕www.ba.com). **China Eastern** (☎021/6268–8899 or 021/8621–95808 ⊕www.ce-air.com). **China Southern Airlines** (☎021/6226–2299 ⊕www.cs-air.com/en). **Hainan Airlines** (☎800/876–8999 ⊕www.hnair.com). **Japan Airlines** (☎021/6288–3000 ⊕www.jal. com). **Northwest Airlines** (☎800/225–2525, 021/6884–6884 in Shanghai ⊕www.nwa. com). **Shanghai Airlines** (☎021/6255–8888 ⊕www.shanghai-air.com). **Singapore Airlines** (☎021/6289–1000 ⊕www.singaporeair. com). **Thai Airways** (☎021/5298–5555 ⊕www.thaiair.com). **United Airlines** (☎800/864–8331 for U.S. reservations, 800/538–2929 for international reservations, 021/3311–4567 in Shanghai ⊕www. united.com). **Virgin Atlantic Airways** (☎021/5353–4600 or 021/5353–4601

⊕www.virgin-atlantic.com). **Xiamen Airways** (☎0592/573–9009 ⊕www.xiamenair.com.cn).

Web Sites C-Trip (⊕english.ctrip.com).**eLong** (⊕www.elong.net).

∎ BY BIKE

Cycling is still the primary form of transportation for many Shanghai residents, despite the government's best efforts to discourage it by banning bikes on main roads. Shanghai's frenzied traffic is not for the faint of heart, though fortunately most secondary streets have wide, well-defined bike lanes. The pancake-flat city landscape means that gears just aren't necessary—take your cue from locals and roll along at a leisurely pace. For relaxed riding, head to the beautiful lanes of the Old French Concession. Pudong roads have far less traffic but also less scenery. If a flat tire or sudden brake failure strikes, seek out the nearest street-side mechanic; they're easily identified by their bike parts and pumps.

Few hotels rent bikes (hostels are usually the exception), but you can inquire at bike shops or even corner stores, where the going rate is around Y30 a day, plus a refundable deposit, which is often high enough to cover the cost of the bike itself. Check the seat and wheels carefully prior to accepting the rental, or else you'll be stopping to fix flats all day.

Bicycle lights are nonexistent, so cycle with caution at night. Most rental bikes come with a lock or two, but they're usually pretty low quality. Instead, leave your wheels at an attended bike park—peace of mind costs a mere Y0.50. Helmets are just about unheard of in Shanghai, though upmarket rental companies like Bodhi Bikes rent them. It charges Y150 or more for its bikes, but its mountain bikes are in great condition. It also organizes mountain-biking tours.

If you're planning a lot of cycling, note that for about Y200 you can buy your own basic bike; expect to pay three or four times that for a mountain bike with all the bells and whistles. Supermarkets like Carrefour or the sports shop Decathlon are good places to buy them.

Bike China Adventures has a 17-day bike trip that includes Shanghai, along with other destinations in China.

Bike Rentals Bohdi Bikes (☎021/5266–9013 or 139/1875–3119 ⊕www.bohdi.com.cn).

Bike Tours Bike China Adventures (☎800/818–1778 ⊕www.bikechina.com).

Shops With Bikes Carrefour (✉2671 Gaoqing Lu, Pudong ☎021/5065–7391 ⊕www. carrefour.com.cn). **Decathlon** (✉393 Yinxiao Lu, Pudong ☎021/5045–3888 ⊕www. decathlon.com.cn).

▌ BY BOAT OR FERRY

WITHIN SHANGHAI

More than 20 ferry lines cross the Huangpu River between Pudong and Puxi. The most convenient ferry for tourists runs daily between the Bund in Puxi and Pudong's terminal just south of the Riverside Promenade. There are no seats, merely an empty lower deck that welcomes the masses with their bikes and scooters. The per-person fare is Y0.50 each way. The ferries leave the dock every 10 minutes, 24 hours a day. Upscale ferries with air-conditioning and seats run from some piers and cost Y2–Y10.

TO & FROM SHANGHAI

Boats leave from Shanghai's Wusong Passenger Terminal for destinations along the Yangzi River such as Wuhan and Chongqing; coastal cities such as Nantong, Dalian, and Ningbo; and the outlying island of Putuoshan. First-class cabins have comfortable beds and their own washbasin.

The Shanghai Ferry Company and the China-Japan International Ferry Company both operate services to Osaka, Japan, from the International Passenger Terminal at Waihongqiao. Boats leave at midday on Tuesday and Saturday, respectively; the trip takes around two days. There are restaurants, a game room, and even karaoke on board.

You can purchase tickets for both international and domestic services (in Chinese) at each terminal, or through China International Travel Service (CITS) for a small surcharge.

Information China International Travel Service (CITS ☎021/6289–8899 ⊕www. cits.com.cn). **China-Japan International Ferry Company** (✉908 Dongdaming Lu, Hongkou ☎021/6595–7988). **Pudong–Puxi ferry** (✉Puxi dock, the Bund at Jinling Lu, Huangpu ✉Pudong dock, 1 Dongchang Lu, south of Binjiang Da Dao, Pudong). **Shanghai Ferry Company** (☎021/6537–5111 or 021/5393–1185 ⊕www.shanghai-ferry.co.jp).

▌ BY BUS

TO SHANGHAI

China has some fabulous, luxury, long-distance buses with air-conditioning and movies. Many intercity services depart more regularly than trains. However, buying tickets for them can be complicated if you don't speak Chinese—you may end up on one of the cramped, old-style, school-bus-type affairs. Drivers don't usually speak English, either. Taking a train or an internal flight is often much easier.

Most of Shanghai's long-distance services leave from the Shanghai Long Distance bus station, across the square from the Shanghai Railway Station in Zhabei. You buy tickets in the massive circular ticket lobby; allow time for the walk to the departure gate. It is usually better to book days or weeks in advance, as seats and berths can fill up, and standing room is an adventure better skipped.

Bus Information Shanghai Long Distance Bus Station (✉North Square, Shanghai

Railway Station, 1662 Zhongxing Lu, Zhabei ☎021/6605–0000).

WITHIN SHANGHAI

Shanghai claims to have more bus lines than any other city on earth—around 1,000—though so much choice probably hinders rather than helps. In fact, unless you know Shanghai well, public buses aren't the best choice for getting around. Although there are more and more air-conditioned services, most buses are hot and crowded in summer and cold and crowded in winter. Just getting on and off can be, quite literally, a fight. Pick-pocketing happens so watch your belongings very carefully. Fares on regular services cost Y1; air-conditioned routes cost Y2 (non–air-conditioned routes are nearly extinct now); longer routes can cost up to Y4. To buy a ticket you drop the right change into the box next to the driver as you get on, or swipe your Jiatong card *(see above)*. If you do decide to take city buses, Micah Sittig's encyclopedic Web site has English translations of all of Shanghai's routes.

There are some easy-to-take buses. Bus route 911 runs down Huaihai Lu through the Old French Concession, with great views over the compound walls of the beautiful old Shanghai buildings that line the thoroughfare and to the Shanghai Zoo and beyond. Route 936 runs between Pudong and Puxi, passing the Shanghai Zoo, and number 20 passes by the Bund, Jing'an Temple, Nanjing Road, and Renmin Square.

Local Bus Information **Micah Sittig's Shanghai Bus Route Translations** (⊕msittig. wubi.org/bus/talk/). **Passenger Hotline** (Chinese only ☎021/1608–8160).

▌BY CAR

Highways connect Shanghai to neighboring cities such as Suzhou and Nanjing in the west, and Hangzhou in the south. However, driving yourself is not a possibility when vacationing in Shanghai, as the only valid driver's licenses are Chinese ones. Neither U.S. licenses nor IDPs are recognized in China. However, this restriction should be cause for relief, as the city traffic is terrible, its drivers manic, and getting lost practically inevitable for first-timers.

Car travel in China, even when you're in the passenger seat, can be frightening. Cars speed to pass one another on one-lane roads, constantly blaring their horns. Taxis and pedicabs pass within inches of each other at intersections. Lanes and traffic rules seem ambiguous to those not accustomed to the Chinese style of driving.

If you want to get around by car, put yourself in the experienced hands of a local driver and sit back and watch them negotiate the traffic jams. All the same, consider your itinerary carefully before doing so—the subway is far quicker for central areas. Save car travel for excursions farther afield.

The quickest way to hire a car and driver is to flag down a taxi and hire it for the day—if you're happy with a driver you've used for a trip around town, ask him. After some negotiating, expect to pay between Y350 and Y600, depending on the type of car. Most hotels can make arrangements for you, though they often charge you double their rate—no prizes for guessing whose pocket the difference goes into. As most drivers do not speak English, it's a good idea to have your destination and hotel names written down in Chinese.

Taxi driver identification numbers can be used to report bad behavior or bad driving, and thus tend to inspire more care. Many taxi drivers are also held liable for the condition of their vehicles, so they are less likely to take dangerous risks.

Another alternative is American car-rental agency Avis, which includes mandatory chauffeurs as part of all rental packages. A car and driver usually cost

Y740 to Y850 ($93 to $110) per day for an economy vehicle. Collision insurance (CDW) is compulsory and included automatically in the rental rate.

If your heart is set on driving, it is possible for foreigners to get a Chinese license, but you need to have a temporary residence permit. Then it takes a week or two and a whole load of paper-pushing.

Major Agencies Avis (☎800/331–1084 ⊕www.avis.com).

▌ BY SUBWAY

Shanghai's quick and efficient subway system—called the Shanghai Metro—is an excellent way to get around town, and the network is growing exponentially.

Line 1 runs north–south, crossing the Former French Concession, with a stop at the Shanghai Railway Station. It intersects with Line 2 at People's Square, a labyrinth of a station with two levels, 20 exits, and *lots* of people. Line 2, which will eventually link Hongqiao International Airport with Pudong International Airport, is an east–west line that runs under Nanjing Lu along part of its length, and crosses to Pudong close to the Bund. You can transfer from it to the MagLev at Longyang Station in Pudong. Line 3 (formerly known as the Pearl Line) starts in north Shanghai and loops around the west of the city center; useful stops include Shanghai South Railway Station. Line 4 is a circle line that goes around Puxi and through Pudong, crossing the Huangpu River at two places. Line 5 is a commuter spur line connecting southwest Shanghai to Line 1.

Subway stations are marked by signs with a jagged red "M" for Metro. Signs are not always obvious, so be prepared to hunt around for entrances or ask directions.

Stations are usually sparklingly clean and safe, as are trains. Navigating the subway is very straightforward: station names are clearly displayed in Chinese and Pinyin.

There are maps in each station, although not all exit signs list their corresponding streets. Once on board, each stop is clearly announced in Chinese and English. Trains get very crowded at rush hour, when pick-pocketing can be a problem.

Fares depend on how far you travel: most trips within the city center cost Y3 to Y5, with the maximum fare at Y8. Ticket machines have instructions in English; press the button for the fare you want then insert your coins. Alternatively, go to the ticket booth where sellers sometimes speak some English. Keep your ticket handy; you'll need to insert it into a second turnstile as you exit at your destination. If you're going to do more than one or two trips on the subway (or on any other form of transportation), get yourself a rechargeable Jiaotong card. It saves you time waiting on line for tickets.

Trains run regularly, with three to six minutes between trains on average. Generally speaking, you can change lines without having to buy a new ticket; changes marked TRANSFER are the exception. The best online guide to the Shanghai Metro is at the *Shanghai Daily* "Live in Shanghai" site, but it is not always entirely up-to-date.

▌TIP→ **For a sci-fi experience, take a ride on the MagLev (magnetic levitation) train, which speeds between Pudong Airport and Longyan Lu subway station in eight minutes at 430 kph (267 mph). Note that you'll end in a remote area and many taxi drivers there are scam artists. It's a great experience but inconvenient for those en route to their hotels from the airport.**

Information MagLev Train (☎021/2890–7777 ⊕www.smtdc.com). **Shanghai Metro Passenger Information** (☎021/6318–9000 ⊕www.shmetro.com).

TAXI TRAVEL

■ Hailing a cab on the street is usually the best (and safest) way to go. Theoretically, taxis can't stop within 100 feet of an intersection, but that never seems to deter anyone.

■ *Never* accept offers of rides from cabbies touting their services outside tourist sights: you're walking into a rip-off. Taxis arranged by your hotel doorman may also have some hidden surcharges. When in doubt, walk out and hail one.

■ Unless you're looking to book a cab all day, the metered rate is always better than negotiating a fixed fare.

■ Avoid taxis during rush hour (7:30 AM–9:30 AM and 4 PM–7 PM). Even if you can find one, traffic will drive up your fare exponentially; walk or take the subway instead.

■ Be meter-conscious: check that the cabbie starts the meter *after* you get in, that it's not in an unusual place (near the floor, for example) and that there's nothing obstructing your view of it.

▌ BY TAXI

Taxis are plentiful, easy to spot, and by far the most comfortable way to get around Shanghai, though increasing traffic means they're not always the fastest. Almost all are Volkswagen Santanas or Passats, and they come in a rainbow of colors, which reflect the company they work for. These include teal (Dazhong; most locals' first choice), green (Bashi), yellow (Qiangsheng), red (Premium cab), dark blue (Blue Union), and white (Jinjiang). All are metered.

There's a base fee of Y11 for the first 3 km (2 mi), then Y2 per km for the next 7 km (4 mi), then Y3 per kilometer thereafter. After 11 PM the base fee goes up to Y14, and there's a 20% surcharge per kilometer. You also pay for waiting time

in traffic. Tipping is unheard of—indeed most taxi drivers return even the smallest change. In compact central Shanghai, outrageous traffic drags out otherwise short cab rides.

Drivers usually know the terrain well, but as most don't speak English, having your destination written in Chinese is a good idea. (Keep a card with the name of your hotel on it handy for the return trip.) Hotel doormen can also help you tell the driver where you're going. It's a good idea to study a map and have some idea where you are, as some drivers will take you for a long ride if they think they can get away with it.

Taxi Companies **Centralized Taxi Reservations** (Chinese only ☎021/96965). **Dazhong Taxi Company** (☎021/96222). **Jinjiang Taxi** (Chinese only ☎021/96961). **Qiangsheng Taxi** (Chinese only ☎021/6258–0000). **Shanghai Taxi Authority** (☎021/6323–2150).

▌ BY TRAIN

China's enormous rail network is one of the world's busiest. Trains are usually safe and run strictly to schedule. Buying tickets can be complicated but trips are generally hassle-free.

Shanghai is connected to many destinations in China by direct train. Regional travel is mostly out of the gleaming new Shanghai South Railway Station. Billed as the world's biggest circular station, it looks more like an airport inside than a train station. It opened in mid-2006 with limited services, but more routes will eventually transfer here. The huge ticketing hall is on the ground floor; the upstairs waiting room can accommodate over 16,000 people. Trains to northern and western China and international destinations like Hong Kong leave from the older Shanghai Railway Station. Both stations have easy transfers to the subway. The best train to catch to Beijing is one of the overnight expresses that leave between 5 and 8 PM and arrive in Beijing early the next morning. The express train for Hong Kong departs around noon and arrives at the Kowloon station 18 hours later.

The train system has four classes, but instead of first class and second class, in China you talk about hard and soft. Hard seats (*yingzuo*) are often rigid benchlike seats guaranteed to numb tushes within seconds; soft seats (*ruanzuo*) are more like the seats in long-distance American trains. Travelers can hard- or soft-seat it even for trips of several days, but the more comfortable budget option is the hard sleeper (*yingwo*), with open bays of six bunks, in two tiers of three. They're cramped, but not uncomfortable; however, you have little privacy and unpleasant toilets. Soft sleepers (*ruanwo*) are more comfortable: their closed compartments have four beds. Power outlets are sometimes included, and the toilets, while also shared with the rest of the car, are fairly tolerable. Trains to Hong Kong, and some to Beijing and Xian, have a deluxe class, with only two berths per compartment and private bathrooms. The nonstop Z-series trains have the same amenities but are generally newer and nicer. Train types are identifiable by the letter preceding the route number: Z is for nonstop, T is for a normal express.

You can now buy most tickets 30 to 60 days in advance; unfortunately, this means scalpers and agencies often snap them all up, so book as early as you can. During the time of the three national holidays—Chinese New Year (two days in mid-January to February), Labor Day (May 1), and National Day (October 1)—tickets sell out weeks in advance. If you must travel then plan early.

The cheapest rates are at the train station itself, where they only accept cash. The rail system runs dozens of ticketing offices around town that have surcharges of only a few kuai; your hotel might recommend one, but most will prefer to direct business to their (more expensive) in-house agencies. Most travel agents, including China International Travel Service (CITS), can book you tickets for a larger surcharge (Y20 to Y50), and save you the hassle of going to the station. You can also buy tickets through online retailers like China Train Ticket. It delivers the tickets to your hotel but you often end up paying much more than the station rate.

Overpriced dining cars serve meals that are often inedible, so you'd do better to make use of the massive thermoses of boiled water in each compartment and take along your own noodles or instant soup, like locals do. Trains are always crowded, but you are guaranteed your designated seat, though not always the overhead luggage rack. Note that theft on trains is increasing; on overnight trains, sleep with your valuables or else keep them on the inside of the bunk.

You can find out just about everything about Chinese train travel at Seat 61's fabulous Web site. China Highlights has a searchable online timetable for major train routes. The tour operator Travel China Guide has an English-language Web site that can help you figure out train schedules and fares.

Note that the operators at train station information numbers don't usually speak English.

Information **China Highlights** (⊕www. chinahighlights.com/china-trains/index.htm). **Seat 61** (⊕www.seat61.com/China.htm). **Shanghai Railway Station** (✉303 Moling Lu, Zhabei ☎021/6317–9090). **Shanghai South Railway Station** (✉Between Liuzhou Lu and Humin Lu, Xuhui ☎021/5435–3535). **Travel China Guide** (⊕www.travelchinaguide.com/ china-trains/index.htm).

ESSENTIALS

▌ BUSINESS SERVICES & FACILITIES

Your hotel (or another nearby mid- to top-end one) is the best place to start looking for business services, including translation. Most are very up-to-speed on businesspeople's needs and can put you in touch with other companies if necessary. Regus and the Executive Centre are international business-services companies with several office locations in Shanghai. They provide secretarial services, meeting and conference facilities, and office rentals. Talking China is a reputable translation and interpretation service.

Contacts The Executive Centre (☎021/5252–4618 ⊕www.executive-centre.com). **Regus** (☎800/819–0091 or 021/6122–1005 ⊕www.regus.cn). **Talking China** (☎021/6279–3688 or 021/6247–4708 ⊕www.talkingchina.com).

▌ COMMUNICATIONS

PHONES

The country code for China is 86; the city code for Shanghai is 21, and 10 for Beijing. To call Shanghai from the United States or Canada, dial the international-access code (011), followed by the country code (86), the city code (21), and the eight-digit phone number.

Numbers beginning with 800 within China are toll-free. Note that a call from China to a toll-free number in the United States or Hong Kong is a full-tariff international call.

CALLING WITHIN CHINA

The Chinese phone system is cheap and efficient. You can make local and long-distance calls from your hotel or any public phone on the street. Shanghai's public phones are usually bright red cabins. Some accept coins, but it's easier to buy an IC (integrated circuit) calling card, available at convenience stores and news-stands (⇨ Calling Cards, below). Local calls are generally free from landlines, though your hotel might charge a nominal rate. Long-distance rates in China are very low. For once, calling from your hotel room is a viable option, as hotels can only add a 15% service charge.

Shanghai's city code is 021, and Shanghai phone numbers have eight digits—you only need to dial these when calling within the city. In general, city codes appear written with a 0 in front of them, and are required when calling another city within China.

For directory assistance, dial 114. If you want information for other cities, dial the city code followed by 114 (note that this is considered a long-distance call). For example, if you're in Shanghai and need directory assistance for a Beijing number, dial 020–114. The operators do not speak English, so if you don't speak Chinese you're best off asking your hotel for help.

To make long-distance calls from a public phone you need an IC card (⇨ Calling Cards, below). To place a long-distance call, dial 0, the city code, and the eight-digit phone number.

Contact Local directory assistance (☎114). **Time** (☎117). **Weather** (☎121).

CALLING OUTSIDE CHINA

To make an international call from within China, dial 00 (the international access code within China) and then the country code, area or city code, and phone number.

The country code for the United States is 1.

IDD (international direct dialing) service is available at all hotels, post offices, major shopping centers, and airports. By international standards prices aren't unreasonable, but it's vastly cheaper to use a long-distance calling card, known as an IP (Internet protocol) card *(See Calling Cards, below)*. These cards' rates also beat AT&T, MCI, and Sprint hands-down. If you do need to use these services, dial 108 (the local operator) and the local access codes from China: 11 for AT&T, 12 for MCI, and 13 for Sprint. Dialing instructions in English will follow.

Access Codes AT&T Direct (☎800/874–4000, 108–11 from China). **MCI WorldPhone** (☎800/444–4444, 108–12 from China). **Sprint International Access** (☎800/793–1153, 108–13 from China).

CALLING CARDS

Calling cards are a key part of the Chinese phone system. There are two kinds: the IC card (integrated circuit; *àicei ka*) for local and domestic long-distance calls on pay phones; and the IP card (Internet protocol; *aipi ka*) for international calls from any phone. You can buy both at post offices, convenience stores, and from street vendors.

IC cards come in denominations of Y20, Y50, and Y100, and can be used in any pay phone with a card slot—most Shanghai pay phones have them. Local calls using them cost around Y0.30 a minute, and less on weekends and after 6 PM.

To use IP cards, you first dial a local access number. This is often free from hotels, while at public phones you need an IC card to do so. You then enter a card number and PIN, and finally the phone number, complete with international dial codes. When calling from a pay phone, both cards' minutes are deducted at the same time, one for local access (IC card) and one for the long-distance call you placed (IP card). There are countless different card brands; China Unicom is one that's usually reliable. IP cards come with face values of Y20, Y30, Y50, and Y100. However, the going rate for them is up to half that, so bargain vendors down.

Y50 gets you around 20 minutes' talking time.

CELL PHONES

If you have a multiband phone (some countries use different frequencies from those used in the United States) and your service provider uses the world-standard GSM network (as do T-Mobile, Cingular, and Verizon), you can probably use your phone abroad. Roaming fees can be steep, however: 99¢ a minute is considered reasonable. And overseas you normally pay the toll charges for incoming calls. It's almost always cheaper to send a text message than to make a call, since text messages have a very low set fee (often less than 5¢).

If you just want to make local calls, consider buying a new SIM card (note that your provider may have to unlock your phone for you to use a different SIM card) and a prepaid service plan in the destination. You'll then have a local number and can make local calls at local rates. If your trip is extensive, you could also simply buy a new cell phone in your destination, as the initial cost will be offset over time.

■TIP➜**If you travel internationally frequently, save one of your old cell phones or buy a cheap one on the Internet; ask your cell-phone company to unlock it for you, and take it with you as a travel phone, buying a new SIM card with pay-as-you-go service in each destination. You can also simply buy a basic phone in China for US$50–$100.**

If you have a tri-band GSM or a CDMA phone, pick up a local SIM card (*sim ka*) from any branch of China Mobile or China Unicom, such as the ones in the arrivals hall at Pudong Airport. You'll be presented with a list of possible phone numbers, with varying prices—an "unlucky" phone number (one with lots of 4s) could be as cheap as Y50, whereas an auspicious one (full of 8s) could fetch Y300 or more. You then buy prepaid cards to charge minutes onto your

LOCAL DO'S & TABOOS

CUSTOMS OF THE COUNTRY

"Face" is the all-important issue in China. A cross between pride and social status, it's all about appearances yet its cultural roots run deep. Shame someone publicly, and you may lose his friendship for life; make him look good, and you'll go far. What makes people lose and gain face is complicated, but respect is the key issue. Don't lose your cool if things go wrong, especially when reserving tickets and hotel rooms. Instead, be stern but friendly—raising your voice and threatening will get you nowhere. Keep facial expressions and hand gestures to a minimum; when pointing, use your whole hand, not a finger.

Locals often seem less than forthcoming when giving information. Be patient, they're not trying to mislead you, but rather keep you happy by telling you what they think you want to hear. Keep asking questions until you find out what you want.

Shanghai is a very cosmopolitan city by Chinese standards, and its residents are used to seeing foreigners. However, you will still be stared at, especially if you're not white. Get used to the cry of laowai (a slightly uncomplimentary word for "foreigner") everywhere you go, too. Simply smile back or ignore it.

GREETINGS

Chinese people aren't very touchy-feely with strangers. Save bear-hugs and cheek-kissing for your friends, and stick to handshakes and low-key greetings when you are first meeting local people. Avoid eye contact with strangers. Always use a person's title and surname until they invite you to do otherwise.

SIGHTSEEING

Shanghai is a crowded city; pushing, nudging, and line-jumping are commonplace. It may be hard to accept, but it's not considered that rude, so avoid overreacting (even verbally) if you're accidentally jostled. More aggressive shoving, though, except on the subway, is considered an uncouth necessity. Follow the crowds, but don't let them trample you. Street and traffic signs are mostly considered optional suggestions.

OUT ON THE TOWN

It's a compliment to be invited to someone's house, so apologize at length if you can't go. Arrive punctually with a small gift for the hosts, preferably a bottle of liquor, dessert, or fruit; there will usually be a place to remove shoes just inside the door. Eating lots is the biggest compliment you can pay the food (and the cook).

Tea, served in all Chinese restaurants, is the common drink at mealtimes. It's quite normal to order other drinks, though, especially alcohol, soda, and bottled water.

Smoking is one of China's greatest vices. No-smoking sections in restaurants are nearly nonexistent, and people light up anywhere they think they can get away with it—including on public transport, at times.

Once taboo, romantic PDAs are increasingly common in China, and any park at dusk will be crammed with adolescents getting to, or going past, second base. Nonetheless, standards are about on par with the United States or Europe, so keep the hot-and-heavy at home. Same-sex physical affection between friends and family, women especially, is normal, so don't mistake an affectionate hand-holding as a pass.

DOING BUSINESS

Time is of the essence when doing business in Shanghai. Make appointments well in advance and be extremely punctual, as this shows respect. Chinese people have a keen sense of hierarchy in the office: if you're visiting in a group, the senior member should lead proceedings.

Suits are still the norm in China, regardless of the outside temperature, although trendy casual is catching on in most professions in Shanghai. Most businesswomen in Shanghai try to replicate the latest China Vogue spreads, regardless of work suitability, but

LOCAL DO'S & TABOOS

international sensibilities hold sway in most foreign companies' offices. Women hold their own in Shanghai business but may be judged by their looks.

Face is ever-important. Never say anything that will make people look bad, especially in front of superiors. Avoid being pushy or overly familiar when negotiating: address people as Mr. or Ms. until they invite you to do otherwise, respect silences in conversation, and don't hurry things or interrupt. When entertaining, local businesspeople may insist on paying: after a slight protest, accept, as this lets them gain face.

Business cards are a big deal: not having one is like not having a personality. If possible, have yours printed in English on one side and Chinese on the other (your hotel can usually arrange this in a matter of hours). Proffer your card with both hands and receive the other person's in the same way, then read it carefully and make an admiring comment about the person's job title or the card design.

Many gifts, like clocks and cutting implements, are considered unlucky in China. Food—especially presented in a showy basket—is always a good gift choice, as are imported spirits. Avoid giving four of anything, as the number is associated with death. Offer gifts with both hands, and don't expect people to open them in your presence.

LANGUAGE

One of the best ways to avoid being an "ugly" American is to learn a little of the local language. You need not strive for fluency; even just mastering a few basic words and terms is bound to make chatting with the locals more rewarding.

Everyone under 40 in Shanghai speaks Putonghua (pu[b]tōnghuà, the "common language") as the standardized national language of China is known. It's written using ideograms, or characters. In 1949 the

government also introduced a phonetic writing system that uses the Roman alphabet. Known as Pinyin, it's widely used to label public buildings and station names, so even if you don't speak or read Chinese, you can easily compare Pinyin names with a map.

Many Shanghai residents also speak the local Chinese dialect, Shanghainese. It uses mostly the same characters as Putonghua for writing, but the pronunciation is so different as to be unintelligible to a Putonghua speaker. While the city government actively discourages the use of Shanghainese in front of visitors, using a few phrases like *nong hao* (hello) and *xia ya nong* (thank you) will endear you immensely and immediately to locals.

Chinese grammar is simple, but a complex tonal system of pronunciation means it usually takes a long time for foreigners to learn Chinese. Making yourself understood can be tricky. However, the Chinese will appreciate your making the effort to speak a few phrases understood almost everywhere. Try "Hello"—"*Ní ha[b]o*" (nee **how**); "Thank you"—"*Xiè xiè*" (shee-**yeh**, shee-**yeh**); and "Good-bye"—"*Zai jian*" (dzai **djan**). When pronouncing words written in Pinyin, remember that "q" and "x" are pronounced like "ch" and "sh," respectively; "zh" is pronounced like the "j" in "just"; "c" is pronounced like "ts."

Not many Shanghainese speak English, though travel agents and the staff in most hotels and upscale restaurants are usually exceptions. If you're lost and need help, look first to someone under 30, who may have studied some English in school. In shops, calculators and hand gestures do most of the talking. While sometimes the "Chinglish" is a good-natured attempt to communicate, often it is intended as mockery of foreigners and its protracted use can signal a forthcoming rip-off or worse. Be wary of vendors who use it. Body language and context matter most for interpreting intent.

SIM—do this straight away as you need credit to receive calls. Local calls to landlines cost Y0.25 a minute, and to cell phones Y0.60. International calls from cell phones are very expensive. Remember to bring an adapter for your phone charger. You can also buy cheap handsets from China Mobile. If you're planning to stay even a couple of days this is probably cheaper than renting a phone.

China Mobile Phones and PandaPhone rent cell phones, which they can deliver to your hotel or the airport. Renting a basic Nokia handset costs US$10 for the first two days, then US$1 per day thereafter. You then pay the same local or international call rates as any other cell-phone user.

Contacts Cellular Abroad
(☎800/287–5072 ⊕www.cellularabroad. com) rents and sells GSM phones and sells SIM cards that work in many countries. **China Mobile Phones** (☎021/5109–7153 ⊕www. china-mobile-phones.com). **China Mobile** (☎1860 English-language assistance ⊕www. chinamobile.com) is China's main mobile-service provider. **China Unicom** (☎1001 English-language assistance) is China's second-largest main cell-phone company. **Mobal** (☎888/888–9162 ⊕www.mobalrental.com) rents mobiles and sells GSM phones (starting at $49) that will operate in 140 countries. Per-call rates vary throughout the world. **PandaPhone** (☎800/820–0293 ⊕www.panda phone.com). **Planet Fone** (☎888/988–4777 ⊕www.planetfone.com) rents cell phones, but the per-minute rates can be as much as $4.

▌CUSTOMS & DUTIES

You're always allowed to bring goods of a certain value back home without having to pay any duty or import tax. But there's a limit on the amount of tobacco and liquor you can bring back duty-free, and some countries have separate limits for perfumes; for exact figures, check with your customs department. The values of so-called "duty-free" goods are included in these amounts. When you shop abroad, save all your receipts, as customs inspectors may ask to see them as well as the items you purchased. If the total value of your goods is more than the duty-free limit, you'll have to pay a tax (most often a flat percentage) on the value of everything beyond that limit.

Except for the usual prohibitions against narcotics, explosives, plant and animal material, firearms, and ammunition you can take anything into China that you plan to take away with you. Cameras, video recorders, GPS equipment, laptops, and the like should pose no problems. However, China is very sensitive about printed matter deemed seditious, such as religious, pornographic, and political items, especially articles, books, and pictures on Tibet. All the same, small amounts of English-language reading materials aren't generally a problem. Customs officials are for the most part easygoing, and visitors are rarely searched. It's not necessary to fill in customs-declaration forms, but if you carry in a large amount of cash, say several thousand dollars, you should declare it upon arrival.

You're not allowed to remove any antiquities dating from before 1795. Antiques from between 1795 and 1949 must have an official red seal attached. Quality antiques shops know this and arrange it.

U.S. Information U.S. Customs and Border Protection (⊕www.cbp.gov).

▌DAY TOURS & GUIDES

You can't turn a corner in Shanghai these days without tripping over tour companies or a guide desperate for your patronage. *Never* accept unsolicited offers of tours, as most are scams.

Although it's true that sightseeing tours often pack a lot in, think carefully before signing up for one, because most Shanghai tours are vastly more expensive than visiting the same sights alone, even if you hire your own car and driver. Well, you're paying for the guide, you say. True, but years of censorship and a limited education system mean that guides often aren't as clued in on places as, say, your guide-book (though they tell charming stories packed with interesting "facts"). Many companies see you as a handy cash cow to be milked all day long—they take substantial cuts at the inevitable shopping stop-offs (mostly rip-offs), and restaurant visits, and through tips, normally not a part of Chinese culture.

Independent sightseeing in Shanghai may seem a daunting prospect, but with a little research it's actually fairly straight-forward. Downtown areas like the Bund, the Old French Concession, and Nanshi are easy to reach and you can see them at your own pace, and you can make out-of-town trips by hiring a car and driver, or taking an air-conditioned bus. If you do decide to go on an organized tour, shop around. The forums on Fodors.com are a great place to see what companies fellow travelers have used recently, how much they paid, and what they thought of them.

The state-run agencies, China Travel Service (CTS) and China International Travel Service (CITS), are usually reliable, though their prices aren't always the cheapest around. At CITS you can arrange private or group tours. China Highlights has a range of Shanghai group-tour packages, some of which include hotels. The shorter tours are reasonably priced (for a tour, that is).

Recommended Tours/Guides **China Highlights** (China: ☎773/283–1999 U.S.: ☎800/268–2918 ⊕www.chinahighlights.com). **China International Travel Service** (Shanghai: ☎021/6289–8899 or 6289–4510 ⊕www.scits.com U.S.: ☎626/568–8993 ⊕www.citsusa.com). **China Travel Service** (Shanghai: ☎021/6247–8888 U.S.: ☎800/899–8618 ⊕www.chinatravelservice.com).

ELECTRICITY

The electrical current in China is 220 volts, 50 cycles alternating current (AC), so most American appliances can't be used without a transformer. A universal adapter is especially useful in China as wall outlets come in a bewildering variety of configurations: two- and three-pronged round plugs, as well as two-pronged flat sockets.

EMERGENCIES

If you lose your passport, contact your consulate immediately.

In a medical emergency don't call for an ambulance. The Shanghai Ambulance Service is merely a transport system that takes you to the closest hospital, not the hospital of your choice. If possible, take a taxi to the hospital; you'll get there faster. The best place to head in a medical emergency is the Shanghai United Family Hospital or the World Link Medical Center, both of which have 24-hour emergency services (including dental) and pharmacy assistance. The Shanghai East International Medical Center has similar services but no dentistry. SOS is an international medical service that arranges Medivac. Huashan and Huadong hospitals are both local hospitals with English-speaking foreigners' clinics. Although cheaper than the international clinics, their hygiene standards aren't as high.

Shanghai has different numbers for each emergency service, but staff often don't speak English. If in doubt, call the U.S. embassy first: staff members are available 24 hours a day to help handle emergencies and facilitate communication with local agencies.

Lifeline, a nonprofit support group for expatriates, operates a counseling hotline daily noon to 8 PM. The clinics and hospitals listed below have a number of English-speaking doctors on hand. At most hospitals, few staff members will speak English.

Medical Services **Huadong Hospital** (⊠Foreigners' Clinic, 2F, 221 Yanan Xi Lu, Jing'an ☎021/6248-3180 Ext. 30106). **Huashan Hospital** (⊠Foreigners' Clinic, 15F, 12 Wulumuqi Zhong Lu, Jing'an ☎021/6248-9999 Ext. 2531 for 24-hour hotline). **Shanghai East International Medical Center** (⊠551 Pudong Nan Lu., Pudong ☎021/5879-9999 ⊕www.seimc.com.cn).

Shanghai United Family Health Center (private; ⊠1139 Xian Zia Lu, Changning ☎021/5133-1900, 021/5133-1999 emergencies ⊕www.unitedfamilyhospitals.com). **SOS International Shanghai Office** (⊠Sun Tong Infoport Plaza, 22nd fl., Unit D-G, 55 Huaihai Xi Lu, Xuhui ☎021/6295-0099 emergencies ⊕www.internationalsos.com).

World Link Medical Center (⊠Room 203, West Tower, Shanghai Center, 1376 Nanjing Xi Lu, Jing'an Hongqiao Clinic; ⊠Mandarin City, 1F, Unit 30, 788 Hongxu Lu, Minhang Jian Qiao Clinic; ⊠51 Hongfeng Lu, Jian Qao, Pudong ☎021/6445-5999).

Foreign Consulates **United States Consulate** (⊠1469 Huaihai Zhong Lu, Xuhui ☎021/6433-6880, 021/6433-3936 after-hours emergencies ⊠Citizen Services Section, Westgate Mall, 8th fl., 1038 Nanjing Xi Lu, Jing'an ☎021/3217-4650 ⊕shanghai.us consulate.gov).

General Emergency Contacts **Fire** (☎119). **International SOS Medical Services 24-hour Alarm Center** (☎021/6295-0099). **Police** (☎110, 021/6357-6666 English). **Shanghai Ambulance Service** (☎120).

Hotline **Lifeline** (☎021/6279-8990).

Pharmacies The most reliable places to buy prescription medication is at the 24-hour pharmacy at the World Link Medical Center and the Shanghai United Family Health Center (⇨ *Medical Services, above).* During the day, the Watson's chain is good for over-the-counter medication but has limited selection and poor service; it has dozens of branches around town. Chinese pharmacies offer a fuller range

of imported over-the-counter drugs and are usually open 24 hours; look for the green cross on a white sign.

Watson's Pharmacy (⊠Westgate Mall, 1038 Nanjing Xi Lu, Jing'an).

▌HEALTH

The most common types of illnesses are caused by contaminated food and water. Especially in developing countries, drink only bottled, boiled, or purified water and drinks; don't drink from public fountains or use ice. Tap water in Shanghai is safe for brushing teeth. However, it contains a high concentration of metals, so you should buy bottled water to drink. Make sure food has been thoroughly cooked and is served to you fresh and hot; avoid vegetables and fruits that you haven't washed (in bottled or purified water) or peeled yourself. If you have problems, mild cases of traveler's diarrhea may respond to Imodium (known generically as loperamide) or Pepto-Bismol. Be sure to drink plenty of fluids; if you can't keep fluids down, seek medical help immediately.

SPECIFIC ISSUES IN SHANGHAI

Pneumonia and influenza are common among travelers returning from China— talk to your doctor about inoculations before you leave. If you need to buy prescription drugs, try to go to the pharmacies of reputable private hospitals like the World Link Medical Center. Do *not* buy them in street-side pharmacies as the quality control is unreliable. Staff at the hospitals listed here *(⇨Emergencies, above)* speak English; indeed many doctors are expats.

OVER-THE-COUNTER REMEDIES

Most pharmacies carry over-the-counter Western medicines and traditional Chinese medicines. By and large, you need to ask for the generic name of the drug you're looking for, not a brand name. Oral contraceptives are also available without prescription, but quality in regular pharmacies varies.

HOURS OF OPERATION

Most offices are open between 9 and 6 on weekdays; most museums keep roughly the same hours but may close Monday or Tuesday. Everything in China grinds to a halt for the first two or three days of Chinese New Year (sometime in mid-January through February), and opening hours are often reduced for the rest of that season.

Banks and government offices are open weekdays 9 to 5 (or as late as 7), although some close for lunch (sometime between noon and 2); they have truncated hours on weekends and holidays. Bank branches and China Travel Service (CTS) tour desks in hotels often keep shorter hours and sometimes close on arbitrary weekdays. Many hotel currency-exchange desks stay open 24 hours.

Pharmacies are open daily from 8:30 or 9 AM to 6 or 7 PM. Some large pharmacies stay open until 9 PM or are staffed 24 hours a day.

Shops and department stores are generally open daily 10 to 10; some stores stay open even later in summer, in popular tourist areas, or during peak tourist season.

HOLIDAYS

National holidays include New Year's Day (January 1); Spring Festival, aka Chinese New Year (late January/early February); Qingming Jie (April 4); International Labor Day (May 1); Dragon Boat Festival (late May/early June); anniversary of the founding of the Communist Party of China (July 1); anniversary of the founding of the Chinese People's Liberation Army (August 1); and National Day—founding of the Peoples Republic of China in 1949 (October 1); Chongyang Jie or Double Ninth Festival (9th day of 9th lunar month).

MAIL

Sending international mail from China is extremely reliable. Airmail letters to any place in the world should take five to 14 days. Express Mail Service (EMS) is available to many international destinations. Letters within Shanghai arrive the next day, and mail to the rest of China takes a day or two longer. Domestic mail can be subject to search so don't send sensitive materials, such as religious or political literature, as you might cause the recipient trouble.

Service is more reliable if you mail letters from post offices rather than mailboxes. Buy envelopes here, too, as there are standardized sizes in China. You need to glue stamps onto envelopes, as they're not self-adhesive. Most post offices are open daily 8 to 7; many keep even longer hours. Your hotel can usually send letters for you, too.

You can use the Roman alphabet to write an address. Do not use red ink, which has a negative connotation. You should also include a six-digit zip code for mail within China. The Shanghai municipality's postal code is 200000, and each of the city's districts differs in the fifth and sixth digits; for example, Xuhui district is 200030.

Sending airmail postcards costs Y4.50 and letters Y5–Y7.

Forest-green signs identify the many branches of China Post in Shanghai. The main post office is at 276 Suzhou Bei Lu, and there are also English-speaking staff at the Shanghai Center and Xuhui branches.

Main Branches **Post Office** (✉ 276 Suzhou Bei Lu, Hongkou ✉ Shanghai Center, 1376 Nanjing Xi Lu, Jing'an ✉ 133 Huaihai Lu, Xuhui ☎ 021/6393–6666 Ext. 00). ✉ 105 Tianping Lu).

SHIPPING PACKAGES

It's easy to ship packages home from China. Take what you want to send *unpacked* to the post office—everything will be sewn up officially into satisfying linen-bound packages, a service which costs a few yuan. You have to fill in lengthy forms, and enclosing a photocopy of receipts for the goods inside isn't a bad idea, as packages may be opened by customs along the line. Large antiques stores often offer reliable shipping services that take care of customs in China. Large international couriers operating in Shanghai include DHL, Federal Express, and UPS. Your hotel can also arrange shipping parcels, but there's usually a hefty markup on postal rates.

Express Services **DHL** (☎800/810–8000 ⊕www.cn.dhl.com). **FedEx** (☎800/988–1888 ⊕www.fedex.com). **UPS** (☎800/820–8388 ⊕www.ups.com).

▌MONEY

The easiest way to obtain Chinese currency in Shanghai is at an ATM. HSBC's machines are the most reliable. Otherwise, the best places to convert your dollars into yuan are at your hotel's front desk or a branch of a major bank, such as Bank of China, CITIC, or HSBC. All these operate with standardized government rates—anything cheaper is illegal, and thus risky. You need to present your passport to change money.

Although credit cards are gaining ground in China, for day-to-day transactions cash is definitely king. Getting change for big notes can be a problem, so try to stock up on tens and twenties when you change money.

▐TIP➔ **Banks never have every foreign currency on hand, and it may take as long as a week to order. If you're planning to exchange funds before leaving home, don't wait until the last minute.**

ITEM	AVERAGE COST
Cup of coffee at Starbucks	Y15
Glass of local beer at a bar	Y30
Cheapest Metro ticket	Y3
1 km (½ mi) taxi ride in Shanghai	Y11
Hour-long foot massage	Y50
Fake Chloé purse	Y200

ATMS & BANKS

Your own bank will probably charge a fee for using ATMs abroad; the foreign bank you use may also charge a fee. Nevertheless, you'll usually get a better rate of exchange at an ATM than you will at a currency-exchange office or even when changing money in a bank. And extracting funds as you need them is a safer option than carrying around a large amount of cash.

▐TIP➔ **PIN numbers with more than four digits are not recognized at ATMs in many countries. If yours has five or more, remember to change it before you leave.**

ATMs are widespread in Shanghai and rates are as good, if not better, than at exchange desks. The most reliable ATMs are HSBC's. They also have the highest withdrawal limit, which offsets the transaction charge. Of the Chinese banks, your best bet for ATMs is the Bank of China, which accepts most foreign cards. That said, machines frequently refuse to give cash for mysterious reasons. Move on and try another. On-screen instructions appear automatically in English.

CREDIT CARDS

In Shanghai, American Express, MasterCard, and Visa are accepted at most major hotels and a growing number of upmarket stores and restaurants. Diners Club is accepted at many hotels and some restaurants.

Throughout this guide, the following abbreviations are used: **AE,** American

Express; **DC,** Diners Club; **MC,** Master-Card; and **V,** Visa.

It's a good idea to inform your credit-card company before you travel, especially if you're going abroad and don't travel internationally very often. Otherwise, the credit-card company might put a hold on your card owing to unusual activity—not a good thing halfway through your trip. Record all your credit-card numbers—as well as the phone numbers to call if your cards are lost or stolen—in a safe place, so you're prepared should something go wrong. Both MasterCard and Visa have general numbers you can call (collect if you're abroad) if your card is lost, but you're better off calling the number of your issuing bank, since Master-Card and Visa usually just transfer you to your bank; your bank's number is usually printed on your card.

If you plan to use your credit card for cash advances, you'll need to apply for a PIN at least two weeks before your trip. Although it's usually cheaper (and safer) to use a credit card abroad for large purchases (so you can cancel payments or be reimbursed if there's a problem), note that some credit-card companies *and* the banks that issue them add substantial percentages to all foreign transactions, whether they're in a foreign currency or not. Check on these fees before leaving home, so there won't be any surprises when you get the bill.

■TIP→ **Before you charge something, ask the merchant whether or not he or she plans to do a dynamic currency conversion (DCC). In such a transaction the credit-card** *processor* **(shop, restaurant, or hotel, not Visa or MasterCard) converts the currency and charges you in dollars. In most cases you'll pay the merchant a 3% fee for this service in addition to any credit-card company and issuing-bank foreign-transaction surcharges.**

Dynamic currency conversion programs are becoming increasingly widespread.

Merchants who participate in them are supposed to ask whether you want to be charged in dollars or the local currency, but they don't always do so. And even if they do offer you a choice, they may well avoid mentioning the additional surcharges. The good news is that you *do* have a choice. And if this practice really gets your goat, you can avoid it entirely thanks to American Express; with its cards, DCC simply isn't an option.

Reporting Lost Cards **American Express** (☎800/992-3404 in the U.S., 336/393-1111 collect from abroad ⊕www.americanexpress.com). **Diners Club** (☎800/234-6377 in the U.S., 303/799-1504 collect from abroad ⊕www.dinersclub.com). **MasterCard** (☎800/622-7747 in the U.S., 636/722-7111 collect from abroad, 010/800-110-7309 in China ⊕www.mastercard.com). **Visa** (☎800/847-2911 in the U.S., 410/581-9994 collect from abroad, 010/800-711-2911 in China ⊕www.visa.com).

CURRENCY & EXCHANGE

The Chinese currency is officially called the yuan (Y), and is also known as *renminbi* (RMB), or "People's Money." You may also hear it called *kuai.* It's pegged to the dollar at around Y6.50.

Both old and new styles of bills circulate simultaneously in China, and many denominations have both coins and bills. The Bank of China issues bills in denominations of 1 (burgundy and green), 5 (brown or purple), 10 (turquoise), 20 (pink), 50 (green or occasionally yellow), and 100 (red or blue). There are 1-yuan coins, too. The yuan subdivides into 10-cent units called *jiao* or *mao*; these come in coins of 1, 2, and 5. The smallest denomination is the *fen,* which comes in coins of 1, 2, and 5, but are almost never used. Counterfeiting is rife in China, and even small stores inspect notes with ultraviolet lamps. Change can be a problem in taxis and small shops—don't expect much success paying for a Y13 purchase with a Y100 note, for example.

WORST CASE SCENARIO

All your money and credit cards have just been stolen. In these days of real-time transactions, this isn't a predicament that should destroy your vacation. First, report the theft of the credit cards. Then get any traveler's checks you were carrying replaced. This can usually be done almost immediately, provided that you kept a record of the serial numbers separate from the checks themselves. If you bank at a large international bank like Citibank or HSBC, go to the closest branch; if you know your account number, chances are you can get a new ATM card and withdraw money right away. **Western Union** (☎ 800/325–6000 ⊕ www. westernunion.com) sends money almost anywhere. Have someone back home order a transfer online, over the phone, or at one of the company's offices, which is the cheapest option. The U.S. State Department's **Overseas Citizens Services** (☎ 202/647–5225) can wire money to any U.S. consulate or embassy abroad for a fee of $30. Just have someone back home wire money or send a money order or cashier's check to the United States Department of State, which will then disburse the funds as soon as the next working day after it receives them.

Exchange rates in China are fixed by the government daily, so it's equally good at branches of the Bank of China, at big department stores, or at your hotel's exchange desk, which has the added advantage of often being open 24 hours a day. Any lower rates are illegal, so you're exposing yourself to scams. A passport is required to change money. Hold on to your exchange receipt, which you need to convert your extra yuan back into dollars.

■ TIP→ **Even if a currency-exchange booth has a sign promising no commission, rest assured that there's some kind of huge, hidden fee. (Oh . . . that's right. The sign didn't say no fee.) And as for rates, you're almost always better off getting foreign currency at an ATM or exchanging money at a bank.**

▌PACKING

GEAR

Forget Paris, New York, and Milan—the new center of the fashion universe is Shanghai. People in the rest of China dress for comfort, but the Shanghainese dress to impress. Although suits are still required for some meetings and business functions, casual apparel is increasingly popular. Slop around in capri pants or Bermuda shorts and white sneakers and you will feel like there's a neon "tourist" sign over your head. Pack jeans or cargo pants for sightseeing—there are plenty of fake handbags around with which to dress them up come dinner.

From May through September it's seriously hot and sticky, but air-conditioning in hotels, restaurants, and museums can be arctic—keep a wrinkle-proof sweater or shawl in your day pack. In October and April, a jacket or sweater should suffice. Temperatures plunge into the 30s and 40s Fahrenheit (0°C–10°C) in November and stay low until mid-March so you'll need a heavy-duty jacket or overcoat. No self-respecting Shanghai resident leaves home each morning without a folding umbrella, nor should you.

That said, in Shanghai you can prepare to be unprepared: the city is a clothing-shopper's paradise. If a bulky jacket's going to put you over the airline limit, buy one for next to nothing in China and leave it behind when you go.

Keep packets of Kleenex and antibacterial hand wipes in your day pack—paper isn't always a feature of Chinese restrooms. Watson's is a pharmacy chain with various branches around town; it stocks international toiletry brands and tampons, which otherwise can be hard to find.

RESTROOMS

Public restrooms abound in Shanghai—the street, parks, restaurants, department stores, and major tourist attractions are all likely locations. Most charge a small fee (usually less than Y1), but seldom provide Western-style facilities or private booths. Instead, expect squat toilets, open troughs, and rusty spigots; WC signs at intersections point the way to these facilities. Toilet paper or tissues and antibacterial hand wipes are good things to have in your day pack. The restrooms in the newest shopping plazas, fast-food outlets, and deluxe restaurants catering to foreigners are generally on par with American restrooms, but sometimes are poorly maintained.

Find a Loo **The Bathroom Diaries** (⊕www.thebathroomdiaries.com) is flush with unsanitized info on restrooms the world over—each one located, reviewed, and rated.

SAFETY

There is little violent crime against tourists in China, partly because the penalties are severe for those who are caught—China's yearly death-sentence tolls run into the thousands. Single women can move about Shanghai without too much hassle. Handbag-snatching and pick-pocketing do happen in markets and on crowded buses or trains—keep an eye open, your bag closed, and your money safe and you should have no problems. Use the safe in your hotel room to store any valuables, but always carry a copy of your passport with you for identification purposes.

Shanghai is full of people looking to make a quick buck. The most common scam involves people persuading you to go with them for a tea ceremony, which is often so pleasant that you don't smell a rat until several hundred dollars appear on your credit-card bill. "Art students" who pressure you into buying work is another common scam. The same rules that apply to hostess bars worldwide are also true in Shanghai. Avoiding such scams is as easy as refusing *all* unsolicited services—be it from taxi or pedicab drivers, tour guides, or potential "friends."

Shanghai traffic is as manic as it looks, and survival of the fittest (or the biggest) is the main rule. Crossing streets can be an extreme sport. Drivers rarely give pedestrians the right-of-way and don't even look for pedestrians when making a right turn on a red light. Cyclists have less power but are just as aggressive.

Shanghai's severely polluted air can bring on, or aggravate, respiratory problems. If you're a sufferer, take the cue from locals, who wear surgical masks, or a scarf or bandana as protection.

■TIP→ **Distribute your cash, credit cards, IDs, and other valuables between a deep front pocket, an inside jacket or vest pocket, and a hidden money pouch. Don't reach for the money pouch once you're in public.**

Safety **Transportation Security Administration** (TSA; ⊕www.tsa.gov).

TAXES

There is no sales tax in China. Hotels charge a 5% tax; bigger, joint-venture hotels also add a 10% to 15% service fee. Some restaurants charge a 10% service fee.

TIME

Shanghai is eight hours ahead of GMT, 13 hours ahead of New York, 14 hours ahead of Chicago, and 16 hours ahead of Los Angeles. There's no daylight saving time, so subtract an hour in summer.

Time Zones **Timeanddate.com** (⊕www.timeanddate.com/worldclock) can help you figure out the correct time anywhere in the world.

▌ TIPPING

Tipping is not done in China. It's officially forbidden by the government, and locals simply don't do it. In general, follow their lead without qualms. Nevertheless, the practice is beginning to catch on, especially among tour guides, who often expect Y10 a day. Official China Travel Service representatives aren't allowed to accept tips, but you can give them candy, T-shirts, and other small gifts. You don't need to tip in restaurants or in taxis—many drivers insist on handing over your change, however small. If the lack of tipping makes you uncomfortable, remember that as a foreigner you are probably already being charged 10%–50% extra for everything, and consider that your "tip."

▌ VISITOR INFORMATION

ONLINE TRAVEL TOOLS

All the Web sites listed below are in English. If you want to read Chinese-only Web sites in English, try using Google's "Translate this page." It might not read like Shakespeare, but you'll get the gist of the information.

All About Shanghai **China Digital Times** (⊕chinadigitaltimes.net/) is an excellent Berkeley-run site tracking China-related news and culture in serious depth. **China National Tourism Office** (⊕www.cnto.org) gives a general overview of traveling in China. **China Travel Services (U.S. site)** (⊕www.chinatravelservice.com), the state-run travel agency, is a helpful starting place. **Chinese Government Portal** (⊕english.gov.cn). **Shanghai City Weekend** (⊕www.cityweekend.com.cn) is an online version of the local magazine with top-notch searchable listings on just about everything in Shanghai. **Shanghai Municipality** (⊕www.shanghai.gov.cn) is the comprehensive (if slightly dry) government guide to the city. **Shanghai Tour** (⊕lyw.sh.gov.cn/en/) is the official government tourism Web site, with advice on sightseeing, hotels, and restaurants.

That's Shanghai (⊕www.urbanatomy.com/thatssh/) is the Web address of Shanghai's old-

est and most in-depth English monthly, with exhaustive arts, events and dining listings.

Business **American Chamber of Commerce in Shanghai** (⊕www.amcham-shanghai.org) has a Web site packed with useful business information and links to other resources. China Business Weekly (⊕www.chinadaily.com.cn/bw/bwtop.html) is a weekly magazine from the China Daily newspaper. **Chinese Government Business Site** (⊕english.gov.cn/business.htm) has news, links, and information on business-related legal issues from the Chinese government.

Culture **China Vista** (⊕www.chinavista.com/experience) has incredibly detailed information on all aspects of Chinese arts and culture. **Chinese Culture** (⊕www.chinaculture.org) is a detailed, searchable database with information on Chinese art, literature, film, history, and more.

Currency Conversion **Google** (⊕www.google.com) does currency conversion. Just type in the amount you want to convert and an explanation of how you want it converted (e.g., "14 Swiss francs in dollars"), and then voilà. **Oanda.com** (⊕www.oanda.com) also allows you to print out a handy table with the current day's conversion rates. **XE.com** (⊕www.xe.com) is a good currency conversion Web site.

Local Insight **Enjoy Shanghai** (⊕www.enjoyshanghai.com) has searchable listings for eating out, shopping, and finding Wi-Fi spots. **Shanghai Expat** (⊕www.shanghaiexpat.com) has advice and listings from foreigners living in Shanghai. **Shanghai-ed** (⊕www.shanghai-ed.com) provides expat expertise on the city. **Shanghaiist** (⊕www.shanghaiist.com) is the city's most popular expat blog, run by the same company as NYC's Gothamist; it gives a different take on what's going down in town. *SH Magazine* (⊕www.asia-city.com) is a quirky weekly rag whose online version gives the lowdown on just about everything happening in town. **Shanghai Eats** (⊕www.shanghai-eats.com) lists hundreds of local restaurants, bars, and clubs, all authoritatively reviewed. That's Shanghai (⊕shanghai.urbanatomy.com/thatssh/) is a glossy local monthly that's also available online.

Newspapers **China Daily** (⊕www.chinadaily. com.cn) is the country's leading English-language daily. **People's Daily** (⊕english.people daily.com.cn) is an English edition of China's most popular—and most propagandistic—local daily. **Shanghai Daily** (⊕english.eastday.com) is the city's English-language newspaper.

Weather **Shanghai Weather** (⊕weather. china.org.cn).

Other Resources **CIA World Factbook** (⊕www.odci.gov/cia/publications/factbook/ index.html) has profiles of every country in the world. It's a good source if you need some quick facts and figures.

VISITOR INFORMATION

For general information before you go, including information about tours, insurance, and safety, call or visit the Web site of the China National Tourist Office.

Shanghai Tour, the government tourism Web site, is a good planning resource. It runs the official Shanghai Tourist Information and Service Centers, which have branches all over town, usually identifiable by big aquamarine signs. Reasonably informed staff dole out free maps and leaflets, and can also book hotels, restaurants, and flights. Compare prices with other travel agencies, as Shanghai Tour is often not the cheapest. The Web site lists branch details.

The two best-known Chinese travel agencies are China International Travel Service (CITS) and China Travel Service (CTS), both under the same government ministry. Although they have some tourist information, they are businesses, so don't expect endless resources if you're not buying a tour or flight through them.

Contacts **China National Tourist Office** (New York: ☎888/760-8218 Los Angeles: ☎800/670-2228 ⊕www.cnto.org). **China International Travel Service** (CITS Shanghai: ☎021/6289-8899 or 021/6289-4510 U.S.: ☎626/568-8993). **China Travel Service**

(CTS Shanghai: ☎021/6247-8888 New York: ☎800/899-8618 ⊕www.chinatravelservice. com). **Shanghai Tour** (☎021/6252-0000 ⊕lyw.sh.gov.cn/en/).

GOVERNMENT ADVISORIES

■TIP→ **If you're a U.S. citizen traveling abroad, consider registering online with the State Department (https://travelregistration.state.gov/ibrs/), so the government will know to look for you should a crisis occur in the country you're visiting.**

General Information & Warnings **Australian Department of Foreign Affairs & Trade** (⊕www.smartraveller.gov.au). **Consular Affairs Bureau of Canada** (⊕www.voyage. gc.ca). **U.K. Foreign & Commonwealth Office** (⊕www.fco.gov.uk/travel). **U.S. Department of State** (⊕www.travel.state.gov).

PASSPORTS & VISAS

All U.S. citizens, even infants, need a valid passport with a tourist visa stamped in it to enter China (except for Hong Kong, where you only need a valid passport). It's always best to have at least six months' validity on your passport before traveling to Asia.

Children traveling with only one parent do not need a notarized letter of permission to enter China. However, as these kinds of policies can change, being overprepared isn't a bad idea.

VISAS

Getting a tourist visa (known as an "L" visa) in the United States is straightforward. Standard visas are for single-entry stays of up to 30 days, and are valid for 90 days from the date of issue (*not* the date of entry), so don't get your visa too far in advance. Costs range from $50 for a tourist visa issued within two to three working days to $80 for a same-day service.

Note: The visa application will ask your occupation. The Chinese don't look favorably upon those who work in publishing or the media. People in these professions routinely state "teacher" under "occupation." Before you go, contact the embassy or consulate of the People's Republic of China to gauge the current mood.

China officially denies visas (and thus entry) to anyone suffering from infectious diseases, including leprosy, AIDS, venereal diseases, and contagious tuberculosis. You must complete information regarding these on applications and on entering the country. However, this information is almost never checked for tourist visas; medical tests are required for longer visas.

Under no circumstances should you overstay your visa. To extend your visa, stop by the Entry and Exit Administration Office of the Shanghai Public Security Bureau a week before your visa expires. The office is known as the PSB or the Foreigner's Police, and is open weekdays 9 to 11:30 and 1:30 to 4:30. It's extremely bureaucratic, but it's usually no problem to get a month's extension on a tourist visa. You need to bring your passport and a registration of temporary residency from your hotel. You generally need to leave your passport for five to seven days, so do any transactions requiring it (and make copies!) beforehand. If you are trying to extend a business visa, you'll need the above items as well as a letter, from the business that originally invited you to China, stating it would like to extend your stay for work reasons. Rules are always changing (Visa to Asia has up-to-date information), so you will probably need to go to the office at least twice to get all your papers in order.

Passport & Visa Information **Chinese Consulate, New York** (New York: ☎212/244–9456 ⊕www.nyconsulate.prchina.org). **U.S. Department of State** (☎877/487–2778 ⊕travel.state.gov/passport). **Visa Office of Chinese Embassy** (☎202/338–6688 ⊕www.china-embassy.org). **Visa to Asia** (⊕www.visatoasia.com/china.html).

U.S. Passport & Visa Expediters **A. Briggs Passport & Visa Expeditors**

(☎800/806–0581 or 202/338–0111 ⊕www.abriggs.com). **American Passport Express** (☎800/455–5166 or 603/559–9888 ⊕www.americanpassport.com). **Passport Express** (☎800/362–8196 or 401/272–4612 ⊕www.passportexpress.com). **Travel Document Systems** (☎800/874–5100 or 202/638–3800 ⊕www.traveldocs.com). **Travel the World Visas** (☎866/886–8472 or 301/495–7700 ⊕www.world-visa.com).

Visa Extensions **Entry and Exit Administration Office, Shanghai Public Security Bureau** (⊠No. 1500, Minsheng Rd., Pudong ☎021/2895–1900 ⊕www.shanghai.gov.cn).

GENERAL REQUIREMENTS FOR SHANGHAI	
Passport	Must be valid for 6 months after date of arrival
Visa	Required for U.S. citizens ($25–$130)
Required Vaccinations	None
Recommended Vaccinations	Hepatitis A and B, typhoid, influenza, boosters for tetanus-diphtheria and measles
Driving	Chinese driver's license required

SHOTS & MEDICATIONS

No immunizations are required for entry into China, but it's a good idea to be immunized against typhoid and hepatitis A and B before traveling to Shanghai, as well as routine tetanus-diphtheria and measles boosters. In winter, a flu vaccination is also smart, especially if you're infection-prone or are a senior citizen. *For more information see Health.*

TRIP INSURANCE

Comprehensive trip insurance is especially valuable if you're booking a very expensive or complicated trip (particularly to an isolated region) or if you're booking far in advance. Who knows what could happen six months down the road? But whether or not you get insurance has more to do with how comfortable you are assuming all that risk yourself.

Comprehensive travel policies typically cover trip-cancellation and interruption, letting you cancel or cut your trip short because of a personal emergency, illness, or, in some cases, acts of terrorism in your destination. Such policies also cover evacuation and medical care. Another type of coverage to look for is financial default—that is, when your trip is disrupted because a tour operator, airline, or cruise line goes out of business.

Consider buying medical-only coverage at the very least. Neither Medicare nor some private insurers cover medical expenses anywhere outside of the United States besides Mexico and Canada (including time aboard a cruise ship, even if it leaves from a U.S. port). Medical-only policies typically reimburse you for medical care (excluding that related to pre-existing conditions) and hospitalization abroad, and provide for evacuation. You still have to pay the bills and await reimbursement from the insurer, though.

■TIP→ Even at Shanghai's public hospitals foreigners need to pay fees to register, to see a doctor, and then for all tests and medication. Prices are cheap compared to the city's fancy foreigner clinics, where you pay $100 to $150 just for a consultation, but most doctors don't speak English and hygiene standards are low even at better public hospitals.

Expect comprehensive travel insurance policies to cost about 4% to 7% of the total price of your trip (it's more like 12% if you're over age 70). A medical-only policy may or may not be cheaper than a comprehensive policy. Always read the fine print of your policy to make sure that you are covered for the risks that are of most concern to you. Compare several policies to make sure you're getting the best price and range of coverage available.

TRIP INSURANCE RESOURCES

Insurance Comparison Sites **Insure My Trip. com** (☎800/487-4722 ⊕www.insuremytrip.

com). **Square Mouth.com** (☎800/240-0369 ⊕www.quotetravelinsurance.com).

Comprehensive Travel Insurers **Access America** (☎800/284-8300 ⊕www.access america.com). **CSA Travel Protection** (☎800/711-1197 ⊕www.csatravelprotection. com). **HTH Worldwide** (☎610/254-8700 or 888/243-2358 ⊕www.hthworldwide. com). **Travelex Insurance** (☎888/457-4602 ⊕www.travelex-insurance.com). **Travel Guard International** (☎715/345-0505 or 800/826-4919 ⊕www.travelguard. com). **Travel Insured International** (☎800/243-3174 ⊕www.travelinsured.com).

Medical-Only Insurers **International Medical Group** (☎800/628-4664 ⊕www.imglobal.com). **International SOS** (☎215/942-8000 or 713/521-7611 ⊕www. internationalsos.com). **Wallach & Company** (☎800/237-6615 or 540/687-3166 ⊕www. wallach.com).

▌VACATION PACKAGES

Packages *are not* guided excursions. Packages combine airfare, accommodations, and perhaps a rental car or other extras (theater tickets, guided excursions, boat trips, reserved entry to popular museums, transit passes), but they let you do your own thing. During busy periods packages may be your only option, as flights and rooms may be sold out otherwise. Packages will definitely save you time. They can also save you money, particularly in peak seasons, but—and this is a really big "but"—you should price each part of the package separately to be sure. And be aware that prices advertised on Web sites and in newspapers rarely include service charges or taxes, which can up your costs by hundreds of dollars.

■TIP→ Some packages and cruises are sold only through travel agents. Don't always assume that you can get the best deal by booking everything yourself.

Each year consumers are stranded or lose their money when packagers—even large ones with excellent reputations—go out of business. How can you protect yourself? First, always pay with a credit card; if you have a problem, your credit-card company may help you resolve it. Second, buy trip insurance that covers default. Third, choose a company that belongs to the United States Tour Operators Association, whose members must set aside funds to cover defaults. Finally, choose a company that also participates in the Tour Operator Program of the American Society of Travel Agents (ASTA), which will act as mediator in any disputes. You can also check on the tour operator's reputation among travelers by posting an inquiry on one of the Fodors.com forums.

A vacation package to Shanghai is unlikely to save you much money over booking things yourself, though it might make things quicker and easier. One of the services the company will provide is arranging your Chinese visa. If you're only staying in Shanghai, it's easy to book your hotel and you really don't need a package for other activities. It's cheaper to book excursions through one of Shanghai's many local tour companies. You can do this before your trip to be sure of a place on the day you want.

∎TIP→ Local tourism boards can provide information about lesser-known and small-niche operators that sell packages to only a few destinations.

Organizations **American Society of Travel Agents** (ASTA ☎703/739–2782 or 800/965–2782 ⊕www.astanet.com). **United States Tour Operators Association** (USTOA ☎212/599–6599 ⊕www.ustoa.com).

∎ GUIDED TOURS

Few companies organize package trips only to Shanghai. It's usually part of a bigger China or Asia multidestination package. You get a day or two in Shanghai, with the same sights featured in most tours. If you want to explore the city in

any kind of depth, you're better doing it by yourself or getting a private guide.

Shopping stops plague China tours, so inquire before booking as to when, where, and how many to expect. Although you're never obliged to buy anything, they can take up big chunks of your valuable travel time, and the products offered are always ridiculously overpriced. Even on the best tours, you can count on having to sit through at least one or two.

Small groups and excellent guides are what Overseas Adventure Travel takes pride in. Two of its China tours include Shanghai. Adventure Center has a huge variety of China packages, including trekking, cycling, and family tours. China Focus Travel has 10 different China tours—it squeezes in a lot for your money. Ritz Tours is a midrange agency specializing in East Asian tours. R. Crusoe & Sons is an offbeat company that organizes small group or tailor-made private tours. For something more mainstream, try Pacific Delight; for serious luxury, head to Artisans of Leisure.

Recommended Companies **Adventure Center** (☎800/228–8747 ⊕www.adventurecenter. com). **Artisans of Leisure** (☎800/214–8144 ⊕www.artisansofleisure.com). **China Focus Travel** (☎800/868–7244 ⊕www.chinafocus travel.com). **Overseas Adventure Travel** (☎800/493–6824 ⊕www.oattravel.com). **Pacific Delight** (☎800/221–7179 ⊕www. pacificdelighttours.com). **R. Crusoe & Sons** (☎800/585–8555 ⊕www.rcrusoe.com). **Ritz Tours** (☎626/289–7777 ⊕www.ritztours. com).

SPECIAL-INTEREST TOURS

BIKING
Bike China Adventures organizes trips of varying length and difficulty all over China—its 17-day tour includes Shanghai. Tours don't include flights.

∎TIP→ Most airlines accommodate bikes as luggage, provided they're dismantled and boxed.

Contacts **Bike China Adventures**
(☎800/818-1778 ⊕www.bikechina.com).

CULINARY
Artisans of Leisure's culinary tour takes in Shanghai and Beijing from the cities' choicest establishments, with prices to match. Intrepid Travel is an Australian company specializing in budget, independent travel. Its China Gourmet Traveller tour includes market visits, cooking demonstrations, and lots of eating at down-to-earth restaurants. Imperial Tours' Culinary Tour combines sightseeing with cooking lectures and demonstrations, and lots of five-star dining. Only Artisans of Leisure's tours include airfare.

Contacts **Artisans of Leisure**
(☎800/214-8144 ⊕www.artisansofleisure. com). **Imperial Tours** (☎888/888-1970 ⊕www.imperialtours.net). **Intrepid Travel** (☎613/9473-2673 or 1300/364-512 ⊕www. intrepidtravel.com).

CULTURE
Local guides are often "creative" when it comes to history and culture, so having an expert with you can make a big difference. Learning is the focus of Smithsonian Journeys' small group tours, which are led by university professors. China

experts also lead National Geographic Expeditions' trips, though all that knowledge doesn't come cheap. Wild China is a local company with some of the most unusual trips around. For example, one of its cultural trips explores China's little-known Jewish history.

Contacts **National Geographic Expeditions** (☎888/966-8687 ⊕www.national geographicexpeditions.com). **Smithsonian Journeys** (☎877/338-8687 ⊕www. smithsonianjourneys.org). **Wild China** (☎010/6465-6602 ⊕www.wildchina.com).

GOLF
China Highlights organizes golf packages that combine Shanghai sightseeing with golfing at the Binhai Golf Club.

Contacts **China Highlights**
(☎800/268-2918 or 800/879-3007 ⊕www. chinahighlights.com).

HIKING
The Adventure Center's Yangtse River Explorer combines hiking in the Three Gorges area with time in Shanghai.

Contacts **Adventure Center** (☎800/228-8747 or 510/654-1879 ⊕www.adventure center.com).

INDEX

NOTES

NOTES

NOTES

NOTES

NOTES

NOTES